THE NORTHERN IRELAND QUESTION

The Northern Ireland Question

Nationalism, unionism and partition

Edited by
PATRICK J. ROCHE
BRIAN BARTON

Ashgate

Aldershot • Brookfield USA • Singapore • Sydney

Published by
Ashgate Publishing Ltd
Gower House
Croft Road
Aldershot
Hants GU11 3HR
England

Ashgate Publishing Company
Old Post Road
Brookfield
Vermont 05036
USA

Ashgate website: http://www.ashgate.com

British Library Cataloguing in Publication Data
The Northern Ireland question : nationalism, Unionism and
    partition
    1. Unionism (Irish politics) 2. Nationalism - Northern
    Ireland
    I. Roche, Patrick J., 1940 - II. Barton, Brian, 1944 -
    320.9'416

Library of Congress Catalog Card Number: 99-73317

ISBN 1 84014 490 4

Printed in Great Britain

Contents

Introduction

Patrick J. Roche and Brian Barton

The objective of this book is to examine the origins, development and ideological basis of the unionist and nationalist movements from the late nineteenth century. This includes an analysis of the political content and mode of thought of these traditionally incompatible forces, consideration of their historical interaction and an assessment of their formative impact on contemporary institutions in Ireland.

The first three essays provide the pre-partition background and framework for those that follow. In chapter 1, Brian Girvan looks at the roots of Irish nationalism and at the nature of the political culture from which it emerged, and sets this within a comparative European framework. It focuses particularly on the role of Daniel O'Connell in shaping a sense of Irish identity, on the impact of the great famine in the process of Ireland's "modernisation" and the significance of the confrontation with unionism over home rule in moulding nationalist aspirations and strategies.

This is balanced in chapter 2, by D George Boyce's analysis of the origins and growth of unionism in Ireland from 1885 to 1921. The writer emphasises especially the central role played by the decisions and rhetoric of W E Gladstone and Charles Steward Parnell in the emergence of the movement. Its mode of argument, its institutional development and its internal tensions are each thoroughly examined, as is its response to successive Home Rule crises.

In chapter 3, Brian Barton reviews the background to the passing of the Government of Ireland Act, 1920, and the reasons for the broad convergence of opinion which emerged at Westminster in support of Irish partition during the period of the First World War. This essay then considers the prospects for the Northern Ireland government in mid 1921, and examines the genuine state of siege which it subsequently experienced, especially during 1921–2, and the enduring impact of this hostile context on its political and judicial structures.

The remaining chapters focus on different aspects of Ireland's political development from partition to the Good Friday Agreement, and beyond. In chapter 4, Dennis Kennedy begins by briefly describing the characteristics of Irish administration pre-partition, before exploring "concepts of the oneness of the island" and seeking "to explain why relations between the two administrations remained almost non-existent" post 1921. It first examines the provisions for a Council of Ireland (1920) and the eventual abandonment of the body, and the implementation and overall significance of the Collins–Craig pacts (1922) and Boundary Agreement (1925). It then details the "broadening gulf" which arose between North and South from the mid 1920s to 1950s. Thereafter, it identifies and dissects a narrowing of this gap, as evidenced by the O'Neill-Lemass meetings (1965), and the Sunningdale, Anglo-Irish and Belfast Agreements of 1973, 1985 and 1998 respectively.

In chapter 5, Graham Gudgin analyses an issue which has been absolutely central to political discourse in Northern Ireland, particularly from the late 1960s – religious discrimination, and the extent to which it was practised by successive unionist governments from 1921 to 1972. He scrutinises the evidence in relation to housing and employment, and also considers the vital question as to whether the distribution and pattern of either is very different now, after the reforms introduced by Westminster in the 1970s and 80s and long after the fall of Stormont. Finally, some reasons are suggested to explain and account for the consistent failure of much academic literature to make an accurate assessment of the actual level of sectarian discrimination in Northern Ireland.

Parallel issues are raised by Sidney Elliot in chapter 6, which looks at the electoral system in Northern Ireland. The nature and development of the franchise locally for Stormont and council elections, 1921–72, is compared with the changes in practice which had meanwhile been introduced at Westminster. The key question is then asked as to whether the decisions taken regionally had any politically partisan impact, either singly or cumulatively. Likewise, the redistribution of local government areas (1920s–'30s), the operation of single member, Stormont constituencies and the various methods of election adopted from 1921 to the present, are looked at and their repercussions on party representation assessed.

In chapter 7, Esmond Birnie considers the contemporary economic context in Ireland, which forms an often neglected but nonetheless vital backdrop to all meaningful political discussion. He reviews the comparative performance of northern and southern Irish economies in the 1990s, and sets both in the context of overall European Union growth rates. He then critically evaluates the economic case for the maintenance of Northern Ireland within the Union and the main flaws in the economic arguments advanced by constitutional nationalist and republican spokespersons.

Finally, in chapter 8, Michael Cunningham highlights and critiques the language of unionism and nationalism in recent years and examines their current proposals for political progress and new constitutional structures. He also analyses what strategies the two principal political identities have adopted in pursuit of their aims in the 1990s. Unionist policies and prescriptions for Northern Ireland's future are scrutinised as are the political language and the structures advocated by the two main nationalist parties.

1   The Making of Irish Nationalism: Between Integration and Independence

Brian Girvan

Introduction

When the First Dáil assembled in 1919, it issued a 'Message to the Free Nations of the World', insisting on Ireland's right to a place at the peace conference on the basis of its nationality. The message itself contains a set of claims which have remained central to the self-image of Irish nationalism ever since, but draw on beliefs which long predate this particular assertion:

> Naturally, the race, the language, the customs and traditions of Ireland are radically distinct from the English. Ireland is one of the most ancient nations in Europe, and she has preserved her national integrity, vigorous and intact, through seven centuries of foreign oppression; she has never relinquished her national rights, and throughout the long era of English usurpation she has in every generation defiantly proclaimed her inalienable right of nationhood down to her last glorious resort to arms in 1916.[1]

These sentiments remained central to Irish nationalist political culture thereafter; remaining largely unchallenged until the 1970s. The 1937 constitution contained the key elements of this assertion, especially in articles 2 and 3 only now amended within the terms of the Belfast Agreement of 10 April 1998.[2] During the 1970s a more critical approach to Irish history and nationalist claims emerged. This led in turn to considerable dispute concerning the origins, nature and objectives of Irish nationalism. Revisionist historians challenged many of the views traditionally associated with Irish nationalism, while traditional historians and publicists insisted on a reaffirmation of the orthodox position. This debate has been informed not only by the normal development of historical analysis, but more potently by the violence in Northern Ireland. This latter conflict has provided an emotive context for historical debate on the republican tradition, unionism and the justification of violence to achieve political ends. As a consequence, the historical debate has overlapped with a political

1

debate about means and ends which makes most historical analysis potentially controversial.[3]

Beliefs about the nation and nationality remain central to self-identity in the modern world, because nationalist belief systems provide the foundation blocs for modern political cultures. In turn, political cultures transmit values, beliefs and attitudes from one generation to the next. For over two hundred years, at least, nationalism, national identity and nationality have edged out alternative and competing forms of political association. Nationalism has become the main mobilising force for political identity at the end of the twentieth century. Nationalism is one of the main components in constructing modern political cultures, indeed it may be the most fundamental one available. The beliefs that nationalists assert need not be true in any objective sense, as in the case cited above for the historic origins of Irish nationalism, but they have to be believed by the people who identify themselves as nationalists. A distinction can be drawn between 'what is', what actually exists, and 'what the individual believes' which may or may not reflect this reality.[4] This describes what R. G. Collingwood called 'absolute presuppositions', those beliefs which people hold so dearly that without them they would be fundamentally different from what they are. The normal rules of falsification do not arise for those who hold such beliefs, for to question them is to undermine their function.[5] Nationalism is the most tenacious absolute presupposition in contemporary politics, but its power has been evident since the eighteenth, if not earlier.[6] In the twentieth century, nationalism and national identify have become the main source of the norms and values in most political systems. Even in multi-national states, such as the United Kingdom and Canada, increasingly the recognition of distinct national identities and loyalties are what matters to the legitimacy and stability of the state.[7] Moreover, there is a growing tension between the claims made by the state and those of the nation if the two are in conflict.

Irish nationalism and the British state

Ireland may not be the oldest nation in Europe in the sense invoked by nationalists, but it is a very early example of a sub-state nationalism within a multi-national state. The evolution of Irish nationalism within the British state, the form it took as a political movement and the subsequent political cleavages which characterised Ireland under the Union, highlight the dynamic content of nationalism as well as the contradictions which it brings with it. Moreover, the divisions opened up in the eighteenth century continue to have an impact on Irish politics in the late twentieth century, as can be seen in current responses to events in Northern Ireland.[8] In Ireland, as elsewhere, the nation contains within it a set of shared memories about its collective past. These are not random events, but recall specific historical events and confrontations. However, each nation remembers or imagines an event is a specific way. The way memory is retrieved by a community provides the building blocks for a political culture. What is unique in each case is how memories are constructed out of the actual past.[9]

The emergence of Irish nationalism as a fully formed political movement in the nineteenth century was, however, neither inevitable nor pre-destined. It was the outcome of a complex historical process, which could have led in other directions. It is one, but not the only, response to the expansion of the English (later the British) state and its drive to integrate the islands of Britain and Ireland politically, administratively and institutionally. In the process, the state encountered a number of sub-cultures across the two islands, each representing different values, loyalties and social organisation. While these sub-cultures were not equivalent to nations, in some cases they provided a substantive basis for them to evolve subsequently. Hugh Kearney has warned that:

> What became later national boundaries were extended backwards into a past where they had little or no relevance, with the consequence that earlier tribal or pre-national societies were lost from sight.[10]

While this has considerable appeal, there is also evidence to suggest that a self-conscious 'English', 'Scottish' and 'Irish' identity existed well before the modern period.[11] In the case of England and Scotland in the medieval period the existence of a state enhanced the sense of identity. However, the absence of a state does not in itself entail the absence of a national or ethnic consciousness. Irish and Welsh identity survived the absence of an independent state, while Scottish identity did not disappear after the Act of Union in 1707.[12]

The Irish case is even more problematic than that of Scotland and Wales. For the most part Scotland, Wales and later Protestant Ulster were integrated into the British state, becoming British in the sense established by Linda Colley. She excludes Ireland (both Catholic and Protestant) from her analysis on the grounds that:

> The invention of Britishness was so closely bound up with Protestantism, with war with France and with the acquisition of empire, that Ireland was never able or willing to play a satisfactory part in it. Its population was more Catholic than Protestant. It was the ideal jumping-off spot for a French invasion of Britain, and both its Catholic and its Protestant dissidents traditionally looked to France for aid.

Much of this is true, but it neglects the extent to which Irish Protestants successfully developed a British identity, almost identical to the one she describes

3

for England, Scotland and Wales.[13] Colley places considerable emphasis on those who were loyal and patriotic, but ignores the extent to which both Catholic and Protestant Irish opinion in the eighteenth century manifested these characteristics. Furthermore, the assumption that the great body of Irish opinion was dissident in the eighteenth century is misleading, as is the quick dismissal that the Catholic Irish could not, under any set of circumstances, have become British.[14]

A considerable amount depends on where the historical focus is concentrated. If it is on the seventeenth century, it is clear that Irish Catholics generally opposed the expansion of English power in Ireland, while during the nineteenth century opposition to the Union distinguished Irish Catholics from Protestants and became the foundation for Irish nationalism. However, the eighteenth century was a somewhat different matter, and there is some evidence that, despite the 1798 uprising, Catholic Ireland was overall loyal to the state, though this does not imply that it was British. The seventeenth century was a particularly vicious one for both islands: rebellion, war, revolution, restoration, attempted counter-revolution followed one another with destructive force.[15] The settlement that followed the Glorious Revolution had a differential impact on the two islands. Notwithstanding the differences between England, Scotland and Wales, William and Mary's success reinforced the dominance of protestantism, but also secured the basis for a new consensual relationship between the monarchy and parliament. The growth of stability in Britain was maintained by this consensus as well as by the political integration of the island.[16] In Ireland, the outcome was quite different. The Penal Laws were expressly anti-Catholic, though as recent research has demonstrated their application after the 1730s was not especially severe or sustained. Nevertheless, the Catholic Irish (and to some extent the Presbyterian Irish also) were an oppressed majority within Ireland and it was their religion which was the primary marker for this distinction. The extension of the British state into Ireland after 1690 is divisive rather than unifying, with the Protestant nature of the state alienating the defeated Catholic majority in Ireland. Outside the north-east, the Anglican ruling elite acted as the repressive apparatus of an alien culture. Church, state and property were controlled by this elite, one which not only excluded Catholics from power but at times actively repressed them through the Penal Laws. Even at the end of this period, at a time when relations between denominations had improved, the Irish Lord Chancellor admitted that: 'When we speak of the people of Ireland it is a melancholy truth that we do not speak of the great body of the people'.[17]

Though the Presbyterian majority in the north-east had a more 'liberal' view of Catholics at times, a deep suspicion existed between the two denominations despite a growing recognition that reform of the relationships was required.[18] The reforms of the late eighteenth century met some of the complaints frequently made by Catholics, but did not resolve the question of iden-

4

tity in Ireland. Among the possible options available between 1760 and 1830, some appear more realistic than others do. One possibility was that the three Irish religious sub-cultures would become British as happened in Scotland and Wales. This would have allowed each sub-group to retain traditional features unique to itself (language, law or religion), but accept a notion of Britishness which would allow all to share in that identity. However, because the Irish did not become British does not mean that they could not have, in fact a significant proportion of those living in Ireland did become British after the Union in a fashion similar to that of Scotland and Wales. At the very least, accommodation was possible between the Catholic aristocracy, the Catholic church in Ireland and sections of the Catholic middle class and more inclusive concepts of Britishness. The moderate and constitutional reformism of mainstream Catholic opinion was maintained into the first decade of the nineteenth century, was noted by Castlereagh in 1801 and reinforced by the public statements and actions of the Catholic hierarchy throughout the period. It is possible that if the British political establishment had acted to relieve Catholics further after the Act of Union, as was expected by most Catholics, this would have generated a quite different situation.[19] The King's refusal to concede Catholic emancipation in 1801 led to the resignation of Pitt, Cornwallis and Castlereagh, though in the short term Catholic opinion remained optimistic that a British government would concede the political demands. Nor can the King's behaviour be taken in isolation from the popular basis of anti-Catholicism in Britain. If opposition had been restricted to the King and his immediate circle, it would have been possible for a politician with Pitt's ability to overcome these reservations.[20] The quarter century after 1800 was crucial because during this time new identities were employed to give force to new forms of mobilisation in Ireland, with long term consequences. Nor was this confined to Ireland, similar developments occur throughout Europe.[21]

If the Protestant nature of the British state in 1800 undermined the possibility of a British identity imprinting itself upon the Catholic Irish, the appeal to a new Irish identity also failed. The best known expression of this view was given by Wolf Tone, who in 1791 argued that Catholic, Protestant and Dissenter had the means to forge a new national identity in Ireland, one which excluded both the British state and British identity from Ireland. Tone's argument is of interest because it has remained a benchmark claim of every generation of Irish republicans since that time. Tone assumed in 1791 that Enlightenment principles were spreading among the Irish, especially among middle class Catholics. He realised that in these circumstances the pope would have little influence on Catholic behaviour, and that the intolerant nature of Catholicism would not undermine the unity of the three religions. Nor was such a hope without foundation, but it was based on false premises. The type of secular, republican nationalism, which Tone promoted, was weak in Ireland, restricted to fairly unrepresentative groups within each religion.[22] An-

5

glican opinion was profoundly hostile to any changes in the status quo which guaranteed them ascendancy, believing that their minority tyranny over Catholics would be replaced by a majority tyranny exercised by Catholics. Anglicans in Ireland as a group in the 1790s choose to commit themselves to the British state in the belief that the armed apparatus of that state would uphold their privileged position. The record of the Anglican political class, despite honourable exceptions, was oppressive in respect of Catholics of all categories. In his well-known speech in opposition to the Act of Union, Daniel O'Connell declared that he would prefer the restoration of the Penal Laws if that would maintain an Irish parliament. Despite O'Connell's later prominence, this was not a representative view among Catholics at this time. Most of his co-religionists despised the use made of its political power by the Anglican political class, which controlled the Dublin parliament, and many welcomed the imposition of direct rule from London.[23]

They expected more, were disappointed when they did not get it, but this should not disguise the popular (pro-state if not pro-British) view among Catholics at the time. There was considerable hostility to the French Revolution among the Irish hierarchy, a view which was shared by many Catholics because of its anti-religious currents. Nor, despite earlier indications, were Presbyterians attracted to an alliance with Catholics to forge a new identity. Though this alliance had more potential than one including Anglicans, it foundered on the political weakness of the United Irishmen, sectarian rural politics in Ulster and the reservations which the Presbyterian middle class had to the French Revolution.[24] It is possible that a revolutionary elite could have broken the link with Britain with French aid, thus establishing an independent Republic. As such an outcome was dependent on French military strength, it is likely that Ireland would have suffered the same reversal as other radical alternatives in Europe once Britain and its allies had defeated the French. It is sometimes forgotten that after 1815, the United States was the only radical republic left intact after the revolutionary wars. It is unlikely that political control by republicans in Ireland would have survived the fall of Napoleon. However, what needs stressing is that the opportunity was available, if in weak form, but was not realised in the political context at the time. The fiasco of 1798 demonstrated the inherent instability of political unity in Ireland. Moreover, the influence of 1798 on Presbyterianism was limited, within a relatively short period of time that community adopted the Union as its own while internalising their historic connections with Scotland and Britain. This east-west channel of communication was of long standing in any event, surviving the north-south possibilities of the 1790s but reinforced by the new economics and politics of the early nineteenth century.[25] The Presbyterians have remained a puzzle for Irish nationalism ever since, but the claims made in the early nineteenth century reflected its distinct historic tradition, especially religious and theological traditions. Outside of Ulster, Anglican identity remained the identity of an oppressive elite, believing in its own innate superiority over a subordinate majority. Anglicans outside of Ulster remained dependent on British power to secure its position of privilege, and consequently remained weak and fearful. In contrast, both Anglicans and Presbyterians in Ulster developed a British identity during the nineteenth century, establishing a distinct frame of reference for themselves that allowed for a separate political evolution from either Irish Catholic or southern Irish Protestants.

O'Connell and Irish identity

In the fluid politics of the late eighteenth century, certain options were formulated but some paths were explored more successfully than others were. By the time of the Act of Union, Catholic Ireland faced a crucial dilemma concerning its future. Its political leadership, both clerical and lay, eschewed the secular republican nationalism of Tone, the United Irishmen and Emmet. Catholic opinion remained cautious and in the main loyal throughout the Napoleonic wars.[26] This loyalism, however, was not evidence for the emergence of Britishness among Irish Catholics, though there was potential for this development. If Irish Catholics had continued to accept the Union the potential for change was considerable, while the possibilities for political integration would have been enhanced. The opportunity to copper fasten Irish Catholics to the Union was quickly lost by the prevarication of the British government and by the behaviour of the Anglican ruling class in Ireland, which took the opportunity of war to enhance its political control and exclude Catholics from influence and power. Catholics, even aristocrats, were suspect in the eyes of the Irish ascendancy because of their Catholicism. Lord Fingal, perhaps the most loyal of the Catholic aristocracy, had to defend himself against charges of disloyalty when he was appointed a Justice of the Peace in 1803, while O'Connell highlighted the partisan nature of the Protestant judiciary on numerous occasions.[27]

The foreclosure of a united Irish identity or the accommodation of Irish Catholics with a British multi-national identity led the search for a distinct political identity into more traditional terrain. Nationalist mobilisation is often prompted by a belief that a dominant but ethnically different group within the state rejects the minority community. This is reinforced by the conviction that the group can run its own affairs separated from the larger group as well as by a fear that the group's distinctiveness would be eroded if it remained in the larger union.[28] Indeed, by the first decade of the nineteenth century each of the sub-cultures was edging towards redefining its identity in terms of historic cultural attachments. The crucial event in Irish Catholic politics between 1800 and 1829 is the mass mobilisation of Catholics around a set of political demands which, though couched in terms of equality, civil rights and toler-

7

ance, actually reflected a new self confidence in a distinct Irish identity. At the heart of this change stands Daniel O'Connell, a deeply ambivalent figure, child of the Enlightenment, successful self-made professional, chieftain and Catholic democrat. O'Connell rejected the radical republicanism of the French Revolution and the violence of the terror, yet he remained attached to the ideals of the Enlightenment. Though a moderate he was a separatist in terms of the politics of the early nineteenth century. This can be seen in this speech against the Union in 1800, but as late as 1810 he could still express a political philosophy quite close to that of Tone:

> The Protestant alone could not expect to liberate his country – the Roman Catholic alone could not do it – neither could the Presbyterian – but amalgamate the three in the Irishman, and the Union is repealed. Learn discretion from your enemies – they have crushed your country by fomenting religious discord – serve her by abandoning it for ever, I require no equivalent from you – whatever course you shall take, my mind is fixed – I trample under foot the Catholic claims, if they can interfere with Repeal.[29]

O'Connell believed that the British government was the cause of Ireland's problems and that once the Union was repealed Irish freedom would be assured. He was genuine in emphasising the primacy of repeal over Catholic objectives, as he was already a nationalist. Yet over the next thirty years O'Connell was to create a political movement acceptable to only one section of the Irish people, the Catholics, and did so by associating it with the aims of one denomination. The three main campaigns organised by O'Connell, the veto, Catholic emancipation and tithes, were Catholic in character. The aim was to gain concessions for Catholics, but also to give Irish Catholics political leverage and independence. The mass mobilisation which O'Connell sustained during these three campaigns and later in repeal, had a number of consequences for Irish politics. The appeal to democratic participation in the campaigns undermined the influence of the Catholic aristocracy on Catholic politics, providing a new middle class leadership. In turn, it brought the Catholic church to the centre of Irish politics. This may have been unintended, but the outcome was that the institutional and organisational influence of the church was harnessed to democratic mass mobilisation. This gave the movement a Catholic character, which was unusual in the politics of the time. It likewise associated denomination quite strongly with the growth of national identity. A Catholic democracy may have been a misnomer in other regions of Europe, but it had a significant impact on Ireland. The basis for Irish democracy and nationalism was laid at the same time and the two not only reacted on one another, but also drew on the emotional power of an oppressed people for its strength. Furthermore, much of this strength is based on the common identity of a shared oppression of Catholics. O'Connell's campaigns did more than this; they disciplined the inchoate 'mob' of people drawn to mass rallies, to the polling booths and to political action. This is not to claim that violence was absent from these campaigns, but O'Connell insisted that discipline was a prerequisite to political victory in the repeal movement and in his earlier campaigns. O'Connell's achievement in reducing violence, while orchestrating mass campaigns is extraordinary when one considers the weak transport infrastructure, the levels of literacy as well as the excitement generated by political mobilisation and sectarian animosity. The growth of the temperance movement and the decline in faction fighting also contributed to this pacification of Irish opinion.[30] The only comparable achievement that I am familiar with is that of Gandhi in the context of the Indian independence movement. Both figures recognised the need for the nation to be self-disciplined and both succeeded to a remarkable degree. Within a fairly short period of time, Irish Catholics had been transformed into a powerful political movement, well organised and with a purposeful political programme. It had coherent objectives expressed by a disciplined mass movement under the control of a self-conscious political elite.[31]

It is unlikely that O'Connell, or those close to him, had sectarian intentions, but in the context of mass mobilisation it is the denominational character of Irish life by the 1830s, which is most pronounced. Henry Inglis, travelling in Ireland in 1834 concluded that the main division was along religious lines:

> There is a Protestant and a Catholic inn – known by these names; the Protestant and Catholic coach, driven by, and supported by, persons of different persuasions; and the very children, playing or squabbling in the street are divided into sects.

He found this represented throughout the island, in urban as well as rural areas. Catholic and Protestant breweries existed in county Wicklow, while a riot followed a horse race when 'Protestant boy' beat 'Daniel O'Connell'.[32] O'Connell increasingly slipped into identifying Irishness with Catholicism:

> The combination of national action – all Catholic Ireland acting as one man – must necessarily have a powerful effect on the minds of the ministry and of the entire British nation. A people who can thus be brought together and by one impulse are too powerful to be neglected and too formidable to be long opposed.[33]

One of the by-products of this mass mobilisation was the alienation of most Protestants from Irish nationalism. As the character of Irish nationalism emerged in the 1820s and 1830s, its most pronounced feature to Protestants, was the close association between Catholicism and nationalism. But this does not entail that Irish nationalism was theocratic or controlled by the church, in fact what occurred was that the Catholic church in Ireland became an Irish church in nationalist terms. While retaining its institutional links with the uni-

9

versal church and the revived papacy, the Irish Catholic church recognised earlier than most that the continuing influence of Catholicism on a people relied upon maintaining and cementing links with the popular forces. This was unusual for most of the nineteenth century and attests to the intelligence of both nationalist leaders and the Catholic hierarchy that the alliance was maintained for so long without serious instability.[34]

By the 1840s, the extent of Irish nationalism as a political movement coincided with Catholicism in Ireland, whether this is measured in demographic terms, by election results or by the failure of O'Connell's repeal movement to attract any significant body of Protestant support in Ulster.[35] Although Ulster Protestant opinion was divided on many issues, on repeal and the Union it was already expressing self-confidence in its separateness from the rest of Ireland as well as its close identity with British identity. Moreover, O'Connell seems to have become more devotedly Catholic by the later stages of his life, at times conflating his personal, political and religious views on issues. In isolation, it is easy to detect these features, but the nature of the British state in Ireland, its sectarian officers as well as the unmitigated suspicion of any Catholic political aims pushed O'Connell closer to the Church and to his own denomination. During the last decade of his life it is more difficult to find evidence of O'Connell's belief that all the Irish could co-operate under repeal and his hostility to Young Ireland reflects the tension within the elderly politician. His parliamentary activities, though supportive of the liberal wing of British politics, had an inevitable denominational character to it. His correspondence contains considerable exchanges with members of the hierarchy emphasising the need for action on Catholic issues in parliament, but also reflects the concerns of the Catholic laity and clergy that though politically equal this remained but a formal right yet to be secured in comprehensive fashion.

In a letter to Paul Cullen in 1842 O'Connell provides a fascinating insight into his mature political mind. O'Connell's was concerned that the Pope would place the Vatican's diplomatic considerations before those of Irish nationalism, with consequent negative consequences for both nationalism and religion in Ireland. In this case O'Connell believed that the proclamation of Charles Acton as Cardinal for England and Wales would have political implications for Ireland. O'Connell condemned Acton's reference to the English, Irish and Scots as British, denying that Ireland could be considered British, 'For we are, thank heaven, a separate nation still and have preserved through ages of persecution – English persecution, political as well as religious – our separate existence.' He insisted on the distinctiveness of the Irish, placing considerable emphasis on the relationship between denomination and nationality. O'Connell argued that the Irish church should define its relationship with the papacy independently of any changes to the English Catholic church. He commended repeal to Cullen on the grounds that it 'would be an event of the most magnificent importance to Catholicity', but could not do so publicly on the grounds that it would increase British hostility to that project. However, he did provide sixteen reasons why the Catholic church should support repeal, the majority of which would secure church authority in Ireland over most of the matters that concerned it. O' Connell believed that the property confiscated from the Catholic church at the time of the Reformation would be returned to its original owners, while his views of protestantism, perhaps reflecting his interaction with them, was decidedly unflattering. Protestants in Ireland were, he affirmed, political rather than religious. Their involvement in religion was a mask for controlling resources and power:

> If the Union were repealed and the exclusive system abolished, the great mass of the Protestant community would with little delay melt into the overwhelming majority of the Irish nation. Protestantism would not survive the repeal ten years. Nothing but persecution would keep it alive and the Irish Catholics are too wise and too good to persecute.

Given the contents of this letter, it was wise of O'Connell to keep his thoughts private, because what he claimed within it was what concerned many Protestants in Ireland.[36] By this time O'Connell, at least at a personal level, had subsumed nationalism and religion under the one heading. But this also reflected the growing symbiosis between the two. The political imperatives of mass mobilisation facilitated this, as did the policy demands of his clerical supporters. But it also responded to the growing identification of religion and nationality among Irish Catholics, especially when Protestants were overwhelmingly hostile to O'Connell's movement and frequently took punitive action against his supporters. During his travels in Ireland in 1835, Alexis de Tocqueville was informed that landlords reorganised their estates to replace Catholic tenants with loyal Protestants in response to the political support given to O'Connell's movement. He also reported the intense hostility to O'Connell and to Catholics generally on the part of Protestant opinion as well as the reciprocal hostility of Catholics to Protestants. A fellow traveller in county Clare recounted in detail the persecutions and the lands confiscated in the past, while on another occasion particular Catholics were identified to de Tocqueville as members of families who had been deprived of their lands in the past.[37] Although sympathetic to the Catholic cause, de Tocqueville was not an uncritical observer. He repeated the view that the church did not wish to be part of the state, but wondered if the church might come to the view that the 'state would do well enough as part of the church.' [38] De Tocqueville's snapshot account is borne out by many other observers. What they report is a society deeply segmented along denominational lines, a church reviving after repression and now articulating self-confidence in respect of the Protestant church in Ireland and the British state. In addition, what is discernible is a people mobilised along democratic lines for the first time, while also identifying with the church as a national movement.[39] The growing overlap between religion and nationalism was a consequence of the nature of O'Connell's political campaigns, but it also reflected the growing polarisation of politics in Ireland. Although, Protestant Ulster evolved separately from the rest of Ireland in the nineteenth century, it shared in this polarisation for similar reasons. In contrast with Britain, liberal politics never dominated either side of the denominational divide, though liberalism had some political success and influence between 1850 and 1870. The primary reason for this is the growth of democratic politics, the heightened sense of national identity based on religion on both sides and the mutual incomprehension expressed by Catholics and Protestants.

The impact of the Famine on Irish nationalism

Nor did the Famine change these contours, indeed it provided a profound basis for reinforcing them. After 1850 Irish nationalism was more cohesive and assertive than before, reflecting a more homogeneous society. O'Connell's pacifism has often been criticised in the face of British government intransigence in the 1840s and again when faced with the Famine. Yet it was also realistic politics, there was no likelihood that a British government would concede any major changes in constitutional arrangements. This applied as much to the demands of the Chartist movement as to repeal. A delicate consensus had emerged within Britain between right and left, one feature of which was that reform was admissible in certain circumstances but root and branch constitutional change not so. In analysing Ireland in the early nineteenth century it is often possible to overlook the changing nature of British politics, which was also in considerable flux. This political compromise, though immensely significant in contributing to the emergence of liberal Britain in the 1860s, was based on a delicate balance between reformists and conservatives in Britain. The new consensus established by Peel and the Whigs excluded the reactionary alternative, which a majority of the Conservative party wanted, but also the root and branch reform desired by radicals. Not only did this preclude major innovation, but it also intensified the focus of British governments on British issues. This consensus was maintained for over thirty years and only began to dissolve during the 1860s.[40]

The actions of Young Ireland in 1848 have often been cited in opposition to O'Connell and constitutionalism, but while violence in the circumstances may have been noble in the light of political circumstances it was fruitless. We have few enough examples at this time for successful secessions by national groups. Those that were successful, such as Belgium and Greece, were achieved due to exceptional circumstances and with the support of the major European powers. There was little likelihood that such circumstances would prevail in Ireland, nor would such a threat have been allowed to upset the balance of power in Europe. Throughout the nineteenth century, Britain retained the capacity and the will to repress secessionist movements within the Empire. In contrast to the physical force tradition in Irish politics, the constitutional alternative developed by O'Connell, and maintained by most nationalist politicians thereafter, was the strategy most likely to achieve the objectives of Irish nationalism.[41] His emphasis on national unity, on the use of mass mobilisation to achieve constitutional aims peacefully and his insistence on the separateness of Ireland from Britain have been key motifs in Irish nationalism ever since. The Catholic church and the Catholic middle classes provide little evidence that they favoured a revolutionary alternative, despite Young Ireland and the Fenians. This is not to deny that the Fenians had popular support, but it was limited and short lived and constitutional options retained the overwhelming support of Irish nationalists. The Famine consolidated the constitutional forces in Irish politics, providing the means for furthering the aims of Irish nationalism within the British state over the next seventy years. Two factors facilitated this. The first was the changing nature of the British state and the inclusion of Ireland in its democratisation process. In contrast to the colonies or the white dominions, Ireland was fully involved in the political modernisation of the United Kingdom of Britain and Ireland in the nineteenth century. It became increasingly possible to formulate nationalist political programmes and to express them in the Imperial Parliament. The second feature was that the Famine changed the nature of Irish nationalist politics. The pre-Famine tensions between Catholics with property and those without was dissolved by the death and emigration of a significant section of landless labourers and cottiers. In its place a confrontation between a Catholic tenant farming majority and a Protestant land owning class came to define the politics of the second half of the century, a less complex cleavage system than previously. In political terms, the Famine demonstrated to Catholic Ireland that they were not British. It is not necessary to claim that the British state's intention during the Famine were malign or genocidal, to accept that there was a degree of neglect on the part of the state. It is true that the crisis in Ireland was immense, but if such a crisis had been faced in Britain the response would have been more adequate. A state is more likely to be positive in response to Famine or other disasters if those suffering share a common identity. When that is not the case, the officials involved treat the issue as one of a number of pressing problems. Britain and Europe between 1845 and 1850 were in turmoil, consequently Ireland was just one, albeit an increasingly serious one, of a number of problems pressing on British officials. What Irish nationalists could do subsequently was blame Britain for its lack of concern at the plight of the Irish and draw the logical nationalist conclusion.[42]

The Famine has frequently been described as a watershed in Irish history, but it may be more accurate to see it as a catalyst. Whether rightly or wrongly Irish nationalists blamed Britain for the catastrophe, insisting that the event demonstrated the uncaring nature of the state. It confirmed for Irish nationalists that they would be better looking after themselves, which reinforced the nationalist appeal. Irish nationalism was in a more propitious position after the Famine. While nationalist politics had been destabilised by the crisis, this had not lead to a weakening of nationalism itself. The new social structure which grew out of the reorganisation of Irish society and its economy during the 1860s was dominated by those groups which had been central to the evolution of nationalism in the first half of the nineteenth century. This new society was more uniformly Catholic, English speaking and middle class than the society that preceded it. Whereas, there had been serious competition for power and resources within the Catholic community in pre-Famine Ireland, the characteristic feature of post famine conflict was competition between the Catholic-nationalist community on the one hand and the British state and Irish landlordism on the other. This reconfiguring was possible because of the virtual disappearance of subsistence farming and the death or dispersal of the cottier and labouring classes in rural Ireland. The demographic toll is but one aspect of the story, more important was the enhanced social weight of the (relatively) prosperous Catholic middle class in town and country, a group that has a tremendous political social influence on post-Famine Ireland.[43] The institution that benefited most from the new circumstances was the Catholic church, which embarked on a radical re-organisation under the leadership of Paul Cullen, who in addition becomes Ireland's first cardinal. This achieved one of the objectives, which O'Connell believed central to avoiding English control of Irish church affairs. The 'Romanisation' of the Irish church was an important feature of this process, involving a 'devotional revolution' which provided an institutional basis for securing the influence of the church for the next 100 years or more.[44] A bourgeois sensibility prevailed in political, economic and social life, achieving hegemonic influence with the formation of the Home Rule Party and the Land League.

Two other forces affected Ireland at this time. The first was the effective integration of the island into the UK state at a political level, even though there was some ambiguity at the institutional level. Though integrated into the state, Ireland was not treated in the same fashion as Scotland and Wales. However, Ireland shared in the liberalisation of the British state as well as its democratisation. Without both of these changes it would be more difficult to have had the disestablishment of the Church of Ireland, the introduction of the Home Rule bills or indeed the resolution of the land conflict on terms favourable to the Irish tenants. The 1851 religious census confirmed that Ireland was the predominantly Catholic region of the UK. Catholics might be a minority in the state, but they were clearly a majority within the island. This numerical majority was turned into an electoral majority as the franchise was extended during the second half of the century. In the context of Ireland, the argument for reform on democratic grounds was unassailable after 1851, but that in itself would not guarantee change. The British state may have become less coercive than its continental counterparts after 1848, but a significant body of opinion remained authoritarian into the 1850s. The emergence of the Liberal party in 1859 resolved the problem for the left, whereas the extension of the franchise in 1867 resolved it for the right.[45] It was only with the liberalisation of the British state (or perhaps more accurately its political system) that reform in Ireland on democratic grounds becomes a possibility. A liberal state may ignore the democratic will expressed through elections, but it does so by endangering its liberalism. This proved a major dilemma for the British state, one that was only partly resolved in 1922 with partition. As a minority within the British state, Irish Catholics could demand reform and relief, while as a majority within Ireland it could demand the recognition of its democratic and national claims.

In a European context, Ireland was unusual. Catholic Ireland was democratic, but was probably less liberal than most other UK regions. More importantly, while Ireland democratised, it did so in a fashion distinct from Britain. It is possible to exaggerate the extent of secularisation among the British public during the second half of the nineteenth century, but there is little disagreement that the society became more tolerant and pluralistic, while some of the state's institutions became non-denominational if not secular. In Britain, liberalism enhanced toleration, pluralism and secularism.[46] In Ireland, democratisation enhanced the denominational basis of political conflict, despite the strong presence of the Liberal and Conservative parties during the 1850s and 1860s. Electoral mobilisation accentuated the differences between religions, as a consequence liberalisation as a social process remained weak. The trends already detectable before the Famine were maintained and in some cases enhanced. The restoration of the Catholic diocesan system in England and Wales divided opinion in Ireland along denominational lines, as did the successive conflicts over education. The tenant right movement, a potential basis for co-operation between Catholics and Protestants, foundered in part because of the different political assumptions of the denominations. The Catholic Defence Association, the 'Irish Brigade' in parliament and the National Association contributed to the growing denominational cleavage in political terms in Ireland. While not all political issues divided Catholics and Protestants, the tendency was for this to become the predominant feature of political behaviour. An issue, such as the unification of Italy, could and did divide opinion clearly along denominational lines. In contrast to most European states, the democratisation of Irish politics did not weaken the close relationship between church and people. This was of particular importance for Irish nationalism, because the papacy and in many cases the national hierarchies elsewhere remained hostile to popular politics and to nationalist movements in particular. The Catholic church in Ireland remained a popular one, one that maintained an effective alliance with popular nationalist forces. This relationship was of fundamental importance in securing the democratic foundations of Irish nationalism during the second half of the nineteenth century, neutralising the physical force tradition in Irish politics and underwriting the almost symbiotic identity between religion and nationalism in the Irish case. The other impact of this identity was to further divide the island along denominational lines and to give a religious flavour to the politics of both nationalism and unionism. Both nationalism and unionism contribute to this outcome, cementing religious identity with that of political behaviour, a phenomenon not unique to Ireland.[47]

Assessing these developments, Lee concluded that 'southern Ireland modernised probably as quickly as any other western European society during this period.' He contrasts this with Belfast, which he considers, fails to achieve this breakthrough; 'rapidly industrialising, yet doggedly defying the pressures of the modernisation process.'[48] There are considerable difficulties with this analysis. In the first place Lee does not compare like with like. Southern Ireland is modern because it became a commercial and market led society, whereas Belfast did not do so because of its sectarian character. The connection between economic change, which occurred in both areas, and political behaviour is in any case causally weak and requires further demonstration. If Belfast (and Northern Ireland) is denied the term modern because of its political divisions, the same could be applied to Glasgow and Liverpool. Historians have systematically underestimated indeed the extent of sectarian politics in such modern economies as Germany, the United States and England. In much the same way, if one wished, southern Ireland could in comparative terms and on the basis of its political behaviour be considered non-modern. There is a more parsimonious approach, which allows for a multi-layered analysis. At the economic level, it can be claimed that Ireland modernised in response to the industrial revolution, but that north and south did so in different ways. One industrialised and integrated into the British market economy in much the same way as Glasgow or Liverpool, the other did so in response to the demand for agricultural products for an expanding urban market in Britain, as did the Netherlands and Denmark at the same time. At the political level, there is no causal relationship between economic change and the form which political behaviour takes. Why should sectarian politics predominate in one area and not in another, why nationalism in one case and integration in another? The answer, it seems to me is associated with notions of identity rather than economic change; though clearly the nature of economic change does provide an environment where particular approaches are worked out.

What is clear is that modernisation, if it involves more than economic change, is never simple and the consequences of modernisation in social, religious and political terms is extremely complex and cannot be restricted to a binary relationship of cause and effect. This is evidently the case when modernity is associated with the Weberian concepts of rationality, urbanisation, secularisation and industrialisation.[49] It is possible for an economy to modernise, while the society retains traditional norms and values, indeed brings these to the core of the social meaning through nationalism. The growth of nationalism in the nineteenth century was not, as some writers suggest, a product of modernity, but a response to the chaos of socio-economic and political change. The rationalist, legal universalist basis of the Enlightenment rests uneasily with the emotional, particularist and organic appeals of nationalism. The former serves the state and the market driven economy, whereas the latter defends the specific, the traditional and the local. In this preservative sense, nationalism is conservative in that it preserves aspects of a society, which is threatened by change and universalism. It is possible to confuse the ideas of nationalism, especially those associated with the French Revolution, with the practise. The secular republican ideal may appear radical, but this is more a product of its destructive power and its willingness to use mass violence to achieve its ends than an inherent radicalism. Nationalism appealed in the nineteenth century because it restructures traditional societies to make them fit to deal with the onset of modernity. Even if a modern secular republican nationalism is considered a possibility, for the most part nationalism in the nineteenth century reflected other and usually more traditional modes of behaviour and belief systems.[50]

As an early version of a nationalism, which was both modern and traditional, but not secular, Irish nationalism (and unionism) is of some significance. The denominational character of Irish nationalism has frequently been identified, though often denied by Irish nationalism. The fact that virtually all Irish nationalists are Catholics is taken to be a coincidence, which has no connection with the political form the movement takes according to Irish nationalist apologists. The implicit logic of this view is that Protestants can with but a little effort be Irish nationalists. Their refusal to be involved can then be attributed to false consciousness, bribery or bigotry. Yet, both historical developments within Ireland as well as the character of the different religions lead to political outcomes, which were never accepted by Irish nationalism. From O'Connell to de Valera and up to the present day, Irish nationalism whether constitutional or militaristic has been united in denying that unionists constitute a distinct and separate identity within Ireland. If nationalism is the determining factor in Irish Catholic political culture what weight should be given to the Catholic church? With very rare instances the relationship between church and nationalism in Ireland has been an intimate one. The controversy over Parnell notwithstanding, Ireland appears remarkably free from anti-clericalism from O'Connell to de Valera. This outcome was contingent on a number of factors, not an inevitable product of the nation's piety. The nation was pious because the relationship between church and nation remained one of intimacy which both parties had to work hard to sustain.

This relationship prevented Ireland from secularising, as was the case in Britain. Secularism is a difficult concept to define, but it is clear that from the beginning of the nineteenth century a process was emerging, 'by which sectors of society and culture are removed from the domination of religious institutions and symbols'. It does not necessarily imply that people cease to be religious but it does mean that the church as an institution ceases to retain individuals as members while its control over areas of policy and certain sectors of society weakened appreciable.[51] If this process was occurring in some regions of Europe during the second half of the nineteenth century, the very opposite was happening in Ireland. Here, religious identification retained its importance while the Catholic church successfully extended its influence and its control over education, medicine and society. In whatever way one measures the process, between the Famine and 1914 nationalist Ireland became more Catholic. Churches were built, education brought under religious control and there was a rapid increase in the numbers entering religious orders.[52]

At the heart of this process stands Paul Cullen, probably the most influential clerical figure in Irish history. In some respects, he is a paradoxical figure. Sent to Ireland by Pius IX to reorganise the church, he remained close to the Pope playing an active role in the Papal defensive war against modernity, which culminated in the Vatican Council of 1869. But he was also of crucial importance in the evolution of Irish politics after the Famine frequently influencing the choices of lay political leaders. As the scourge of the Fenians he is remembered with hostility by radical republicans, yet he remained a nationalist throughout his life. Some of the paradoxes are apparent in the overlap between his role in the universal church and his position at the centre of Irish Catholicism. While Cullen defended the papacy actively, he is sometimes take to be a liberal. His advocacy of a separation of church and state, of toleration as well as his support for the Liberal party seems to place him among the liberal Catholics condemned by the Pope. The Syllabus of Errors condemned *inter alia* religious toleration, liberalism and the separation of church and state. Yet it is mistaken to conclude from this that Cullen and the Irish church were liberals in the sense defined by John Stuart Mill or generally accepted in Europe at the time. When the Liberal party criticised the Pope or Vatican policy, Cullen was quick to condemn them, and was quite dismissive of Gladstone on this account. He continuously condemned mixed education and reiterated the Church's opposition to the so-called 'godless' colleges. Moreover, Cullen was prepared to explicitly endorse the Syllabus of Errors on specific topics.[53] On education, on the Church of Ireland and on the role of the Vatican Cullen was orthodox and conservative, yet on political matters there is some doubt. During the 1868 election Cullen advised Catholics to vote against 'the orange ascendancy', while a little later he described his own preferences in the election:

> Dr Corrigan the Liberal candidate, formerly a great advocate of mixed educa-
> tion, denounced the Queen's College most vehemently and declared for Catho-
> lic education. Pim the Quaker went on in the same strain. The Tories declared
> for the Protestant Church and mixed education ... I voted [today] for Pim and
> Corrigan. I suppose no cardinal ever voted for a Quaker before. The contest is
> very close and it is impossible to know who will win. ... If the Liberals get a
> large majority, the poor [established] Church will soon count her last days.[54]

Does this make Cullen a liberal? It certainly makes him a supporter of the
Liberal party on this and other occasions, but for what reasons? In the first
place, the electorate was quite limited but liberal candidates were in a position
to defeat conservatives. Furthermore, the liberal candidates accepted the need
for disestablishment, a major objective for Cullen. He had a keen political
sense, both in respect of Rome and of Irish politics. His alliance with the
Liberal party was based on the view that this was the best method of achieving the political objectives of both the church and the nation. If this was rather
an unorthodox position for a cardinal to take, it was a realistic one for an Irish
cleric to adopt at this time. Cullen's theological conservatism protected him
in Rome, allowing him flexibility in his dealings with Britain. This approach
was generally maintained by his successors. Cullen was illiberal in religious
matters, but his political views were more complex. Though conservative he
was not theocratic and accepted the limited nature of representative government without being an enthusiast for democracy. Cullen's attitude to the clergy's involvement in politics was a cautious one, but one which clearly
recognised that Irish priests would also be nationalists.[55] This approach was
adopted also by his successors, presupposing the existence of a national identity distinct from the state. Matters distinct from the church should normally
be left to the politicians and the will of the people. It is also possible that
Cullen recognised, as de Tocqueville had in his examination of the position of
Catholics in the United States, that democracy would aid rather than hinder
the advance of Catholicism:

> The Catholics are in a minority, and it is important for them that all rights be
> respected so that they can be sure to enjoy their own in freedom. For these two
> reasons they are led, perhaps in spite of themselves, towards political doctrines
> which, maybe, they would adopt with less zeal were they rich and predomi-
> nant.[56]

Although this recognition was implicit rather than explicit in Ireland, Cullen's
activities and those of his successors contributed to the further democratisation of Irish politics. By the time the franchise was again extended in 1884
(after Cullen's death) the new mass electorate had before it powerful influences; an Irish nationalist party, a tradition of constitutional action and a vital
national church extending into all aspects of Irish social life.[57]

Home rule and the limits of constitutional politics

By the time the Home Rule party was formed in 1874, the main features of Irish nationalism had been established. Among its characteristics were a belief in the unity of Ireland politically and culturally, its distinctiveness from Britain, a complex identification between the Catholic church and nationalist politics, a reluctance to embrace the social attributes of modernity and a determination to wrest control from the Protestant elite in Ireland. Increasingly, the political and institutional relationship between Britain and Ireland was considered an oppressive one by nationalists, a view reinforced by the Land War and the campaign for Home Rule. At the centre of conflict in Ireland up to 1922, and thereafter in Northern Ireland, has been religion. This formed the primary political cleavage within the island for both nationalist and unionists, voting patterns tended to follow those of denomination as was also the case in a number of European states.[58] Both nationalist and unionist political culture were linked inexorably with denomination. For Protestants, whether Anglican or Presbyterian, religion provided a link to the British majority while also assuring their distinctiveness from the Catholic Irish. Catholicism also provided Irish nationalism with a distinctive feature within the UK, setting them apart from their Protestant counterparts. It also provided the leverage to separate Ireland from the UK, a feature that was reinforced by historical memory, the land struggle and a distinct cultural evolution. George Boyce has asked why Irish MPs, even before mass politics of the 1880s, did not, 'fulfil the same role as Scottish politicians and simply act as some sort of geographical expression of political representation.' In large part the answer to this lay in the unique relationship which existed between religion and politics in Ireland, especially the way in which religion became the dividing line between the political communities.[59]

However, what gave Irish nationalism its cutting edge in the 1880s was the expansion of the electorate, the successful mobilisation of this electorate in support of the Home Rule party and the identification of this mass political movement with Catholicism, self-determination and possession of the land. This changed the focus of British politics as well as Irish. The Liberal party found it increasingly difficult to ignore the democratically expressed demands of the majority of Irish people. This is not to claim that the British state or indeed even the Liberal party, as can be seen in the case of Chamberlain's defection in 1886, was enthusiastic for change in Ireland. But, without a reversion to autocratic repression the state had to come to terms with the main demands of Irish nationalism. The defeat of the first home rule bill simply postponed the issues, as can be appreciated from the return of the issue again in 1892 and 1912. Despite the divisions prompted by the Parnell split, Irish nationalism showed little sign of weakening during the following decades. Indeed the 1898 reform of local government extended nationalist political influence significantly by gaining control of the sub-national administrative structure outside of Protestant Ulster. Likewise, the Wyndham Land Act (1903) destroyed the social influence of the Protestant landlord class in much the same way as the reform of local government had done so in political terms. Furthermore, the agreement to establish the National University of Ireland in 1908 reflected the expanding political and social influence of nationalism. A similar pattern can also be identified within Unionism in northern Ireland, but less attention has been paid to that.

By 1910, all but one of the main demands made by Irish nationalism had been realised. The land question had been resolved to the satisfaction of most, if not all, of those involved in the conflict. The (re) possession of the land by Catholic tenants was as much a political act as an economic one. The role of the Catholic church in the educational system and in medicine had been reinforced by this time, confirming the essentially denominational basis of education and health in Ireland. These concessions also reflected the great social power accumulated by the church during the latter half of the nineteenth century, a power sustained and endorsed by the nationalist political culture. In political terms Irish nationalists had also gained much. The advance of popular politics after the second and third reform acts confirmed electorally that Catholic Ireland was in broad measure also nationalist Ireland. The one demand which remained elusive by 1910 was home rule, though nationalists were optimistic after the second general election in 1910 that this goal was now within their reach.

The confrontation over home rule between 1911 and 1914 established the context for the militarisation of Irish politics, for 1916 and eventually for partition itself. This is not to say that each of these outcomes was inevitable, but increasingly the polarisation of opinion within nationalist and unionist Ireland reduced the possibility of a constitutional outcome. Nationalist Ireland in the immediate pre-1914 decades was a self-assured society, confident in its superiority over the British and over Irish unionism. Yet Irish unionism was the weak link in the Irish nationalist political strategy. The success of Irish nationalist politics after 1869 in undermining the economic, political and religious dominance of Irish unionism in the south of the country disguised the continuing strength of unionism in Ulster. Irish nationalists assumed that unionism (north and south) would accept the parliamentary outcome in respect of home rule. Yet they also choose to ignore the consistent opposition of Ulster unionism to it[60] Irish nationalists knew virtually nothing about unionism outside Catholic Ireland, and based its view of Ulster unionism on its experiences of dealing with the southern version of the political form. The threat of home rule after 1910 to the Union generated two responses on the part of Irish unionism. Southern unionists eventually sought the most favourable terms possible within a home rule Ireland, whereas Ulster unionists insisted on its right to opt out of any settlement. Ironically, the Ulster unionists used many of the same arguments against Irish nationalists as the nationalists had used against the British and the Union. Ulster unionism appears in response to home rule as a self assured and confident political community, asserting its right to determine its own future. In this both Ulster unionism and Irish nationalism were similar.

The confrontation between unionism and nationalism over home rule was in essence a conflict over national identity and the extent to which the territorial aspects of home rule should reflect each political community. If Irish nationalism had accepted partition at any time up to 1914, then 1916 and the violence that followed the end of the war might have been avoided. Southern Irish unionists accepted that the new institutional arrangements would reflect democratic reality. Yet Irish nationalists would not accept that the same criteria should apply in northern Ireland where nationalists were in the minority. All Irish nationalists were insistent that the democratic measure should be the island of Ireland and that simple majorities should define the political outcome. This is but one example of a central feature of secessionist movements in the twentieth century. Irish nationalists argued that all those who lived on the island were members of the Irish nation, refusing to acknowledge the counter-argument that Ulster unionists also constituted a distinct national grouping within the island.[61] It is this basic difference which led to the crisis in Irish politics after 1911, to the organisation of the UVF and the Irish Volunteers and subsequently to the 1916 rising. The Ulster unionists decision to mobilise against home rule has been the recourse of all nationalist groups concerned by the threat to their identity by another (larger numerically) national group.[62] This, in turn, led Irish nationalist to eschew constitutional politics before 1914 and to move decisively towards coercion. home rule could have been achieved constitutionally without Ulster, but a united home rule Ireland could only have been achieved through coercion. It is sometimes remarked that Ulster unionism destroyed constitutional politics in Ireland by organising a paramilitary organisation to challenge the will of the majority in parliament. This is in part true, but ignores the autonomous nature of the nation. Ulster Unionism certainly withdrew consent from the British parliament on the grounds that this institution could not legislate away the rights of British people in Ireland. When parliament appeared to be ignoring them, Ulster unionists did what all nationalists have done, rejected the authority of the state and organised politically to deny that authority within its territory. But Irish nationalism did precisely the same. Irish nationalism never gave unqualified consent to British parliamentary majorities; they did so when that majority favoured the political objectives of the Irish nation but not when they did not concur.[63]

By 1914 neither nationalism nor unionism were giving consent to Parliamentary majorities in the UK parliament, especially if the majority did not agree with what nationalism or unionism wanted. It was a zero-sum game. If

22

there was a parliamentary majority for a united Ireland, the unionists would reject it, while if partition was supported by a majority this would be unacceptable to nationalists. The absence of consensus is striking and it is what has been missing in most national conflicts ever since. With the notable, but exceptional, case of Norway and Sweden national differences and secession are extremely difficult to resolve. In the case of Norway and Sweden, it was a close run thing to achieve consensus.[64] Elsewhere, violence has more often been the outcome. The reason for this is that consensus can only be achieved when all participants agree on notions of political order. Majorities can only be invoked when there is agreement on political order, authority and legitimacy. If this is achieved and a consensus on the issues arrived at, then the majorities can be utilised to achieve agreed outcomes. Those in a minority accept outcomes because they have previously agreed to the arrangements that establish political order. Consensual politics is based on the possibility of agreement, not on the absence of conflict. But conflict can be resolved in a consensual context because all parties accept the rules of the political game, giving their consent to outcomes which they might vote against – for example a general election or the devolution referendum in Scotland. Ireland in 1914 did not have consensus, because two political communities existed which were internally consensual but not in agreement with the other. Indeed, each community's concept of political order was in conflict with the other over the very notion of what constituted the national community. 'Normal' political competition is not possible in these circumstances and consequently the willingness to withdraw consent from parliamentary institutions and the possible use of violence is enhanced.[65]

The first world war postponed the political conflict between nationalists and unionists, but the response of both confirmed the existence of two distinct communities. Both participated in the war to further their national ends. Within nationalism, there was disagreement with a small minority rejecting the pro-war position of Redmond and the Irish Parliamentary Party. Yet nationalist support for the war remained contingent on the state delivering home rule. Until 1916, Redmond's position remained the dominant one, though there was growing pressure on the Parliamentary Party by then.[66] The 1916 rebellion undermined the fragile consensus within nationalism, though it did not at first lead to the collapse of constitutional politics. Irish nationalists generally opposed the rising, but a significant body of opinion admired the bravery of those who fought. The failure to achieve a home rule settlement in 1916 and the threat of partition contributed to the alienation of former supporters of Redmond's party. What happened in 1917 is not an explicit endorsement of the 1916 Rising, but a shift within electoral politics towards the reorganised Sinn Fein. The electoral victories of 1917 indicated that a significant proportion of constitutional opinion was now prepared to support a more radical electoral challenge to the British state in Ireland. Sinn Fein's successes in

1917 and 1918 were based on attracting voters on the existing (restricted electoral register, indicating that even without the expansion of the electorate in 1918 a Sinn Fein victory at the general election might well have occurred. Indeed, the internal consensus shifted decidedly in 1918, from one where the Irish Parliamentary Party received overwhelming support from the nation to one where there was effective competition. Competitive politics was only permissible where nationalism was dominant; in Northern Ireland an election pact was brokered by the Catholic church between Sinn Fein and the Parliamentary Party to prevent safe nationalist seats from going to unionists in the event of competition within nationalism. The Catholic church was faced with a very complex situation between 1916 and 1922, seeking to maintain the constitutional consensus while recognising that a new style of politics was on offer to nationalists. The price paid by Sinn Fein in 1917 and 1918 for, at the very least, benign neutrality on the part of the church was an acceptance of constitutional methods of political action. The political re-organisation of 1917, the central role in the anti-conscription campaign, the mobilisation of the vote for the general election, as well as the establishment of the First Dáil all fell within constitutionalism.

William O'Brien MP insisted in December 1917 that Sinn Fein was a constitutional party by this stage and in his opinion offered the best prospect for the future.[67] Yet the commitment of the Sinn Fein leadership to constitutional politics did not exclude a more militant assertion of nationalist demands than that expressed by Redmond. The demand for a republic, the abstentionist policy and the use of extra-parliamentary methods to challenge the British state marked a significant departure in the strategy of Irish nationalism. Sinn Fein's success in the 1918 election was an endorsement of this strategy. The general election of 1918 changed the leadership of Irish nationalism, giving the movement a mandate to negotiate secession from Britain. The refusal of the British state to acknowledge the right to self determination of Irish nationalism after the explicit support given to Sinn Fein's programme undermined what remaining legitimacy the British state had for many nationalists in Ireland and this gave nationalist military action during the War of Independence a degree of legitimacy not available in 1916 because the IRA leadership had the de facto, if not *de jure*, authority of the representative government of nationalist Ireland. In this context what mattered was not whether the British state considered the actions legitimate, but whether the nation did. The 1916 rising never received either the de facto or de jure legitimacy based on the electoral or political support of the nation, despite what the survivors claimed later. Nor did military action by the IRA receive uncritical support from the nationalist community. The hierarchy and the clergy were distinctly uneasy about the use of violence, as it was a break with the constitutional consensus, which had prevailed for over a century. In addition, public opinion was never fully reconciled to the violence and constrained the actions of the volunteers as a consequence. Yet, despite this both the church and public opinion were far more hostile to the actions of the British state than they were to those of the IRA.[68]

The nature of Irish nationalism between 1918 and 1921 imposed considerable constraints on the use of violence. The support base for Sinn Fein in 1918 was not an unadulterated republican or revolutionary majority. It consisted of former Redmondites as well as new voters, radicals and trade unionists, many of whom continued to value constitutional methods of politics. In addition, Sinn Fein had to return to the electorate for a further mandate on a number of occasions during the years of military action. These factors were recognised by the leadership, if not always by the active service units and the flying columns, which were frequently outside the control of any external authority.[69] What Sinn Fein supporters shared were their nationalism and a commitment to some form of self-government, many other issues divided them. Sinn Fein's strength was based on a successful strategy of integrating the various social strands within Irish nationalism into a single movement, a coalition that in fact held together until 1922. Only in Northern Ireland and there for special reasons was this consensus absent. Although the treaty settlement divided this coalition, the establishment of the Irish Free State marked the end of a significant period for Irish nationalism. Irish self-government had been achieved, even though it dissatisfied a significant minority. Partition created problems, which were to remain important for Irish nationalism until the 1990s. Most significant was the quick return to constitutional politics and the rule of law after 1922. The new government was able to impose its will on those who refused to recognise the state, with the support of a majority of public opinion. This was possible because of the strength of constitutional political culture in nationalist Ireland, but also because public opinion applied a different notion of legitimacy to its own state than that which had been used in respect of Britain. An Irish government could apply sanctions to its recalcitrant minority, which would have been seen as oppressive if applied by Britain. The effectiveness of this 'constitutional tradition' was such that the new state stabilised fairly quickly and even its most severe critics not only came to terms with it but provided its governments for most of the time after 1932.

References

1. *Message to the Free Nations of the World*, issued in Irish, English and French by Dáil Éireann, 21 January 1919, cited in D. Macardle, *The Irish Republic,* Corgi Books, London, 1968 (original edition 1937), pp. 850–51.
2. Nor is contemporary Ireland immune from these influences. The difficulty which Fianna Fáil has had in persuading its members to amend articles 2 and 3 of the 1937 constitution in the interests of the peace agreement in Northern Ireland provides some evidence of this, *Irish Times*, 16 April 1998.

3. F. Gallagher, *The Indivisible Island: The History of Partition in Ireland,* Gollancz, London 1957 is an expression of the official consensus and is a semi-official history used by the Department of External Affairs in negotiations with the United Kingdom after its publication. However, in many respects it was the last such uncritical approach to these questions. The most influential 'revisionist' history of Ireland is R. F. Foster, *Modern Ireland 1600–1972,* Allen Lane, London, 1988; see also the contributions to C. Brady (ed), *Interpreting Irish History: The Debate on Historical Revisionism,* Irish Academic Press, Dublin, 1994: a volume that provides an overview of opinion on this issue. The orthodoxy is reasserted by D. Fennell, 'Against Revisionism' and B. Bradshaw, 'Nationalism and Historical Scholarship in Modern Ireland', both reprinted in C. Brady, op.cit., pp. 181–216. In Irish politics these views are most readily held by members of Fianna Fáil, the Social Democratic and Labour Party and Sinn Fein, though members of other nationalist political parties also shore some if not all of the views. The Supreme Court decision in the McGimpsey case can be found in The Irish Law Reports 1990, volume 1, pp. 110–25.

4. S. Verba, 'Comparative Political Culture' in L.W. Pye and S.Verba (eds.), *Political Culture and Political Development,* Princeton University Press, Princeton, 1965, pp. 512–60, quotation at p. 516.

5. R. G. Collingwood, *An Essay on Metaphysics,* Clarendon, Oxford, 1940.

6. A. Heraclides, 'Ethnicity, secessionist conflict and the international society: towards normative paradigm shift' *Nations and Nationalism,* vol. 3, no. 4, pp. 493–520.

7. A. D. Smith, *National Identity,* Penguin, London, 1991; J.Hutchinson, *Modern Nationalism,* Fontana, London, 1994; M.Keating, 'Canada and Quebec: Two Nationalisms in the Global Age', *Scottish Affairs.* vol. 11, 1995, pp. 14–30.

8. I have examined the continuity of this conflict in B. Girvin, 'Nationalism and the Continuation of Political Violence in Ireland' in A. Heath, R. Breen and C. T. Whelan (eds.), *Ireland: North and South,* Oxford University Press, Oxford, forthcoming 1998.

9. The complexity of how the past is remembered can be seen in the way in which Oliver Cromwell is recalled in Ireland, England and the United States.

10. H. Kearney, *The British Isles: A History of Four Nations*, Cambridge University Press, Cambridge, 1989, p. 3.

11. P. Wormald, 'The Making of England' *History Today,* February 1995; D. Broun, 'When did Scotland Become Scotland', *History Today,* October 1996, pp. 16–21; *The Declaration of Arbroath* (1320) is often presented as evidence for nationalist consciousness in Scotland, a view rejected by C. J. Berry, 'Nations and Norms', *The Review of Politics,* vol. 43, 1981, pp. 75–87.

12. M. Lynch, *Scotland: A New History,* Pimlico, London, 1991, pp. 51–110.

13. L. Colley, *Britons: Forging the Nation 1707–1837*, Yale University Press, New Haven, 1992, pp. 8, 5.

14. D. Hempton, *Religion and Political Culture in Britain and Ireland,* Cambridge University Press, Cambridge, 1996, pp. 143–48; I. McBride, 'Ulster and the British Problem' in R. English and G. Walker (eds.), *Unionism in Modern Ireland*, Gill and Macmillan, Dublin, 1996, pp. 1–18.

15. J. Ohlmeyer (ed.), *Ireland from Independence to Occupation 1641–1660*, Cambridge University Press, Cambridge, 1994; B. Fitzpatrick, *Seventeenth-Century Ireland: The War of Religions,* Gill and Macmillan, Dublin, 1988.

16. L. Colley, op. cit., pp. 11–54; H.Kearney, op. cit., pp. 129–40.

17. Cited in W. Hinde, *Castlereagh,* London 1981, p. 21; J. Kelly, 'The Genesis of the "Protestant Ascendancy"', in G. O'Brien (ed.), *Parliament, Politics and People*, Gill and Macmillan, Dublin 1989, pp. 93–128; T. Bartlett, *The Fall and Rise of the Irish Nation: The Catholic Question 1690–1830*, Gill and Macmillan, Dublin, 1992, pp. 30–65; S. J. Connolly, *Religion, Law and Power: The Making of Protestant Ireland 1660–1760,* Oxford University Press, Oxford, 1992.

18. A. T. Q. Stewart, *A Deeper Silence: The Hidden Origins of the United Ireland Movement*, Faber and Faber, London, 1993.

19. This is discussed in detail in B. Girvin, 'The Act of Union, Nationalism and Religion: 1780–1850' in Jürgen Elvert, *Nordirland in Geschichte und Gegenwart/Northern Ireland – Past and Present*, Franz Steiner Verlag, Stuttgart, 1994, pp. 53–81.

20. B. Girvin, op. cit., for a discussion of this; T. Bartlett, op. cit., pp. 202–267; B. McDermott (ed.), *The Catholic Question in England and Ireland: The Papers of Denys Scully*, Dublin,1988.

21. M. Teich and R. Porter (eds.), *The National Question in Europe in Historical Context*, Cambridge University Press, Cambridge, 1993.

22. Wolf Tone, *An Argument on Behalf of the Catholics of Ireland*, BICO, Belfast, 1973, original edition 1791, pp. 25–6; M. Elliot, *Wolf Tone: Prophet of Irish Independence*, Yale University Press, New Haven, 1989; T. Bartlett, 'The Burden of the Present: Theobald Wolf Tone, Republican and Separatist', in Dickson, Keogh and Whelan, op. cit., pp. 1–14; The emphasis on continuity can be found in Padraig Pearse, 'Ghosts'.

23. Speech at the Catholic Meeting, Royal Exchange Hall, 13 January 1800, cited in John O'Connell (ed.), *The Life and Speeches of Daniel O'Connell, MP*, Dublin, 1846, two volumes, volume 1, pp. 22–3; Denys Scully, *An Irish Catholic's Advice to his Brethren*, Dublin, 1803, for a Catholic critique of the Irish parliament; Edmund Burke shared the deep suspicion of an Irish parliament controlled by Anglicans, see Conor Cruise O'Brien, *The Great Melody: A Thematic Biography of Edmund Burke*, Sinclair-Stevenson, London, 1992.

24. D. Miller, *Queen's Rebels*, Gill and Macmillan, Dublin, 1978; P. Brooke, *Ulster Presbyterianism*, Gill and Macmillan, Dublin, 1987; N. J. Curtin, *The United Irishmen: Popular Politics in Ulster and Dublin 1791–1798*, Clarendon, Oxford, 1994; D. Hempton, *Religion and Political Culture in Britain and Ireland: From Glorious Revolution to the Decline of Empire*, Cambridge University Press, Cambridge, 1996, pp. 93–116.

25. B. Walker, *Dancing to History's Tune: History, Myth and Politics in Ireland*, Institute of Irish Studies, Belfast, 1996, pp. 1–14; G. Walker, *Intimate Strangers: Political and Cultural Interaction Between Scotland and Ulster in Modern Times*, John Donald, Edinburgh, 1995, pp. 1–16.

26. A. Houston, *Daniel O'Connell: His Early Life and Journal, 1795–1802*, London, 1906; Denys Scully, *An Irish Catholic's Advice to his Brethren*, Dublin, 1803.

27. M. O'Connell, *The Correspondence of Daniel O'Connell*, 8 Volumes, Vol., 1, p. 299; *Memoirs and Correspondence of Viscount Castlereagh*, , vol. Iv, London, 1849, pp. 298–313.

28. S. Dion, 'The re-emergence of secessionism: lessons from Quebec', in A. Breton, G. Galeotti, P. Salmon and R. Wintrobe (eds.), *Nationalism and Rationality*, Cambridge University Press, Cambridge, 1995, pp. 116–42, for a discussion of these themes.

29. J. O'Connell, op. cit., vol. 1., pp. 34–52 for the speech.

30. Alexis De Tocqueville, *Journeys to England and Ireland*, edited by J. P. Mayer, Faber and Faber London,, 1958, pp. 118–96 for a contemporary description of Irish social and political life.

31. B. Girvin, 'Political Independence and Democratic Consolidation', in M. Holmes and D. Holmes (eds.), *Ireland and India*, Folens, Dublin, 1997, pp. 120–44; R. Kumar (ed.), *Essays on Gandhian Politics: The Rowlatt Satagraha of 1919*, Clarendon, Oxford, 1971; D. Dalton, *Mahatma Gandhi: Non-violent Power in Action*, Columbia University Press, New York, 1993).

32. H. D. Inglis, *A Journey Throughout Ireland During the Spring, Summer and Autumn of 1834*, London, 1834, 2 volumes, vol. 1, pp. 24–6, 343–5, 40.

33. O'Connell to Bishop Doyle, 29 December 1827, in Correspondence vol. III, pp. 372–3.

34. The Irish case can be usefully compared with that of Belgium and Poland where similar adjustments were taking place in the nineteenth century. I am also grateful to Hilda Faloon for discussing the liberal aspects of O'Connell with me.

35. Girvin, 'The Act of Union...' pp. 75–8 for a discussion.

36. O'Connell to Paul Cullen, 5 May 1842, in Maurice O'Connell (ed.), *The Correspondence of Daniel O'Connell*, vol. 7, 1841–1845, Blackwater Press, N.D., Dublin, pp. 155–61.

37. De Tocqueville, op. cit., pp. 141, 174–8.

38. Ibid., pp. 140, 181–2.

39. E. Burke, "The Irishman is no *lazzarone*': German travel writers in Ireland 1828–1850", *History Ireland*, vol. 5, no. 3, 1997, pp. 21–5.

40. B. Girvin, *The Right in the Twentieth Century*, Pinter, London, 1994, pp. 41–5.

41. A. J. Ward, *The Irish Constitutional Tradition: Responsible Government and Modern Ireland*, Irish Academic Press, Dublin, 1994, pp. 50–100.

42. The literature on the famine and its consequences is immense. For a representative sample of approaches see Cathal Póirtéir (ed.), *The Great Irish Famine*, RTE/Mercier, Cork, 1995. A contemporary approach to famine can be found in Amartya Sen, *Poverty and Famines: An Essay on Entitlement and Deprivation*, Oxford University Press, Oxford, 1981.

43. D. G.Boyce, *Nineteenth-Century Ireland: The Search for Stability*, Gill and Macmillan, Dublin, 1990, pp. 154–76.

44. T. Inglis, *Moral Monopoly: The Rise and Fall of the Catholic Church in Modern Ireland*, University College Dublin Press, Dublin, 1998, pp. 129–200; E. Larkin, *The Roman Catholic Church and the Creation of the Modern Irish State 1878–1886*, Gill and Macmillan, Dublin, 1975.

45. B. Girvin, *The Right in the Twentieth Century*, Pinter, London, 1994, pp. 44–5; B. Coleman, *Conservatism and the Conservative Party in Nineteenth Century Britain*, Edward Arnold, London, 1988.

46. O. Chadwick, *The Secularisation of the European Mind in the Nineteenth Century*, Cambridge University Press Cambridge, 1975; H. McLeod, *Religion and the People of Western Europe*, 1789–1970, Oxford University Press, Oxford, 1981.

47. This has been discussed by D. Martin, *A General Theory of Secularisation*, Basil Blackwell, 1978).

48. J. Lee, *The Modernisation of Irish Society 1848–1918*, Gill and Macmillan, Dublin, 1973, pp. 168, 52.

49. E. Gellner, *Plough, Sword and Book: The Structure of Human History*, Paladin, London, 1988, pp. 205–60.

50. R. Eatwell (ed.), *European Political Cultures Conflict or Convergence?*, Routledge, London, 1997; M. Teich and R. Porter, (eds.), *The National Question in Europe in Historical Context*, Cambridge University Press, Cambridge, 1993, for discussion and examples.

51. P. Berger, *The Social Reality of Religion*, Penguin, Harmondsworth, 1973, p. 113.

52. T. Inglis, op.cit., for a full discussion of this as applied to Ireland.

53. P. MacSuibhne, (ed.) *Paul Cullen and His Contemporaries*, Leinster Leader, 5 volumes, 1961–77,vol. 5, Naas, Co.Kildare, pp. 246, 16; *Freeman's Journal*, 31 January 1865 for Cullen's pastoral letter;

54. Cullen to Kirby, 18 November 1868 in P. MacSuibhne, op. cit., vol. 4., p. 243; K. T. Hoppen, *Elections, Politics and Society in Ireland, 1832–1885*, Oxford University Press, Oxford, 1984.

55. P. MacSuibhne, ibid., vol. 1., pp. 394–5 for a report of Cullen's view on this relationship; for a critical biography of Cullen see, D. Bowen, *Paul Cullen and the Shaping of Modern Irish Catholicism*, Gill and Macmillan, Dublin, 1883, pp. 245–81.

56. Alexis de Tocqueville, *Democracy in America*, Doubleday, Garden City, New York, 1969, pp. 288–9; 442–49.

57. These issues are discussed by E. Larkin, op. cit., and T. Inglis, op. cit.
58. K.T.Hoppen, op. cit., for an evaluation; Brian Walker, 'The 1885 and 1886 General Elections – A Milestone in Irish History' in B. Walker, *Dancing to History's Tune: History, Myth and Politics in Ireland,* Institute of Irish Studies, Belfast, 1996, pp. 15–33.
59. D.G. Boyce, op. cit., p. 130; D. Hempton, op. cit., pp. 72–116.
60. A.J.Ward, op. cit., pp. 90–4; M. W. Heslinga, *The Irish Border as a Cultural Divide,* Van Gorcum, Assen, 1962; David Pringle, *One Island, Two Nations: A Political Geographical Analysis of the National Conflict in Northern Ireland,* Research Studies Press, Letchworth, 1985.
61. I. McBride, 'Ulster and the British Problem', in R. English and G. Walker (eds.), *Unionism in Modern Ireland,* Gill and Macmillan, Dublin, 1996, pp. 1–18; as well as other essays in that volume.
62. This is a recurring problem in contemporary politics as can be seen in the partition of India, Cyprus and Yugoslavia, although in each case the political literature tends to stress the uniqueness of the conflict.
63. T. Garvin, 'The Rising and Irish Democracy', in Máirín Ní Dhonnchada and T. Dorgan (eds.), *Revising the Rising,* Field Day, Derry, 1991, pp. 21–8.
64. R. E. Lindgren, *Norway-Sweden: Union, Disunion, and Scandinavian Integration,* Princeton University Press, Princeton, New Jersey, 1959.
65. B. Girvin, 'Change and Continuity in Liberal Democratic Political Culture', in John R. Gibbins (ed.), *Contemporary Political Culture,* Sage, London, 1989, pp. 31–51; Mahmood Mamdani, 'From Conquest to Consent as the Basis of State Formation: Reflections on Rwanda', *New Left Review,* no. 216, March/April 1996, pp. 3–36 for some similar observations applied to the Rwanda situation, pp. 17, 31.
66. P. Bew, *Ideology and the Irish Question: Ulster Unionism and Irish Nationalism 1912–1916,* Clarendon Press, Oxford, 1994, pp. 117–52.
67. *O'Brien Papers,* University College, Cork: AS 222, Letter to *The Times,* 26 December 1917; see also O'Brien to Frank Gallagher, 3 January 1918 AS 226.
68. J. Augusteijn, *From Public Defiance to Guerrilla Warfare,* Irish Academic Press, Dublin, 1996, pp. 251–334; D. W. Miller, *Church, State and Nation in Ireland, 1898–1921,* Gill and Macmillan, Dublin, 1978, pp. 452–84.
69. J. Augusteijn, op. cit. pp. 124–85; P. Hart, 'The Protestant Experience of Revolution in Southern Ireland', in R. English and G. Walker, op. cit., pp. 81–98. For a consideration of the issue of whether the war of independence was a just war see D. Millar, op. cit., and P. Coffey. 'The Conscription Menace in Ireland and Some Issues Raised By It', *Irish Ecclesiastical Record,* vol. XI, 1918, pp. 484–98. See also A. Mitchell, *Revolutionary Government in Ireland: Dáil Éireann; 1919–1922,* Gill and Macmillan, Dublin 1995.

2 Ulster Unionism: Great Britain and Ireland, 1885-1921

D. George Boyce

It is hard to disentangle myth from history in Irish unionism, not least because unionism is itself often dismissed as myth: as the manufactured product of exaggerated fears by Protestants of their destruction at the hands of Roman Catholics, less perjoratively, as a necessary ideology for those who, for reasons of their own, needed to invent the idea of the 'whole Protestant community', united in its determination to defeat home rule.[1] Before the pioneering work of Patrick Buckland, whose research on Irish unionism revealed new dimensions,[2] unionism in the west and south of Ireland was regarded as, at best marginal, at worse not even worthy of study. Unionism in Ulster was regarded as synonymous with unionism in the six counties that comprised Northern Ireland, even though Colonel Saunderson, Irish unionist leader between 1886 and 1906 had his family home in County Cavan. Indeed, it could be argued that few movements have set out so resolutely, not only to misinterpret their past to others, but also to themselves, so that unionism has accepted the given image as narrow, negative and nasty, comforting itself with the reflection that it has at least developed a stout carapace in the process.

But even if this view of unionism is accepted – and some will accept it readily – it stands oddly beside the history of Irish and Ulster Protestants before the coming of the home rule crisis in 1886. The Protestants of Ireland were themselves the product of a diverse history; indeed, their very origins, in the Protestant Reformation, were bound to render them diverse also, for the divisions between Anglican and Presbyterian (not to mention other denominations such as Methodists, Baptists and a whole host of smaller sects) grew from the very principles of the Reformation, that no institution could stand between an individual and God, and that those who chose to do so could organise their religious worship and government as they wished, and as it pleased God for them to do so. Anglican strove for mastery over Dissenter; dissent provoked more dissent; freedom of conscience, while it might not stretch to granting others, especially Roman Catholics, the same freedom, nonetheless pitted man against the state. And then there were social divisions: landlord and tenant, which in most of Ulster and in other parts of Ireland as well, could mean Protestant landlord against Protestant or Presbyterian tenant. With the industrialisation of east Ulster in the second half of the nineteenth century came conflict between employer and worker. Regionalism worked its impact also: while, in the end, Protestant and Protestant might see eye to eye on the question of Irish nationalism, yet the southern Protestant experience was different: sectarian flash-points, though possible in some areas where there were reasonably substantial collections of both religions in close proximity, were rare. In the north, they were not unlikely. City and countryside in Ulster might produce different perspectives: the landlord-tenant question, so important in rural Antrim or Down, would mean nothing to the working class of Belfast or Lisburn.[3]

Yet there was another view. When it came to the constitution – when it came to a major, permanent change in the way that Ireland was governed and when a Catholic leader emerged who seemed bent on raising his people at the direct expense of the Protestants – then indeed the view that sectarianism drove Irish, and especially Ulster politics, and that there was a certain inevitability about it all, was persuasive. Examples could be found to illustrate, if not prove, this more deterministic theory long before the fault line of 1886. When Dr Henry Cooke rallied the Protestants of Ulster against the forces of Daniel O'Connell and his attempt to make common cause with the English Whigs in 1834, he spoke of the 'banns of marriage' between the two churches.[4] And in 1882, when the Irish National League sought to organise demonstrations in Ulster it was met by counter demonstrations which involved Orangeman and Protestant landlords, some of whom were magistrates, and with the claim that this was a pan-Protestant front of no classes and all classes.[5] Ulster Protestants were united against the common foe.

But too much must not be made out of these manifestations; suspicion and doubt about the fundamental character of Catholic political ambitions created a febrile atmosphere from time to time, but the nature of Irish political dispute was too varied to be encapsulated in a simple formula that would see Irish unionism as the inevitable outcome of Ireland's sectarian past – a sort of re-run of the wars of religion of the seventeenth century. Dublin Protestants for example, took some time to abandon their doubts about the legislative Union of 1800.[6] The Irish Tenant League, founded in 1850 to secure tenants better terms in their relations with landlords, sought, and to an extent succeeded in bridging the religious/political divide, though the *Londonderry Sentinel*, for its part, warned against any association of the League and its aims with the (by now largely defunct) cause of repeal of the Union.[7] Irish political representation was divided between whigs (later liberals) and conservatives, with a short-lived experiment of independent opposition pursued by the 'Irish Brigade', the representatives of tenant right in Parliament. Conservatives, it is

31

true, were solidly Protestant; whigs and liberals, however, were cross confessional, with Catholics and Presbyterians sharing the party label, but all had in common a certain political frustration: they could bring only very limited pressure to bear on their parent parties in Westminster – for which their parent parties were duly thankful. A National Association, founded in 1864 with the support of Cardinal Cullen, seeking to advance Catholic aims and especially the disestablishment of the Church of Ireland, hardly merits a page in the history books.[8] Landlords and tenants were at odds; but in much, perhaps most, of Ireland, they still could rely on a community of interest, as those who lived on the land, though the cold breath of criticism of their right to be on the land at all was beginning to be felt.

Yet there were other cross currents. The so-called 'devotional revolution' of the early nineteenth century, by which the Catholic church strove to assert its authority and social control over its flock, must frighten Protestants; the great religious, evangelical revival of 1859, which reminded Protestants of their fundamental tenet that to be 'saved' meant accepting God personally and individually, and all His example in word and deed, rendered Roman Catholics as even more wilfully blind to the truth than they already were.[9] For Catholics, the spread of education by the Christian Brothers,[10] an organisation with a strong anti-Protestant and anti-English point of view, alarmed Protestants. Catholic confidence and the search for their place in the Union, though it was still within the Union, alarmed the Church of Ireland, an institution most vulnerable to the claim that it was a minority church feeding on a majority of the population. The census of Ireland in 1861 confirmed that the Catholics were the majority in Ireland, and that the denominational positions had not been altered by the ravages of the Great Famine. There were complaints from Protestant newspapers about the absurdity of Presbyterians marching to vote for liberals alongside Catholics; it was not natural; and Catholic voices, too, echoed the notion that such alliances were unnatural. Even the disestablishment of the Church of Ireland by Gladstone in 1869, though balm alike to Presbyterian and Catholic, provoked some unease amongst the former, for after all the Church and the Union had been created as mutually supportive bonds between Great Britain and Ireland. And Gladstone, for his part, noted at the end of the 1860s that 'the most apparent characteristic of ... Christians' in Ireland was 'their fear of each other'.[11]

It is not surprising, therefore, that the foundation of the Home Government Association by Isaac Butt, a Protestant and former conservative, should have fallen with considerable force on this society and its politics; and yet, still, the division did not become as stark as might be expected. The *Dublin University Magazine*, the mouthpiece of educated and in many ways patriotic southern Irish Protestant opinion, warned in 1874 that the home rule agitation was 'as wicked and demoralising as O'Connell's was, and avowedly constructed with the very same end in view – the dismemberment of the Empire',[12] but the spread of the home rulers through Ireland in the 1870s did not provoke a sense of crisis in Protestant Ireland. This was because home rule was associated with tenant right, and while Protestant and Presbyterian tenant farmers were not minded to support home rule, they were interested in tenant right, and would still vote for liberal candidates.[13] In 1873 in county Fermanagh the Orange Order took up the cause of tenant right against Captain Henry Lowry Corry, the conservative candidate; the land question intruded into a by-election in county Tyrone in 1874, and in county Down in May 1878.[14] In the general election of 1880, liberals won eight seats (with two seats each of the county constituencies of Londonderry, Donegal and Monaghan, and one each in county Armagh and Tyrone), and again the land question (and Catholic acquiescence in non-Catholic political candidature) was significant. The activities of the Land League, formed in 1879 to defend tenants' interests by vigorous direct action, also had an impact in Ulster, so much so that landlords wished it settled by British legislation so that they clear the way for a reassertion of their influence over their tenants.[15]

But this still fluid, if coalescing, political picture was to be ended by 1885; and the reason was the decisions and rhetoric of Gladstone and Charles Steward Parnell. Parnell achieved the leadership of the Home Rule Party in May 1880, and he did so with a reputation as a man willing to ride the tiger of Land League agitation, and defy the British in their own parliament. His essentially conservative nationalist views were not borne out by his association with 'Captain Moonlight' and by his strident rhetoric about the need to take power from the British and 'transfer it to the hands of our own people'. Parnell was a Protestant, and his most insightful biographer has stressed that his real aim was not to destroy, but preserve the landlord class from which he came, through settling the land question, establishing a home rule parliament in Dublin, and finding political space for landlords in the new Ireland.[16] But to do this he had to make his peace with the Roman Catholic church, radical nationalists such as the Fenians, Irish Americans, and the lively tradition of anti-English Irish nationalist discourse. This led him into paths that seemed to stray far from those of moderation, reconciliation, the need to treat all Irishmen as brothers.

Parnell, like any political leader, was obliged to speak in nuanced, qualified ways, while at the same time responding to his audience's need for exciting claims for the Irish nation that must be. It is not surprising, therefore, that he found it necessary to approach the question of Irish and Ulster Protestants in a fashion that would make light of their fears of home rule, make it clear that these fears could not stand in the way of progress, and insist that their proper place was in the nation.[17] These nuances were more frightening, or at least unsettling, than downright hostility to unionists; there was behind them the belief that unionists were not a monolithic group, that when it came to the point of crisis, some, perhaps most, maybe even all would capitulate, and that if they did not, then the British government would oblige them to do so. And this question of the role of the British government was vital. The shock of Gladstone's conversion to home rule cannot be exaggerated. Here was the head of the great liberal party, with members and followers amongst the Presbyterians of Ulster, accepting the logic of Irish self-government, and, moreover, dismissing unionist fears as easily overcome. The British parliament would ensure that they would not be persecuted in a home rule Ireland; and they had no more right to be considered as a separate or distinct people than the highlanders of Scotland: both were minority groups within a nation.[18]

This double blow, of Parnell's rise and especially his triumph in the general election of 1885 when the home rulers won 17 of the 33 seats in Ulster, forged a unionist alliance that, though subject to stress and strain, nonetheless survived until the first world war, and then retreated into its local and regional stronghold of unionist Ulster. But, again, it is important to recognise that there were stresses and strains. Southern unionists could hardly expect to win a seat, outside the representation of Trinity College Dublin; even in Ulster, it took time for unionists to create a common front: In the general election of 1885 an Orange candidate successfully opposed a conservative in East Belfast. There were mutterings about 'rotten Protestants' who would not turn out to do their duty. Liberal Ulster did not finally break with Gladstone until the details of his home rule scheme became known.[19]

What held unionism together, until the pressure of politics drove wedges, first between northern and southern unionism, then between the unionists of the six counties that eventually became Northern Ireland, was the common fear of nationalism. The power, money and political expertise of the Ulster business classes, their educational as well as economic and social background, offered a coherence to unionism in Ulster.[20] Landlords counted for much, of course; landlords dominated southern unionism, and had important links with the British unionist party; English landlords had estates in Ireland.[21] But the Ulster business classes gave organisation and finance to the anti-home rule campaign, and also contributed to the idea that Ulster was a business and industrial complex, and thus quite marked off from rural, nationalist Ireland. At a lower level, too, there was in Ulster the Orange Order, staffed mainly by working class men in the towns and cities, and agricultural workers and farmers in their rural areas, which provided common ground for the business classes, landlords and the lower orders to meet, socialise, and band together against home rule. Unionism in Ulster, thought that if it came to the point, it could stand on its own two feet against home rule – though no-one yet thought seriously of armed rebellion against Gladstone. Southern unionism depended more openly on British unionist help. But both were operating within the context of British politics, and both needed British support for their chances of success. They got this support between 1886 and 1914, though by 1914 the British unionists were starting to show great concern about the consequences of the Ulster unionist preparations for revolt against Asquith's third home rule bill.[22] And this dimension is worth dwelling on: to put it simply, and obviously, the unionists depended on the Union; without that context, their politics would be the politics of a minority. Southern unionists had, arguably, been minoritised between 1800 and 1886; their power had been eaten into by land acts and disestablishment. But still, if they remained in a United Kingdom context, their politics could rest upon a wider base; they enjoyed the privileges of a majority, even if they were no longer one. Ulster unionists could comfort themselves with the reflection that they were not a minority, but a local majority, whose writ ran in most areas of Ulster. Yet they too depended on the Union for their fundamental political securities. To remove that context, even by means of a measure of home rule that seemed, and nowadays seems even more, a very modest, compromising constitutional change.

The struggle over the first home rule bill had another, and sustained, impact on unionist politics. It was now easy (and of course necessary) to gloss over the divisions between Protestants in the past, social divisions, religious disagreement. Now the fight against home rule can be summed up in the words of the French statesman, Clemenceau, who in 1891 declared that 'it is always the same men struggling with the same enemies ... what our forefathers wanted we still want'.[23] Or, in the unionist case, what their forefathers did not want, unionists still did not want – Roman Catholic domination and minority status. They developed the idea that there were two Irelands, theirs and a bad one.[24] An Ireland of smiling prosperity and firm social peace, and an Ireland of murder and expropriation. Of course, when the Irish unionist MPs encountered their nationalist opponents in the precincts of the House of Commons, they acknowledged that they were not the hosts of good arrayed against those of evil; but at home they spoke as if they were. At the Ulster unionist convention held in Belfast on 17 June 1892, one speaker urged the 'men of Ulster' to trust in God, and the tempest would soon cease

> No Surrender! Men of Ulster!
> Till the peril pass away;
> Man the walls of truth and freedom.
> Trust in God, and watch and pray.
> Forward in the cause of Union,
> Trust in God, and plan and do;
> Look! The banner floats above you!
> The same that o'er your fathers flew.[25]

But unionism, in Ulster and elsewhere, did not only deploy this kind of historical and emotional language. Unionists went out of their way to insist that they were engaged in a defence of the rights of citizenship of all the people of Ireland; Ulster unionists stressed too their determination to defeat home rule for the sake of Catholics as well as Protestants in Ulster. In the 1892 Convention the Duke of Abercorn referred to loyal Catholics, warning his audience that Protestants must not think that they had a monopoly of loyalty in Ulster.[26] Another speaker, Sir W. Q. Ewart stressed that unionists had no hostile feeling towards 'our Roman Catholic fellow-countrymen' and that unionists claimed 'for them the same religious freedom that we claim for ourselves'.[27] Another speaker denied that Ulster was making any claim for a Protestant ascendancy: was it likely that 'we, who as members of the Liberal party, worked heart and soul in alliance with our Roman Catholic countrymen for the redress of civil and religious inequalities, are now about to demand their re-imposition?'. Thanks to 'our common contendings', all their children, Catholic or Protestant, were 'born into the enjoyment of electoral freedom, and of a religious equality, and an agricultural emancipation unknown in England and Scotland'. Those who demanded home rule were led astray by 'unscrupulous agitators'.[28] The reverend Dr McCutcheon, President of the Methodist College, said that the unionists desired that all men stand equal before the law.[29]

There was still, in 1892, a firm conviction that unionism in Ireland was a seamless garment; that, the Rev. James Cregan

> put it we have promised before God, angels, and men to be loyal to the position we have taken up, to the British throne, to each other, to our fellow unionists throughout Ireland, and to our own beloved country – the country we love so dearly … .[30].

The Presbyterian Rev. Dr Lynd also assured southern unionists that they 'may rest assured that our strength is their strength, that our heart is their heart, that their interests are our interests, and that our hand shall be as swift to strike for them as for ourselves'. And all their rights could only be assured under the British constitution.[31] The Rev. Dr Kane, grand master of the Orange Order, warned his listeners against too narrow an interpretation of the struggle.

> It is quite possible to write the word Ulster too large in this controversy. This Convention is assembled to protest most solemnly against any kind of dismemberment of the United Kingdom … no conceivable arrangement for Ulster would meet our objections to a Dublin parliament, to which our brethren in the other provinces in Ireland should be subject.

The people of Cork and Middlesex should all be subject to the same laws. Unionism, others stressed, was not merely orangeism; nor was it confined to particular classes or religious denominations; it was in the interests of all the people of Ireland.[32]

The stress laid upon the way in which unionism straddled all creeds and classes gives rise to the suspicion that it was precisely because unionism did not fully overcome class divisions at least that the convention delegates found it essential to re-state the case for the unity of unionism. T. W. Russell, who made a rousing speech at the convention, was within a few years at odds with landlords in Ulster over the demand by tenant farmers to be allowed compulsory purchase of their land.[33] In quiet times, after the defeat by the House of Lords of the second home rule bill in 1893, unionism lost its momentum. And the question of what should be done if the British parliament were indeed to pass a home rule bill was as yet unclear. In 1892 one speaker declared that 'firm and unchangeable determination of the people of Ulster to resist by constitutional means and, if need be, by force the passing of the home rule bill into law'.[34] Another speaker warned that the resources of civilisation were not yet exhausted, but when they were 'it remained for them, as loyal sons of sires agone, to find out how they might resist the resolution of the imperial parliament to hand them neck and heel to a tyranny that was beyond the conception of the English electorate.[35] A speaker warned that the cause for which blood had been shed in the past might need to be fought for again.[36] But these words seemed far away from action. C. Lytton Faulkner, an historian of Ireland, claimed that the best weapon was the ballot box – 'a peaceful weapon ... a weapon the constitution provided them with'.[37] The *Irish Times* commented that there had been 'no threat, no boast, no bluster. The purpose was, that more than a million of the people of Ireland should say simply no'.[38] Even Gladstone, referring to the convention in a meeting with nonconformists on 18 June, spoke of the 'comparative moderation' which 'did honour to the Ulster Protestants', especially in the light of threats uttered by leaders of the political opposition against home rule.[39]

Unionists, at the great convention and elsewhere, used the general language of British patriotism and imperial sentiment, bonded by the common heritage of Protestantism, the religion that most centrally defined British national identity. They asked if the great British empire was to be smashed between the mill-stones of 'English atheism and Irish romanism', with the victories of Marlborough, Wellington and Nelson 'blotted out'.[40] James Loughlin has argued convincingly that Ulster unionists did place themselves firmly in the centre of a British national identity and a British imperial mission,[41] Alvin Jackson argues, again with excellent evidence, that Ulster unionists were always more pragmatic, more particularist in the basis of their political mobilisation.[42]

It would be surprising, however, if Ulster unionists did not call upon a multiple nationality; certainly, they stressed the identity issue more strongly in 1892 than they had done in their earlier encounters with Daniel O'Connell and his repeal movement. In 1840-41 the reverend Thomas Cooke, rallying his Presbyterians against repeal of the Union, spoke primarily in religious terms: 1841 might be another 1641, another attack upon the Protestants of Ulster.[43] Now, however, the question of British national identity was brought forward as central to the unionist case against home rule. The 1892 convention has been described by Peter Gibbon as the foundation of an Ulster nationalism:[44] but he cannot have read the speeches. The Duke of Abercorn managed to describe himself and his people, in a few sentences, as 'descendants of English puritans' and also of Scottish presbyterians, as members of a great empire and as 'Irishmen' whom England must not desert.[45] Dr Rentoul, MP, declared that the empire was 'not made by Englishmen in the past, nor by Scotchmen, nor by Irishmen, but it was made by the union of English pluck and Scottish prudence, and Irish enthusiasm (great cheers) ...'[46] But the heart of the matter was this: as one speaker put it

> It is easy for you, gentlemen of England and Scotland, in your armchairs, to contemplate the effect of what you consider only a party question; but to us it is a matter of life and death, a matter of hearth and home, a matter of religion and freedom, a matter of peace and prosperity.[47]

As another unionist source put it, referring to the Roman Catholics, the 'hereditary racial and religious foes' of Protestants 'would be our governors'.[48] Threats of this kind cause a community to define themselves, to discover or create bonds of unity, to search for boundaries and parameters within which they can feel safe, and for Ulster (and southern Irish) unionists, the safety lay in British identity; and, after all, if nationalists insisted on equating Irishness with nationalism – certainly a short-handed language to say the least – then Protestants and unionists must express the identity with which they felt comfortable, and through which their safety might be assured. This was not merely an expedient, though expediency drove them forward. Rather it was the outcome of their special history, their position as a minority in Ireland but a majority in the United Kingdom; a minority in the south of Ireland, but a majority in the province of Ulster. Now the threat to Ulster unionists in particular was that they would be made a helpless minority in their own part of the British kingdom.

Nowhere was this more keenly felt than in the area of local government, which saw the first elections under the reformed system in 1899. The massive injection of democratisation in urban, rural and county councils offered new areas of contention, especially in Ulster, where unionists had not been obliged to subject themselves to the dismal spectacle of nationalists ruling the roost. It was all very well for southern Protestants to accept the inevitable; they were used to living on a kind of nationalist sufferance since the 1840s. But in Ulster the recognition that each community's representatives looked after it own was now given local administrative shape. Moreover, such a system enabled a minority in Ulster (the nationalist/catholic people) the chance to feel what it would be like if they ever were part of an overall Irish nationalist majority; it also gave Ulster unionists (the majority in Ulster as a whole) the chance to experience the disagreeable sensation of what it would be like to live as a minority in the whole of Ireland.[49] Local competition was, in many ways, felt more keenly even than competition at the national level: jeers and cheers, triumphalism and dismay, flag-waving and the like, all took on an even sharper edge when those who taunted each other, or aspired to dominate each other, lived side by side. On both the local and the general plane, therefore, battle was joined.

This accounts for the rapid demise of liberal unionism in Ireland, and especially in Ulster, following the sudden announcement of Gladstone's conversion to home rule, and the crisis over the first home rule bill. The liberal unionists traced their own sad history, in a commissioned volume, *The Ulster Liberal Unionist Association: A Sketch of its History, 1885-1914*.[50] Significantly, its two line summary of its contents placed 'how it has opposed home rule' above 'and what it has done for remedial legislation for Ireland'. Liberals in 1885 found themselves 'confronted with a painful choice'.[51] Having defended liberal causes, such as Catholic emancipation and the Ballot Act, liberals now found themselves called upon by Gladstone to 'adore what they had burned and to burn what they had adored'.[52] J. R. Fisher declared in his introduction to the book that liberal causes had been maintained: 'a record of constant striving after agricultural, industrial, and social reforms for the benefit of the entire country'.[53] In the book itself, liberal unionists claimed also that they had kept the lamp of liberalism burning brightly in the north, despite 'the great betrayal'.[54] The liberal unionist difficulty in finding a suitable middle ground in a polarised political atmosphere was expressed in their attitude to the riots that accompanied the crisis over the first home rule bill.

> Although it was impossible to justify the stupid way in which the Orange masses and the police were actually set at each other's throats by the want of official tact and patience, the liberal unionists of the city, while strongly condemning the methods adopted of dealing with a terribly excited populace used all their influence in the interests of order and peace and in support of lawful authority in the suppression of turbulence and rowdyism'.[55]

In the discussion of the role of the English liberal unionists in British politics, the Ulster branch drew attention, perhaps unwittingly, to their own plight: they complained about Lord Salisbury's ignoring the liberal unionist contribution to the defeat of the first home rule bill;[56] but it was just this sense of marginalisation, and reality of marginalisation, that would undermine their own ambitions to play an independent role in a unionist alliance. When home rule was the key to British and especially Irish politics, then a party that lost its distinctive voice would find it hard to get a hearing.

But even in quieter times, liberal unionism found it hard to make a distinctive mark. After the defeat of the 1893 home rule bill, when, as the liberal unionists put it, 'home rule was now voted dead',[57] and a conservative/unionist government came to power, liberal unionists seemed to anticipate a chance to move back to their reforming programme; and indeed they claimed that much government reform was due to their impatience with the slow progress of change. But their main concern was to prevent what they called 'cleavage' in unionist ranks over the phenomenon of 'Russellism',[58] that is, the attempts by T.W. Russell to combine nationalist and unionist in the cause of land reform. As Russell 'fomented' agitation, and put up a 'unionist independent land reformer' in the East Down by-election in 1902, followed by another candidature (and another victory) in North Fermanagh, defeating Captain James Craig,[59] the liberal unionists cut a rather sorry figure. On their own admission the Ulster Liberal Unionist Association took no part in these contests, but merely used 'all its influence to maintain the alliance of the two wings of the unionist army, believing that the trend of affairs in connection with the radical party in England warranted the assumption that the party would bid strongly for nationalist support could they obtain even a nominal majority at the next election'.[60]

It is important to note that some twenty years separated the second home rule bill from the third which Asquith for the liberals introduced in April 1912. New men emerged, very different from those essentially respectable citizens who met at the great unionist convention in Belfast in 1892. They had spoken of using force if need to be defend themselves; but they had not spoken with one voice, and it is hard to resist the impression that they were, essentially, moderate and constitutional men. Sir Edward Carson, the hero of Ulster unionism's stand against home rule between 1912 and 1914 bridged the generation gap; but although he placed himself at the head of unionist resistance, his heart was never in the fight – that is, in the idea of a real war of guns as well as words and actions. It has been suggested that their experience in the real war of South Africa, 1899-1902, helped shift some important Ulster unionists, James Craig, Fred Crawford, towards a more resolute militancy;[61] and there may be much truth in the idea of a new, and more dangerous atmosphere in Ireland, Britain and Europe generally on the eve of the great war that helped break down the inhibitions and constraints of bourgeois Europe of the nineteenth century.

An equally significant development was the foundation of the Ulster unionist council in 1905, following the scare over the attempt by Lord Dunraven, and the under-secretary in Dublin castle, Anthony MacDonnell, to break the home rule versus Union deadlock with a modest scheme of devolution in 1904. As far as unionists were concerned, there was no such thing as modest devolution; devolution was another word for home rule.[62] This crisis encouraged Ulster unionists to pull together, banish 'Russellism' from the province, and appeal to the whole Protestant Ulster people – though they had not yet given up the fight against home rule for the whole of Ireland.[63] There was also a quickening of the sectarian atmosphere in Ireland at this time, fostered by the Roman Catholic church's issuing of the *Ne Temere* decree which proclaimed that the children of mixed marriages must be brought up as Catholics. A Presbyterian convention held in Belfast in 1912 declared that under home rule, 'the parliament and executive alike are certain to be controlled by a majority subject to the direction of the *Ne Temere* and *Muto Propio* decrees against whose domination all safeguards designed for the protection of a Protestant minority [...] would be wholly useless'.[64] Actions reinforced words when, on 29 June 1912 a Presbyterian Sunday School excursion mainly consisting of women and children was attacked by nationalists; a fracas ensued, with the incident being fanned into a kind of brush fire of sectarianism, as trouble spread to the Belfast shipyards; the annual twelfth of July celebrations by the Orange Order heightened tension further, causing some southern unionists to acknowledge their distinction from such wild emotions.[65]

This raises a central question about unionism: was it essentially a claim for citizenship, as its adherents insisted, and indeed announced in their *Solemn League and Covenant* of September 1912; or was it driven by deeper, more atavistic forces, forces that persuaded men and women to prepare themselves, if need be, for war with the British government? Were these forces essentially religious in origin, drawn from the deeper wells of the wars of religion of the seventeenth century, or were they the product of the crisis over home rule, with its polarising impact on Irish and especially Ulster politics?

Protestant-Catholic relations, always fragile, were at least manageable throughout most of the nineteenth century; co-existence, peaceful exchange, the ordinary decencies of life were never absent. But before the home rule crisis Protestant, Catholic and Dissenter had defined their self-interest in terms of their denominational allegiance; and, although co-existence was not difficult, it could hardly stand the test of a serious constitutional change – a kind of revolution. In these circumstances older ideas of the 'Catholic threat', the 'Protestant tyranny' could easily resurface and be used as political slogans and persuaders. Some would perceive this as a religious issue; some as a political issue with religion as the badge of ideology; others might think in terms of citizenship, Irish versus British. But none could forget that the strong sense of purpose that the home rule movement gave to the idea that to be Irish and Catholic were synonymous, and the strong sense of purpose that the unionist movement gave to the idea that to be Protestant was to be British, formed the dividing line that few in Irish politics ever crossed.

It was to defend this line that Ulster unionists formed their Ulster volunteer force army to defeat home rule for Ireland and Ulster; and this line could not be crossed, even in wartime, even if nationalist and unionist served in a common enterprise in the British army as it engaged in protracted total war with the German army.[66] Even that most common of experiences, fear and wounds in battle, or the mourning of families for those killed in battle, could not break the mould: on the contrary, wartime experiences only polarised the two sides further, with Ulster unionists claiming that their 'blood sacrifice' at the battle of the Somme in July 1916 entitled them to special treatment as a distinct people, and denouncing also the 1916 Easter Rising in Dublin as a stab in the back for the British army of which they were a part – vindication, even, of their repeated claims that all nationalists were fundamentally enemies of Britain and the British empire, whose true colours had been revealed at last.[67] The war even exposed essential differences between northern and southern unionists. There was a discernible shift in southern unionist thinking after 1914, as unionists began to reconsider their (by now increasingly doubtful) opposition to home rule.[68] Southern unionist losses in the war, in an already small community, amounted to something like a lost generation. And although Lloyd George's attempt to square the circle of unionism and nationalism immediately after the Easter Rising by offering the exclusion of six Ulster counties (Antrim, Armagh, Down, Fermanagh, Londonderry and Tyrone) for an indeterminate period was brought down by determined southern unionist pressure, and supported by key figures in the British cabinet,[69] it proved to be the last fling of the southern unionists. Sir Edward Carson, himself a typical southern unionist, not only accepted the six county exclusion plan, but urged this on the Ulster unionists; Andrew Bonar Law, who was the most determined British politician who opposed home rule before 1914, likewise advocated acceptance.[70] The concern lest the granting of a home rule parliament to John Redmond that would be the prey of separatist nationalists and pro-Germans, that helped defeat the 1916 Lloyd George plan, was overtaken by events in 1917, particularly by the decision of the United States to enter the war on the allies' side. Total war must push the Irish question aside, and the decline of southern unionist opposition after 1917 made some kind of partition solution more likely.

The road to partition was not yet a straight one. It must not be supposed that the partition of Ireland was an easy option: the idea of permanent partition was never accepted by the British government, let alone Irish nationalists, as the preferred policy. But it was clear that the Irish Convention that met to try to thrash out a solution between July 1917 and January 1918 could not overcome unionist Ulster's determination to defend their own people.[71] It was certain that no British government could coerce unionist Ulster, as the Lloyd George coalition stated in its election manifesto in December 1918.[72] But, still, the Lloyd George government's Irish situation committee was reluctant to make partition permanent; and did not want to grapple unionist Ulster firmly to Great Britain. The result was a compromise: Ulster, or six counties of it, would have home rule, thus removing any accusation that Britain was trying to hold any part of Ireland against its will. There would be a nine-county Northern Ireland, the better to protect the Roman Catholic minority that would be stranded within its borders – a design that was frustrated by Ulster unionist insistence that they would not accept their part of the bargain unless they were given only six counties, areas which they could control.[73] There would be a council of Ireland to provide a meeting ground between the two states of northern and southern Ireland, an institution that might help the two states to work towards an agreed united Ireland.[74] No Ulster unionist voted for any part of the government of Ireland bill as it passed through parliament, though they were aware of its benefits, especially the control of the police. Yet their reluctance to vote may also be taken as a sign that they were reluctant to stand before the bar of history as the only Irishmen who stood up and were counted in support of the partition of Ireland.

The last stages of Ulster and Irish unionist resistance to home rule were indeed paradoxical. Ulster unionists accepted that form of government whose justice and rightness they had always denied. Southern unionists divided, with some trying to hold out against the inevitable, while others, most numerous, accepted that the game was up, and that they must make the best they could of the new Ireland: but with some concern about the implications of partition for their position in the south.[75] The British government, in 1921 anxious for a settlement with Sinn Fein, proved reluctant friends of the embryo Northern Ireland government, and was slow to hand over powers under the Government of Ireland Act to Sir James Craig.[76] Craig, for his part, came under severe pressure from the British government in November 1921 to place his home rule parliament under an Irish dominion parliament and government in Dublin, and seems nearly to have succumbed, before being strengthened in his resolve by his own cabinet.[77] When, finally, Lloyd George and the Sinn Fein plenipotentiaries agreed on a settlement in December 1921, they could only set aside the Northern Ireland issue for another day, with a boundary commission (oddly enough, first suggested by Sir James Craig as a means of meeting Roman Catholic objections to inclusion in Northern Ireland)[78] as either a settlement possibility – or a necessary fudge, necessary even for Sinn Fein.

Ulster unionists now set themselves the priority of 'restoring order' and made internal security their priority, which was hardly surprising in the light, not only of political disorder from within, but a determined IRA assault on the new state.[79] Southern unionists set themselves the task of learning to live in the new Irish Free State, and of living down their unionism – unionism that must exclude them from full membership of the Irish state, at least as far as emotional and symbolic ties were concerned, ties that had bound them to Britain for many years.[80] It was indeed a long way from the earnest men and women who gathered together in 1892 at the great unionist convention in Belfast to witness against home rule, or from those Protestants who in 1886 suddenly awoke to the realisation that Gladstone had decided that home rule was the only way to settle the Irish question. Violent confrontation, world war, and the deeply altered post-war world were the chief landmarks on the way to that most curious of solutions: an Ulster unionist home rule state, governed by the very people who had declared their eternal opposition to home rule. And while the idea of the 'whole Protestant community', put forward in 1886, endorsed in 1892 and reaffirmed in 1912 may have been a myth, the institutions that represented its northern Irish component emphatically were no myth, but were a real means of shaping and supporting solidarity among the unionist community. But these institutions also erected barriers, not only between Northern Ireland and the south, but between the unionists and the British state whose political unity and multi-national identities they had fought so hard to maintain.

References

1. Brian Walker, *Dancing to History's Tune: History, Myth, and Politics in Ireland,* Institute of Irish Studies, Belfast, 1996, pp 9-11, discusses the Unionist version of history; D. G. Boyce, *Nationalism in Ireland,* (3rd ed), Routledge, London, 1995, pp 220-221 considers nationalist dismissal of unionism.
2. Patrick Buckland, *Irish Unionism One: The Anglo-Irish and the New Ireland,* Gill and Macmillan, Dublin, 1972; *Irish Unionism Two: Ulster Unionism and the Origins of Northern Ireland, 1886-1932,* Gill and Macmillan, Dublin, 1973.
3. D G Boyce, *Nineteenth Century Ireland : The Search for Stability,* Gill & Macmillan, Dublin, 1990, pp 186-191, 201-4.
4. Frank Wright, *Two Lands on One Soil: Ulster Politics before Home Rule,* Gill & Macmillan, New York, 1996, p. 69.
5. Ibid., p. 477.
6. Jacqueline Hill, *From Patriots to Unionists: Dublin City Politics and Irish Protestant Patriotism, 1660-1840,* Oxford University Press, 1997, pp. 264-80.
7. D. G. Boyce, *Nineteenth Century Ireland; The Search for Stability,* Gill and Macmillan, Dublin, 1990, p. 127.
8. D. G. Boyce, *Nationalism in Ireland,* Routledge, London, 1995, p. 187.
9. D. G. Boyce, *Nineteenth Century Ireland: The Search for Stability,* Gill and Macmillan, Dublin, 1990, pp. 133-4.
10. F. Wright, op. cit., p. 392.
11. D. G. Boyce, op. cit., p. 153.
12. Ibid., p. 185.
13. F. Wright, op. cit., pp. 469-71.
14. D. G. Boyce, op cit., pp. 189-92.
15. Ibid., pp. 190-2.
16. P. Bew, *C. S. Parnell,* Gill and MacMillan, Dublin, 1980.
17. Pauric Travers, 'Parnell and the Ulster Question', in D. McCartney (ed.), *Parnell: the Politics of Power,* Wolfhound Press, Dublin, 1991 , pp 57-71.
18. D. G. Boyce, *The Irish Question in British Politics, 1868-1996,* Macmillan, London, 1996 ed., p. 35.
19. D. G. Boyce, op. cit., p. 197. For the 1885 election see Brian Walker, *Ulster Politics: The Formative Years, 1868-1886,* Ulster Historical Foundation, Belfast, 1989, ch. 1v.
20. Martin Kavanagh, 'An Analysis of the Economic, Social and Political Power in Ulster/ Northern Ireland, c. 1910-1937', PhD thesis, University of Ulster, 1995, ch. 2.
21. Patrick Buckland, *Irish Unionism One: The Anglo-Irish and the New Ireland,* Gill and Macmillan, Dublin, 1972, pp. xiii-xxvii.

22. D. G. Boyce, *The Crisis of British Unionism : Lord Selborne's Political Papers, 1885-1922*, Historians' Press, London, 1971 , pp. 102-13.

23. Robert Tombs, *France 1814-1914*, Longman, London, 1996, p. 145.

24. Ibid., p. 145, quoting the Bishop of Amiens, 1895.

25. *The Ulster Unionist Convention, 17th June 1892*, Belfast, n.d., 1892?, p. 86.

26. Ibid., pp. 20-21.

27. Ibid., p. 25.

28. Ibid., pp. 6-7.

29. Ibid., p. 29.

30. Ibid., p. 30.

31. Ibid., p. 34.

32. Ibid., p. 36; see also p. 40.

33. Ibid., pp. 78-9.

34. Ibid., p. 79.

35. Ibid., p. 81.

36. Ibid., p. 85.

37. Ibid., p. 86.

38. Ibid., p. 105.

39. Ibid., p. 113.

40. Ibid., p. 89.

41. James Loughlin, *Ulster Unionism and British National Identity since 1885,* Pinter, London, 1995, ch. 2.

42. Alvin Jackson, *The Ulster Party: Irish Unionists in the House of Commons, 1884-1911*, Oxford University Press, Oxford, 1989, pp. 8-10.

43. J. L. Porter, *The Life and Times of Henry Cooke,* John Murray, London, 1871, pp. 411-16.

44. P. Gibbon, *The Origins of Ulster Unionism,* Manchester University Press, Manchester, 1975, pp. 130-6.

45. *Proceedings of the Ulster Unionist Convention,* p.23.

46. Ibid., p. 90.

47. Ibid., p. 35.

48. Ibid., pp. 97-9. For a fuller discussion of similar points see Ian McBride, 'Ulster and the British Problem', in R. English and G. Walker (eds.), *Unionism in Modern Ireland,* Macmillan, Basingstoke, 1996, pp. 1-15.

49. D. Burnett, 'The Modernisation of Unionism, 1892-1914?', in R. English and G. Walker, op. cit., pp. 48-52.

50. *The Ulster Liberal Unionist Association: A Sketch of its History, 1885-1914*, Belfast 1914.

51. Ibid., p. iii.

52. Ibid., p. iii.

53. Ibid., p. v.

54. Ibid., p. 9.

55. Ibid., p. 27.

56. Ibid., pp. 31-2.

57. Ibid., p. 39.

58. Ibid., pp. 39-41.

59. Ibid., pp. 40-41.

60. Ibid., p.41.

61. Alvin Jackson, 'Unionists and the Empire, 1880-1920', in K. Jeffrey (ed.), *An Irish Empire?: Aspects of Ireland and the British Empire,* Manchester University Press, Manchester, 1996, pp. 132-8.

62. D. G. Boyce, *Nineteenth Century Ireland: The Search for Stability,* Gill and Macmillan, Dublin, 1990, pp. 227-8.

63. A. Jackson, *The Ulster Party: Irish Unionists in the House of Commons, 1884-1911,* Oxford University Press, Oxford, 1989, ch. 6.

64 D. G. . Boyce, op. cit., p. 231.

65. P. Bew, *Ideology and the Irish Question: Ulster Unionism and Irish Nationalism, 1912-1916,* Oxford University Press, Oxford, 1994, pp. 56-9.

66. D. FitzPatrick, 'Militarism in Ireland', in T. Bartlett and K. Jeffrey (eds.), *A Military History of Ireland,* Cambridge University Press, Cambridge, 1996, pp. 386-92.

67. D. G. Boyce, op. cit., , p. 251.

68. P. Buckland, op. cit., , pp. 83-90.

69. D. G. Boyce, 'British Opinion, Ireland and the War, 1916-1918', in *Historical Journal, vol.* XVII, no. 3, 1974, pp. 575-93, at pp. 579-84.

70. Ibid., pp. 580-1, 585. See also D. G. Boyce, *Crisis of British Unionism; Lord Selborne's Political Papers, 1885-1922,* Historians' Press, London, 1971, pp. 183-4.

71. P. Buckland, op. cit., pp. 103-4, 113-14, 121-2.

72. D. G. Boyce, 'British Opinion, Ireland and the War', *Historical Journal,* vol.xvii, no. 3, 1974, p. 592.

73. D. G. Boyce, 'Northern Ireland: the Origins of the State', in P. Catterall and S. McDougal (eds.), *The Northern Ireland Question in British Politics,* Macmillan, Basingstoke, 1996, pp. 18-19.

74. Ibid., p. 17.

75. P. Buckland, op. cit., pp. 219-22, 146-72.

76. D. G. Boyce, 'Origins of the State' in P. Catterall and S. McDougal, op. cit., pp. 21-22.

77. Ibid., p. 22.

78. *Cabinet Conclusions,* 15 December 1919, Cab. 23/18.

79. B. A. Follis, *A State under Siege: The Establishment of Northern Ireland, 1920-25,* Clarendon Press, Oxford, 1995, pp. 82-115.

80. P. Hart, 'The Protestant Experience of Revolution in Southern Ireland', in R. English and G. Walter (eds.) op. cit., , pp. 81-98; Jane Leonard, 'The Twinge of Memory: Armistice Day and Remembrance Sunday in Dublin since 1919', Ibid., pp. 99-114.

3   Partition: Origins and Implementation

Brian Barton

The causes of partition have been variously interpreted. It has been castigated as a characteristic creation of British imperialism, with its devious strategies of 'divide and rule'. Once the inevitability of Irish self-government had been accepted at Westminster, it is alleged that right wing elements fomented opposition to it in Ulster, so ultimately enabling Britain to preserve its toe-hold in Ireland. Others have seen partition as the product of the manipulative skills of the northern capitalist class, who cynically waved an orange flag in the face of Belfast's poor, and so successfully cloaked from them the extent of their exploitation. Alternatively, the creation of two Irish states in 1921–22 has been portrayed as a reasonable and just compromise; a symptom, but not the cause of Ireland's divisions, an institutional recognition that in it there exists two nations, whose roots can be traced to the Plantation or even Strongbow's Norman knights. These issues will be considered in this chapter.

Soon after its emergence in the mid-1880s, the Ulster unionist movement established itself as the most significant, counter-revolutionary force in Irish political life. Its members were motivated by a desire to maintain the Union and a yet deeper determination to resist the authority of any future Dublin parliament. During the immediate pre-war years, they responded energetically and effectively to their first substantial challenge – the third home rule bill. Subsequently, despite their apparent wartime quiescence there was no abatement in the intensity of their opposition to all-Ireland institutions. Indeed during the course of the conflict they succeeded in defending and, arguably, consolidating their negotiating position.

Meanwhile, between 1915–19, a convergence of opinion occurred at the highest level in British political life, with regard to the Irish question; it found expression in the content of the Government of Ireland Act, in 1920. This provided for the formation of devolved governments in both northern and southern Ireland, each to be responsible for 'peace, order and good government' within their respective jurisdictions. Ireland was to remain an integral part of the United Kingdom and the sovereignty of Westminster was to be undiminished. Whilst the Sinn Fein leadership used the procedures laid down by the measure as an opportunity to renew their electoral mandate, in Northern Ireland its terms were implemented. In due course, an executive, comprised of seven departments, was formed, and also a bi-cameral parliament, whose legislative powers differed, in practice, little from those of a dominion and whose procedures broadly replicated those existing in London.

The decision to establish a regional government in Belfast arose from the anxiety of imperial ministers to legislate in a way which would redeem former pledges to unionists and yet be relatively acceptable to nationalists. Thus in an attempt to minimize the gravity of partition, direct rule was terminated; it was considered that no one could therefore legitimately claim Britain was ruling the northern minority against its will or actively supporting unionists in their refusal to unite with the south. Westminster's implicit objective was the creation of a united Ireland, formed with Ulster's consent, governed by a single, separate parliament and bound closely to Britain. The category of 'reserved' powers was devised to provide an inducement towards this goal; they were to be transferred once unity had been achieved. It was also hoped that the Council of Ireland might serve as the dynamic institutional framework through which the two governments might ultimately coalesce. These policy assumptions were mistaken and expectations unfulfilled. Regional institutions merely strengthened and confirmed the sense of separate identity shared by Ulster unionists whilst direct rule would have been more acceptable to northern nationalists than local dominion by their political opponents.

The unionist movement succeeded in determining the fact but not the form of partition. Its members would have preferred another Cromwell but, unlike their conservative diehard supporters, they did not vote against the measure during commons divisions. Their leaders' protestations that acceptance of a Belfast parliament represented a supreme sacrifice on their part were made largely for tactical reasons; they were responding to pressure from Lloyd George to make concessions during the Anglo-Irish talks. Meanwhile they publicly acknowledged the additional security which resulted from devolution. Craig and his colleagues had earlier with some success striven to amend the Government of Ireland Bill so ensuring that the incipient institutions were more amenable to unionist control They helped define the boundary of the excluded area, a majority of the Ulster Unionist Council preferring six counties to the nine initially proposed by British ministers. They supported an amendment which provided that the composition of the northern senate would precisely reflect the relative strength of the political parties in the lower house. They attempted but failed to weaken the proposed Council of Ireland and to eliminate proportional representation from local parliamentary elections. Nonetheless, Northern Ireland's first election, on 24th May 1921, was a Unionist

Party triumph. It won forty of the fifty-two commons seats; all of its candidates were successful.

There were some grounds for optimism when, on 22 June, George V formally opened the new parliament in Belfast. His speech presaged the Anglo-Irish truce. Moreover, early in the subsequent negotiations, de Valera indicated that Sinn Fein would not attempt to coerce the six counties into a united Ireland. Meanwhile, Sir James Craig expressed his belief that the devolved institutions were regarded as sacrosanct in London. In such circumstances, it seemed possible that a secure, unionist government might prove willing to broaden its programme rather than act merely as an instrument for the maintenance of the Protestant ascendancy. Contemporary speeches by party leaders were optimistic in tone and suggested both an awareness of their responsibilities and consciousness of their opportunities. Craig himself stated: 'God grant that our footsteps may never be diverted from the path of honour,' he promised 'to look to the people as a whole,' to be 'absolutely fair in administering the law' and appealed for friendship with the south.[1] It was reasonable to anticipate that these generous impulses would be reinforced and guided by Westminster and also by the cadre of competent, high-ranking civil servants who transferred to Belfast from Whitehall and Dublin Castle.

Overall, it seemed possible that class issues might eventually transcend the traditionally sectarian basis of local politics. There were some indications that this process had already begun. In June 1918 the Unionist Party had formed the Ulster Unionist Labour Association, mainly as a means of counteracting the appeal of socialism to its erstwhile working class supporters. The success of labour party candidates in municipal elections two years later clearly indicated that this initiative had been inadequate; they polled 10,000 Protestant votes in Belfast alone and were supported by one-fifth of the Catholic electorate in the west of the city. If these trends were sustained unionist ministers might be constrained to reconsider their policies and nationalist MPs also feel obliged to respond, possibly by abandoning recent electoral pledges to abstain from the Belfast parliament.[2]

Hopes of a stable province, led by an effective even-handed, regional government, living in harmony with its southern neighbours, proved to be both illusory and short-lived. In part, this failure was rooted in the content of the 1920 Act; its main terms were divorced from the realities of Irish life. Arguably, its gravest defect lay not in its institutionalization of partition, but rather in the type of government which it provided for Northern Ireland. Local ministers found their political options nullified by the 'excepted' and 're-served' powers retained at Westminster. Those relating to finance reduced them to impotence. As a consequence, they lacked the freedom of action necessary to instigate distinctive and relevant regional programmes. In addition, no consideration was given to the distribution of powers within Northern Ireland. The new government was particularly constricted by being forced to share responsibility for services with the seventy-five local authorities which formed part of its inheritance; non-unionist representation on these bodies had substantially increased due to the introduction of proportional representation into local government elections in 1919.

From the outset, Craig and his colleagues were confronted by awesome political problems. Inevitably Northern Ireland became an Irish irredenta; in 1921 Dail Eireann refused to recognize its existence. Thereafter, southern attitudes and policies consistently reduced the likelihood that devolution would succeed. They reinforced the unionist sense of seige, largely determined security policy within the six counties and exacerbated minority hostility towards the new government. In any case, northern nationalists felt vulnerable and resentful after the passing of the 1920 Act; they had somewhat naively assumed that Sinn Fein would overcome unionist demands for separate treatment. Though deeply split, since mid-1916, between Devlinites in east Ulster and Sinn Fein supporters in border areas, they shared a derisive contempt for partition. Both groupings fought the 1921 election on an uncompromising policy of abstention from the commons and non-recognition of the Belfast government. Hierarchical endorsement of this strategy was highlighted by Cardinal Logue's refusal to attend the state opening of parliament.

Over the previous twelve months, the prolonged political uncertainty and an upsurge in IRA activity in the north had sharpened sectarian feeling. Serious eruptions of violence resulted, especially in Belfast, Lisburn and Londonderry. In July 1920, the Royal Irish Constabulary (RIC) reported the rounding up and expulsion of Catholic workers from Belfast's two shipyards. This prompted a retaliatory Dail boycott of northern goods. Earlier, unionist's doubts as to the will and the ability of Dublin Castle to preserve law and order had contributed to a revival of the Ulster Volunteer Force (in June 1920); its function remained to preserve unionist discipline, protect property and ultimately defend the Union. In early September 1920, Westminster reluctantly agreed officially to recognize this force by recruiting its members into a legally constituted special constabulary; details of the scheme were published on 23 October. The decision to proceed was taken in response to sustained unionist agitation and also to eliminate the risk of a clash between crown forces and paramilitary elements and ease pressure on the already over-stretched local military presence. Though the specials were to have been raised from loyal citizens throughout Ireland, in practice, they were organized exclusively in Ulster, by the newly appointed assistant under-secretary in Belfast, Sir Ernest Clark; his instructions were to lay the foundations for the Northern Ireland government.[3]

The formation of the new force helped assauge Protestant anxieties but it exacerbated minority feelings of alienation, as much for its success against the IRA as for its excesses. Joseph Devlin accused Britain of arming 'pogromists to murder Catholics'.[4] In January 1921, the IRA launched an offensive against its members, whom it described as 'traitors to the republic'.[5] Their campaign provoked further sectarian violence – both spontaneous outbursts and more calculated revenge killings. Thus levels of violence remained high; on some estimates twenty-six died and one hundred and forty were wounded in Belfast alone during July 1921.[6] Unionists anticipated that their newly elected government would take all the steps deemed necessary to restore order.

These wide-ranging, deep rooted and volatile problems, required sensitivity and clear thinking on the part of those politicians responsible; but this was not forthcoming under the system of government obtaining in 1921–22. During this crucial, formative period, the attitude of the imperial authorities towards Northern Ireland was determined by their overriding desire to arrive at and maintain a settlement with the south. When, in mid-October, the Anglo-Irish negotiations began in earnest, partition was a central issue. The Sinn Fein delegates exploited it as a bargaining point, though they lacked a coherent strategy to avert it and independence remained their priority throughout. For their part, British ministers were concerned that the discussions should not founder on the Ulster questions and hoped that Craig could be cajoled into playing a conciliatory role. Thus, in early November 1921, Lloyd George pressed him to concede 'essential unity'. Residual Conservative Party sympathy helped stiffen the resistance of unionist leaders and confirm their refusal to capitulate. Bonar Law commented: 'what is asked of them is not concessions but the surrender of everything for which they have been fighting for thirty-five years'.[7]

The negotiations directly affected the position of the Northern Ireland government in other ways. Their initiation raised minority hopes to a zenith. It encouraged and appeared to vindicate the refusal by nationalists to recognize the infant parliament. Their initial hopes and expectations were shaken in July by publication of the British government's proposals for a settlement. Later, de Valera's statements that no coercion would be used against the north and that individual counties might opt out of a future self-governing Ireland, also caused deep unease. Both developments helped precipitate a spate of nationalist deputations to Dublin and of political resolutions passed by bodies which they controlled in the north-east. Their common concern was to reaffirm Sinn Fein opposition to partition and, as far as possible, to strengthen its bargaining position. The actions taken by Tyrone and Fermanagh county councils were particularly effective; they impressed Lloyd George and alarmed and embarrassed northern unionists.[8]

In the meantime, the minority derived some reassurance from Westminster's apparent reluctance to implement fully the terms of the 1920 Act. For more than five months after the truce no major powers were transferred to the new government. Imperial ministers were concerned not to prejudice or predetermine the outcome of the negotiations; whilst these were in progress, they claimed that the 'legal difficulties involved 'in devolving any responsibilities were 'insuperable'.[9] The delay had particularly grave repercussions with regard to security policy. Local ministers faced the problem of suppressing violence aimed at their overthrow or immobilization as well as that of preventing outbreaks of sectarian conflict. It was clearly a matter of the utmost urgency to establish quickly a system of law enforcement and for the administration of justice which would have the confidence of both communities.

In late June 1921, the cabinet was encouraged to believe that the transfer of policing powers was imminent and that swingeing measures were being prepared, which would break the IRA campaign. Neither materialized. Until 22 November, law and order matters remained exclusively a Westminster responsibility. Meanwhile, unionist distrust of the security forces was confirmed by a decision, taken at Dublin Castle, to apply the terms of the truce to the six counties. This was done in order to facilitate the Anglo-Irish negotiations and without consulting the northern administration. Thus, with no prior warning, the 20,000 members of the special constabulary were immobilized, raising Protestant fears of total disbandment. Military units stationed locally were relegated to a peripheral, peace keeping role; their emergency powers lapsed into abeyance. Police raids and searches ceased. Most galling, from the unionist government's perspective, was the official recognition simultaneously accorded to the IRA. As a consequence, its liaison officers negotiated with representatives of crown forces on equal terms and it was provided with an opportunity to regroup and reorganize. Instantly its activities increased, general headquarters in Dublin providing arms, training and finance. It exploited fully its enhanced status and rapidly expanded its support in Catholic areas so, in Craig's phrase 'gravely imperilling the position of Ulster'.[10] It was, along with the Sinn Fein party, the chief beneficiary of the truce. Traditional popular movements, such as the United Irish League and the Ancient Order of Hibernians, seemed increasingly irrelevant to their erstwhile supporters. Only in west Belfast did constitutional nationalism, under Joseph Devlin's leadership, survive as a credible force.

The unsatisfactory security implications of these developments were immediately evident from the confused response by crown forces to three severe outbreaks of rioting in Belfast, between July-September 1921. During the first of these, in mid-July, the northern cabinet requested General Sir Nevil Macready (GOC British forces in Ireland) to restore the peace preservation measures in operation prior to the truce. Subsequently, additional troops were dispatched, but their actions were still to be guided by the spirit of the agreement. Ministers were also assured that sufficient forces and powers were available to deal with any situation that might arise.

Further severe rioting occurred in late August; on this occasion high initial casualty figures might well have been reduced had troops been dispatched promptly after being requisitioned by J F Gelston, the city's police commissioner. Once again, though more vigorously than before, the Northern Ireland government pressed for firm security measures. It was conscious of mounting criticisms of its apparent impotence from its supporters and stressed the 'danger of the loyalist element getting out of hand'. It demanded the mobilization of the special constabulary, full use by crown forces of their emergency powers 'on the advice of the [local] cabinet' and a display of military force to restore public confidence. It claimed that laxity in security matters had 'provided Sinn Fein with the opportunity to bring additional men and arms' into Belfast.[11]

With great difficulty the semblance of a coherent law and order policy emerged from repeated discussions held during the following weeks. The military and civil authorities in Dublin not only contradicted local political, army and police advice, but also disagreed amongst themselves. There was division in principle over the nature of the violence, as to whether it was political or sectarian in character. There was no consensus either over the appropriate security response – whether troop reinforcements were required, emergency powers could be utilized, the special constabulary should be mobilized or the regular police force placed under army command. One positive decision resulted from these deliberations; the military commander in charge of Belfast, colonel G Carter-Campbell, assured the cabinet that he would dispatch troops more quickly in future and maintain fixed military posts and patrols in affected areas after peace was restored. Other issues, however, remained unresolved. Police authorities in the city forcefully resisted any suggestion that they should be placed under military control. A W Cope, (assistant under-secretary for Ireland) indicated that, despite the truce, authority could and would be given to hold suspects without trial, but stipulated that both sides would have to be interned as both sides were involved in acts of violence. However, a promised, written assurance from him, which would have enabled the arrests to proceed, had not been received by 12 September. On that day increasingly demoralized local ministers discussed the impact of the continuing drift in security policy on public confidence.

Nonetheless when further serious disorders occurred in Belfast during late September, crown forces responded promptly and with vigour. Acting on representations from local politicians and security advisers Dublin Castle agreed to a partial mobilization of the special constabulary, on condition that the patrolling of Catholic areas was entrusted solely to the army and regular police. When violence persisted, Carter-Campbell assumed control of all constabulary personnel in the city. Also troops acting under the Restoration of Order in Ireland Act, made a number of arrests and proscribed assemblies of three or more persons in effected areas.[12]

In nationalist communities these measures reinforced their tendency to look to the IRA rather than crown forces for protection. At the same time, unionists regarded them as inadequate, even inappropriate. They criticized the continuing failure to remobilize the special constabulary at full strength, complete with arms and the recurring imputation in military communiques that the disorder was sectarian rather than political in character with the consequence that when emergency powers were utilized Protestants as well as Catholics had been arrested. Progressively their feelings of optimism and expectation in June 1921 had been replaced by a deepening sense of betrayal and disillusion. Local ministers were castigated for their unwillingness or inability to take effective security measures and for their alleged over-confidence in the British government. Special constables complained bitterly that the IRA's organization for attack was being perfected without hindrance. These sentiments were rendered more volatile by the context of economic recession, trade boycott and political uncertainty. Progressively from July onwards they were reflected in the proliferation of loyalist paramilitary organizations and, later a revival of the UVF throughout much of the province; the cabinet hoped that the latter with its traditions and discipline might contain the discontent. Total membership of these unofficial forces was estimated at 21,000 by mid November 1921.[13]

Later that month, orders in council were issued, fixing appointed days for the formal handing over of powers to the Northern Ireland government under the terms of the 1920 act. On 21 November, it assumed responsibility for maintaining law and order and, on 1 December, control of local government services was transferred. Craig and his supporters viewed these developments with profound relief. To the northern minority, they were cause for trepidation. The extension of executive powers generated the sudden realization that the long derided unionist administration might emerge from the negotiations in London with its position substantially intact. In response, by 7 December, nine local authorities with Sinn Fein – nationalist party majorities, had repudiated its encroaching jurisdiction and defiantly pledged allegiance to Dail Eireann.

It at first seemed possible that the transfer of power might ease the local security problem at least, by enabling a more prompt and considered response to such disorder as might arise. However, though the regional government had at last been granted formal responsibility, it still lacked the financial, legal and physical resources to develop a response, independent of Westminster. Also the experience of the previous five months further restricted its freedom of manoeuvre. Its supporters demanded that it 'deal seriously with the sinn feiners in Ulster' and end the perceived policy of drift both in relation to law and order and local government.[14]

Unionist distrust of Britain was strengthened, in early December, by publication of the Anglo-Irish Treaty. Its terms formally recognized partition, but nonetheless clearly envisaged Ireland as a single entity, even if the 'assertion of the principle was accompanied by no prospect of a practical realization'.[15] The Sinn Fein leadership was firmly convinced that as a consequence of the agreement 'essential unity' had been achieved; at the time this view was broadly shared by the imperial delegation. Article 12 was the main source of these expectations; it stated that if Northern Ireland excluded itself from the Free State, (by passing a special address through both houses of its legislature), its frontiers were to be revised by a Boundary Commission. This provision prolonged the political uncertainty regarding the future of the province; Craig later described it as the 'predominant danger' facing his government and a surrender to Sinn Fein.[16] Unionists, especially west of the Bann, feared that it would result in the transference of substantial portions of the six counties to the south.

Meanwhile, the Boundary Commission became the focal point of the minority's hopes and almost seemed designed to perpetuate its divisions. Article 12 was greeted with particular enthusiasm by border nationalists, where the Sinn Fein party was strongest and where it was believed that the greater part of Fermanagh and Tyrone at least would ultimately be included in the Free State. In contrast, Devlinite nationalists to the east of the province strongly opposed re-partition. Instead they hoped for a revised settlement which would enhance the prospects of national unity and provide, in the interim, guarantees for northern Catholics with regard to policing, education and equitable representation.

All nationalists, especially those in the west, favoured continuing with the policy of non-recognition towards the unionist government.[17] Also, despite its obvious, limitations, neither of the two minority groups considered that there was any viable alternative to the Treaty. To resist it could place the Boundary Commission in jeopardy. Division over its terms would inevitably distract attention from the position of the half million nationalists in the north. Civil conflict would justify and confirm unionist opposition to unification.

Overall, it was in exceptionally difficult circumstances that the Northern Ireland government first sought to exercise its authority in December 1921. Inside its still indeterminate jurisdiction a substantial and embittered minority refused to recognize its existence and had reason to hope that the new institutions would not survive. Across the border, the hostile Sinn Fein leadership helped initiate this response and shared this expectation. More extreme nationalists, north and south, were also prepared to give sustenance to a physical force campaign aimed at achieving unity. As a consequence of the truce the IRA had become better prepared and organized; its membership in the six counties numbered 8,500 by early 1922. Yet despite the formidable problems which northern ministers faced imperial government support remained uncertain, its attitude was still determined by the exigencies of its larger Irish policy. Conditions in the province required generous, sustained and imaginative measures, directed towards winning over the nationalist community and assuaging its suspicions and fears. No such strategy was adapted. Rather, the traditional, unionist siege mentality was accentuated by the context of actual siege. The circumstances of Northern Ireland's birth permanently distorted its political structures. The process was gradual and had begun before powers were transferred.

On 1 December the cabinet considered how best to respond to those recalcitrant nationalist controlled councils, whose activities had caused it embarrassment virtually from the outset of the Anglo-Irish negotiations. It decided to dissolve any that persisted in rejecting its authority and to replace them with paid commissioners. Emergency legislation to this effect was introduced into the commons next day and within three weeks had received the royal assent; the measure was regarded as more urgent once the terms of the Treaty had become known. Meanwhile, some effort was made to establish cordial relations with all councils; 'flamboyant [verbal] effusions' by political opponents were ignored.[18] Some authorities staged a strategic retreat. On 7 December, Tyrone county council resolved that it would loyally carry out the terms of the Treaty so, in effect, giving de jure recognition to the northern government. Most members were anxious to avoid dissolution so that they would be in a position to articulate nationalist claims for inclusion in the south when Article 12 was implemented. A number of other local elected bodies, however, continued to defy 'the partition parliament'; by March 1922, over twenty of these, including Fermanagh county council, had been suspended initially for a period of one year. Craig may have hoped that in the longer term border adjustments would ease his local government difficulties; in early January, the cabinet considered appointing Sir Edward Carson as the province's representative on the Boundary Commission.[19]

During the months which followed ministerial unease at the prospect of boundary revision was overshadowed by absorption in security matters; these became the government's overriding concern. Its policy priorities bore the clear imprint of its experience since the truce. Distrust of Westminster was reflected in its urgent efforts to achieve independence from the imperial military establishment in all circumstances short of an invasion of the six counties or cross border raids in force; the cabinet unanimously agreed that 'the safety of Ulster must come first'. This was balanced by a fixed desire to 'bring the British government along with us'; it was after all the irreplaceable source of troops and finance and the font of sovereign power. At the same time, ministers were concerned that they should 'maintain the confidence of our [ie the Unionist] people'.[20] This was to be achieved through the energetic adoption of the policies thought necessary to restore law and order; liaison arrangements between crown forces and the IRA were terminated as soon as powers were transferred. The pace and intensity of the measures taken subsequently were largely determined by the unpredictable flow of events in early 1922, in particular, the progressive deterioration in relations with the south.

Craig met Collins on 21 January 1922; he later explained to colleagues that he had been anxious to ascertain whether the Sinn Fein government 'intended to declare peace or war with Northern Ireland'.[21] The meeting was arranged by Winston Churchill, secretary of state for the colonies, partly out of concern at recent rioting in Belfast following the release of 130 northern, republican prisoners by the imperial authorities. Discussions between the two leaders were protracted, cordial and wide ranging. They considered the Sinn Fein boycott, the position of expelled Catholic shipyard workers, the release of political prisoners, the boundary question and the Council of Ireland. Afterwards, Craig expressed satisfaction. Remarks made by Collins suggested that he did not regard the treaty as inviolate and he appeared to accept that Ulster could not be coerced into a united Ireland; his attendance in itself implied recognition of the northern government. However, when they met again on 2 February, it was evident that they held mutually irreconcilable views, regarding the release of political prisoners, and above all, the function of the Boundary Commission. Craig would only consider minor boundary rectification. In contrast Collins sought substantial transfers of territory; he argued that 'majorities must rule'[22] and anticipated that if this principle was applied the viability of Northern Ireland might well be undermined. He was dismayed, when days later, during a commons debate at Westminster, Churchill dismissed such an interpretation of Article 12 as 'absurd'.[23]

Nonetheless, Britain's acute concern that the Treaty should be implemented and therefore that the provisional government should establish its authority enabled the southern leadership to exercise a degree of influence over Northern Ireland affairs. As the split within the Sinn Fein movement deepened, partition emerged as an obvious issue on which to attack supporters of the recent settlement. It was also tempting in response to seek to preserve unity and perhaps avoid civil war by diverting attention towards the six counties. Collins took a keen personal interest in the minority, much more so than his cabinet colleagues; he quickly emerged as its spokesman, acted as its protector and successfully exploited the favourable circumstances in which to press his views and demands on Westminster. His role throughout was an ambivalent one and, in the final analysis, subordinate to his primary political tasks and responsibilities in Dublin. Whilst negotiating with Craig in apparent good faith, he consistently supported the minority tactic of non-recognition and himself 'initiated policies of obstruction with every single governmental agency through which the north dealt with the south'.[24] From January, he also covertly provided the IRA's northern divisions with rifles and revolvers 'called in' from Liam Lynch's irregulars and personally authorized cross border raids and kidnappings. His intention was not only to protect the interests of northern nationalists; he also aimed to destabilize the province, to provide evidence that large areas were disaffected and ungovernable and ultimately to achieve unity using any and every means.

A succession of border incidents, during the spring of 1922, contributed to an alarming deterioration in north-south relations and heightened sectarian bitterness in the province. On 8 February, an IRA column, based in county Monaghan and acting on Collin's covert authority, kidnapped 42 leading unionists and special constables in Fermanagh and Tyrone. The probable objective of this, and at least one earlier, operation was to effect the release of three republican prisoners, arrested before the truce and held under imminent death sentence in Londonderry. Next day, the viceroy intervened and issued a reprieve, hours before the time of execution. On 12 February, 'A' special reinforcements dispatched by rail to Enniskillen clashed violently with an IRA unit at Clones station; as a consequence five deaths occurred. The resulting communal tension helped precipitate further outbreaks of rioting in Belfast, which local ministers regarded as 'very adverse to the loyalist cause'.[25] The city had, as Churchill stated an 'underworld ... with deadly forces of its own'.[26]

The northern government perceived this border violence to be part of an organized campaign aimed at its overthrow. Complicity and bad faith on the part of the Dublin leadership were assumed; Craig therefore felt justified in declaring with reference to the Boundary Commission: 'what we have now we hold' and 'not an inch'.[27] The imperial authorities were also denounced for allegedly suspending the rule of law since the truce. Their reprieve of the three prisoners in Londonderry had incensed unionist opinion; Sir James had himself considered resignation. He and his colleagues proceeded to introduce far reaching security measures. 'A' and 'B' class specials were fully mobilized for the first time in almost eight months; the premier claimed in concurrent negotiations with the Treasury that they had 'justified their existence'.[28] The constabulary establishment was raised, partly as a means of absorbing and disciplining Protestant paramilitary organizations. Also with this in mind, a new C1 class was planned, in essence a territorial army; it had been under consideration prior to powers being transferred. In addition, preparations were made for the formation of a new police force. In March, Craig invited field marshall Sir Henry Wilson, the former CIGS, to advise on security matters. On his suggestion a military adviser, major-general Sir Arthur Solly Flood, was appointed; he assumed overall responsibility for maintaining law and order in Northern Ireland, on 7 April, and was supported by officers, on loan from the War Office. In London, this may have been regarded as a means of bringing the special constabulary under a measure of military discipline. Meanwhile, the Civil Authorities (Special Powers) Bill was drafted. Its terms were less far-reaching than those contained in the ROIA, but it nonetheless equipped the ministry of home affairs with extensive emergency powers. These the minister was authorized to delegate to his parliamentary secretary or even to a police officer. It provided for the death penalty or flogging to be applied in a range of political offences and under its specific regulations, internment could be introduced. Craig regarded it as a vital weapon in 'breaking the power of the IRA in the six counties'.[29]

Though these initiatives were intended to provide a greater measure of regional self-reliance, Sir James remained conscious of the province's ultimate dependence on Britain in security matters. He himself noted that it could not survive in a 'campaign of atrocity' with the south.[30] In order to increase moral and financial support for Ulster he therefore launched an energetic propaganda campaign both in the United Kingdom and the colonies. He also consistently rejected appeals for the introduction of martial law mainly because he feared that, if imposed, it would seem in England that 'one side was as bad as the other'.[31] His frequent visits to London to explain and justify policies adopted had the unfortunate consequence of allowing sensitive issues to be determined by uncompromising and partisan colleagues.

The British cabinet was largely uninterested in Northern Ireland's problems, but it was responsive to southern claims and criticisms and therefore wary of taking any action which could be interpreted as a breach of the spirit of the Treaty. Its members therefore felt especially uneasy at the expansion of the special constabulary. It was widely regarded as 'unnecessary' and 'very dangerous to peace'.[32] Moreover, there was concern that it would, 'in certain eventualities, be turned against'[33] the imperial government. Nonetheless British ministers did not themselves undertake responsibility for developing a satisfactory system of law enforcement in the province; Craig suspected that they would have welcomed an opportunity to 'wash their hands of the whole affair'.[34] Despite his protests they refused to halt the disbandment of the RIC; recruitment ended with the truce and the force was dissolved on 31 May 1922. Their support was unobtrusive as well as uncertain; in order to avoid parliamentary controversy, grants towards the upkeep of the special constabulary were concealed in a general subsidy to Northern Ireland. Though additional troops were despatched, they continued to adopt a peripheral, security role. From February 1922 onwards, border defence became the exclusive responsibility of the special constabulary despite the likelihood that this would make future frontier revision more problematical and the grave risks of a collision with regular or irregular forces. More active military involvement was avoided as it might suggest that partition was being imposed and would certainly have increased the danger of a confrontation with the IRA, even of a revival of the Anglo-Irish war.

Churchill's response to the IRA's border offensive, the deepening north-south hostility and continuing sectarian atrocities in Belfast was to organize a further meeting between Collins and Craig. Representatives of the British and both Irish governments met together for the first time on 30 March and after discussions, signed the Collins-Craig Pact. It opened with a dramatic, Churchillian flourish: 'Peace is today declared'. It contained a number of specific commitments: IRA activity in the six counties was to cease, northern political prisoners to be released and expelled, Catholic shipyard workers in Belfast to be returned to their former employment. Other provisions were intended to promote minority confidence in the regional government and to elicit their co-operation in security matters. No-jury courts were to be established for cases of serious crime; an inter-community conciliation committee was to be formed to investigate reports of outrages and complaints of intimidation and an all-Catholic advisory body was to be appointed to select suitable recruits from amongst its co-religionists for service in the special constabulary. In addition, police personnel were to display official identification numbers when on patrol and to hand in their arms before going off duty.[35]

Implementation of these terms was rendered more difficult by the context of political uncertainty in both northern and southern Ireland and the persistence of violence, especially in Belfast, where 21% of the labour force was unemployed. Given the depth of the slump throughout the province and an acute housing shortage, any suggestion that those expelled from their workplaces or homes would be speedily returned merely raised expectations which could not be realized. In any case, the Northern Ireland government showed neither imagination nor urgency regarding its obligations under the pact; had it done so it would have undermined its credibility with most members of the unionist movement. To the party rank and file, the agreement seemed designed to tarnish the reputation of the province's legal system and of its special constabulary, to facilitate the assassination of policemen both on and off duty and, overall, to weaken the forces of law and order with the ultimate objective of making the area ungovernable.

Local ministers, officials and the military adviser sympathized with such views. Craig, acting under pressure from colleagues, interpreted the security clauses narrowly. Thus, he released only a small number of political prisoners and exclusively those charged with technical offences; he himself always regarded convicted republicans as a 'trump card to be played' in negotiations with the south.[36] Characteristically, Dawson Bates took advantage of his leader's frequent absences to subvert implementation of other provisions. In particular he delayed convening the inter-communal investigative committee; its activities had lapsed completely by mid-May.[37] The advisory body to select Catholic recruits for the special constabulary was similarly unproductive owing to ministerial indifference, IRA intimidation and minority alienation; the attitude of border nationalists was governed mainly by the assumption that they would be transferred to the south by the boundary commission.

For his part, Collins appeared strongly to favour conciliation and overtly seemed anxious to fulfil the terms of the agreement. At the same time, however, he made cynical use of its terms to advance southern grievances in London and Belfast. He also secretly participated in pro-Treaty IRA preparations for an offensive against the north. It was to appear as 'a defensive operation, a reaction against the activities of the specials';[38] its purpose was to wreak such havoc and destruction in the province that the unionist leadership would be compelled to seek an accommodation with himself. He had, in any case, little influence with the irregulars unless it was exercised towards war; during late March, they successfully revived the Belfast boycott without his approval. Overall, British government recognition of Collins as the accredited custodian of the minority not only exasperated Craig's supporters but also did much to strengthen the position of more uncompromising nationalists. Thus, within Northern Ireland, the successive inter-governmental agreements conferred credibility and prestige on Sinn Fein and the IRA. As a consequence, the Devlinites, who favoured recognition of the northern parliament and the formation of a broadly based nationalist-labour coalition found their position repeatedly undermined.

An abrupt exchange of letters between Collins and Craig in late April effectively signalled the demise of their March pact;[39] subsequently, as Churchill noted ruefully, the two sides drifted even further apart than before. The level of violence in the north rose due to the mounting IRA campaign, sectarian clashes and disillusion resulting from the repeated failure of negotiations. In response, the special constabulary was maintained at full strength and its establishment further increased. The special powers act was hurriedly passed through parliament; it received the royal assent on 11 April. Also legislation was prepared which provided for the formation of the Royal Ulster Constabulary; in the disturbed conditions then obtaining, the government's initial intention to ensure that one-third of recruits to the new force were from the minority, was jettisoned. Nonetheless, 400 of the 1,100 men who had enlisted by mid-1922, were Catholics.[40]

When considering the measures to be taken, the cabinet remained alert to the sensibilities of imperial ministers and was therefore reluctant either to aggregate to itself the fullest powers or even to make optimum use of those it already possessed. Thus, though it was forewarned by the local police authorities that a major terrorist offensive was being planned, it rejected their recommendation that suspects should be interned. Instead, it decided merely to make lists of those of 'evil designs' so that they could be dealt with 'instantly if the crisis arises'.[41] Similarly ministers rejected the suggestion that special courts should be established for those charged with serious political crimes as they were concerned that such an initiative would not be understood in England. The ostentatious security preparations recommended by Solly Flood were likewise ignored; he had advised equipping the special constabulary with aircraft, tanks and bombs.[42]

Subsequently, as anticipated, the level of violence reached its zenith. In May alone an estimated seventy-five murders took place in Belfast, forty-two of the victims were Catholic. Between 10–25 May, forty-one fires occurred mainly at Protestant owned, business premises in Catholic districts.[43] IRA operations were predominantly conducted by indigenous, pro-treaty units, acting under authority from southern head-quarters. Their campaign was fully unleashed on 18 May and helped provoke a severe sectarian backlash. Alarm amongst northern ministers at the rising toll of death and destruction, was

61

heightened by the signing of the de Valera-Collins electoral pact, on 20 May. Like Churchill, they regarded this as an ominous portent, which would probably presage a concerted attack on the six counties. The agreement had in part, been prompted by a minority delegation to Dublin, two days earlier. Its members had warned the Sinn Fein leadership that civil conflict in the south might well render partition permanent and would certainly leave northern nationalists exposed and unprotected. At the Sinn Fein Ard Fheis days later, Collins stated that the agreement would enable him to concentrate on the affairs of the province.

The escalating violence in the north and news of the pact in Dublin prompted Craig and his colleagues to take full advantage of their emergency powers. On 22 May, a number of extreme nationalist movements were proclaimed, including the IRA, IRB and Cumann-na-mBan. Also on that day internment was introduced and enforced against those 'endeavouring to subvert our parliament'.[44] During the following weeks, over 500 IRA suspects and sympathisers were arrested and held on the Argenta, a ship moored off Larne. Lord Fitzalan, the lord lieutenant, who had initially been reluctant to give his approval, did so unilaterally after the assassination of a unionist MP, William Twaddell and the incineration of Shane's Castle; its proprietor, Lord O'Neill, was father of the speaker of the Northern Ireland house of commons. Both incidents highlight the essentially political nature of the disorder. In early June, the imposition of a curfew, covering the entire six counties, and the application of exclusion orders effectively curtailed large-scale IRA operations in rural areas. The cabinet underlined its commitment to the restoration of order by agreeing 'to stand over [ie indemnify] any action' taken by crown forces. In addition, it fully endorsed a suggestion made by the military advisor that the 'time had arrived when the shooting from across the border should be replied to'.[45]

The increasing turmoil in the province and the government's extensive counter-measures coincided with delicate discussions between London and Dublin over the draft Irish constitution; these had begun on 27 May. From the outset, imperial ministers were concerned that the Sinn Fein leadership would exploit recent developments in the six counties to justify non-compliance with the Treaty, and perhaps even to break off the negotiations. On 30 May, both Collins and Griffith raised the political situation in the north; the former alleged that Catholics were being exterminated there and claimed that members of the special constabulary were implicated. He argued that these circumstances were the responsibility of the British government as it had transferred security powers to Craig and had sanctioned, financed and equipped the specials. He suggested that martial law should be imposed and that an impartial enquiry should be held into the actions taken by the unionist leadership.

By late May the imperial cabinet had itself become acutely uneasy about the measures being adopted in Northern Ireland and also its own role in the region's affairs, particularly in relation to the special constabulary. George's opinion, 'the Ulster difficulty [...] was the weakest part of ish case'. He observed that 'the first murders were of Catholics,' yet had been punished. We had made no inquiry, we had armed 48,000 tants'.[46] The consensus reached by British ministers was that an initiative should be taken which would eliminate the Ulster question from their discussions with the south and so clarify the essential issue of 'republic versus empire'. The imposition of martial law was rejected on the grounds that it was unlikely to be effective, could lead to confrontation with republican forces and was in any case, unacceptable to Craig. Most cabinet members favoured holding a judicial inquiry into Northern Ireland; Lloyd George himself considered that it might at least create a lull in the violence and so facilitate a satisfactory resolution of his negotiations with the provisional government.

Before Craig could be summoned to discuss these matters a new security crisis arose suddenly along the Fermanagh border. On 27 May, pro-Treaty IRA forces occupied the Belleek-Pettigo salient, a remote triangular area, sough of Lough Erne and entirely cut off by the lakes from direct land contact with the remainder of the six counties. The motivation for the incursion is unclear; whether it was a final, desperate bid to avoid civil war in the south by provoking a renewal of the Anglo-Irish war or a protest against the security measures being implemented in the north or alternatively due to the arrival of a new and more forceful regular commandant into this volatile region.

On 30 May, Craig sent a telegram to Churchill to request that imperial troops recapture the two villages; he claimed that Strabane and Londonderry were also at risk from southern invasion. He was not hopeful of a favourable outcome. In fact, the colonial secretary responded promptly and sympathetically and would have resigned had other imperial ministers not supported a positive riposte. He was anxious to reassure border unionists and convinced that military intervention would have a salutary effect on the provisional government. He attributed the violence in the province to the actions of local IRA divisions and the efforts of extreme partisans in the south to break down the devolved institutions. After seeking assurances from Collins that his forces were not responsible for the attack and receiving the approval of reluctant cabinet colleagues, he instructed local army units to clear the occupied area and 'to inflict the greatest loss on the enemy'.[47] It was the first direct confrontation between the British troops and the IRA since the truce, which was still nominally operative. By 8 June the action had been successfully completed with only minor casualties. Whilst Collins protested that southern territory had been violated, Lloyd George celebrated, with genuine relief, the 'great bloodless battle of Belleek'.[48]

Meanwhile, during talks with imperial ministers five days earlier, Craig had aggressively defended his government's record; he protested that the IRA covertly supported by the authorities in Dublin, was seeking to destroy Ulster.

He reiterated his opposition to martial law, but stated that he would accept a judicial enquiry, if it was presented to the public as having been held at his own request. However, when his colleagues were consulted they strongly deprecated this suggestion. Dawson Bates urged: 'You cannot try a government responsible to a parliament by a commission of judges'; he claimed that such a procedure would gravely compromise the cabinet's 'independence' and weaken its authority.[49] During a second and decisive meeting at Westminster on 16 June, Sir James therefore argued that this proposal was inopportune. He suggested as an alternative the sending of a 'trustworthy agent to Belfast who would be given every facility by the Northern government and who could furnish an unbiased report'.[50] Imperial ministers themselves recognized that a judicial inquiry might weaken the authority of the unionist administration and were aware that, if attempted, it could cause Craig and his colleagues to resign. Finally, and with reluctance, they agreed to an official investigation which was to be conducted by colonel Stephen Tallents, private secretary to Lord Fitzalan. His function was to report on whether a full public enquiry should be held to ascertain the reasons for the collapse of Collins and Craig pact and the eruption of violence which followed.

Tallents visited the province between 21 June–1 July 1922. Though his subsequent report did contain criticisms of the Northern Ireland government, especially the ministry of home affairs, its overall conclusions were broadly favourable.[51] It attributed the recent disorder in Belfast partly to the context of political uncertainty and economic recession. It also blamed an organized conspiracy by the IRA, conducted with southern support. There is evidence that Collins' 'hand in glove' involvement was suppressed in order not to provide conservative diehards with ammunition with which to attack the Treaty.[52] The IRA campaign was a flagrant breach of the pact and according to Tallents the main cause of its failure; it had incited retaliatory outrages and reprisals. He recommended that a permanent representative of the British government should be appointed to Belfast to liaise between the two administrations; he himself took up this office in October 1922. He concluded that any additional enquiry would be unhelpful as 'inadvertantly it would encourage ... Catholics in their refusal to recognize' the Northern Ireland government and inevitably revive nationalist propaganda about past events now 'best forgotten'. He observed that if a later and critical investigation was held and Craig was forced to resign: 'you get not a man like Pollock but an extremist like Wilson'.[53]

Given Tallents' recommendations and the significant decline in levels of violence which coincided with his inquiry, no further action was taken by the cabinet at Westminster. During June, IRA ambushes and arson attacks gradually petered out and the number of deaths in Belfast, attributable to the 'troubles', dropped to twenty-five. Extreme Protestant organizations bent on the extermination of Catholics became the main focus of governmental concern. The overall improvement in security was persistent and province-wide and partly due to the sweeping measures taken by local ministers over previous weeks. By mid-1922, the special constabulary had an establishment of 42,250 and an actual strength of 32,000. Its operating costs reached £2.7m for the financial year 1922–23; though a transferred service it continued to be financed and equipped by the imperial exchequer. In June 1922, the RUC numbered 1,100 roughly one-third of its recruitment target; its upper ranks were experienced men drawn from the recently suspended RIC. The combined total of regular and part-time police officers then stood at a ratio of one for every six families in Northern Ireland.[54]

In addition, the government had exercised its emergency powers with considerable effect: republican organizations had been proclaimed, a six county curfew imposed, most border roads closed, exclusion orders issued and, above all, internment applied. Between May 1922-December 1924, 728 suspects were arrested; the disruptive impact of this action was enhanced by the discovery earlier of lists of names of republican activists during a security force raid on St Mary's Hall, the IRA liaison office in Belfast, on 18 March 1922.[55] The persistent haemorrhage of key personnel dealt a crippling blow to the Sinn Fein organization. Its impact on the IRA was more limited but still severe. Nonetheless, acknowledging the cumulative effect of the various measures adopted and of the outbreaks of sectarian violence Seamus Woods, (officer commanding the northern divisions), noted: 'our position is hopeless'.[56]

Simultaneously, the deepening split in the south and the outbreak of civil war devastated the IRA's northern campaign and eliminated any prospect of a concerted assault on Ulster. Ineluctably, Collins was compelled to concentrate on stabilizing his own government and therefore to pursue, at least temporarily, a 'peace policy' towards the province. It was not, he observed, the time 'to take on war' with Great Britain and Northern Ireland.[57] Before the attack on the Four Courts, he was reassured by Churchill that the offensive would 'have a tremendous effect on Craig and put me in a position to require from him action of the utmost vigour against the murder of Roman Catholics in the north'.[58] On 3 June, the southern cabinet had already decided that for the foreseeable future, no regular troops would be permitted to cross the border. In due course, all units involved in the six counties campaign were instructed to suspend their activities; their officers were encouraged to believe that they would start again when circumstances were more favourable. In early August, some leading Free State politicians expressed support for a more comprehensive change in strategy towards the north; they proposed that the partition government should be granted official recognition in the belief that the unification process would be accelerated by fostering harmonious relations between Dublin and Belfast.[59]

In part, the shifting emphasis in Collins' policy was prompted by operations reports he had received from northern IRA commanders. From early June, they had progressively and unilaterally reduced the scale of their operations. Increasingly, they themselves favoured calling off the campaign temporarily at least. Their numbers were being depleted by the constant drift of volunteers south to join the regulars and by internment. They were dispirited by the deepening Sinn Fein split and by the imminence of civil war. Their supplies of arms and equipment were inadequate as a growing proportion was diverted to other areas. Also, crucially, they were aware of the diminishing support for physical force amongst northern nationalists; one local commander conceded that the national spirit was 'practically dead'.[60] As a consequence, information was being passed on to the special constabulary, arms dumps were being uncovered and men forced to go on the run.

This changing mood was shared and articulated by members of the Catholic hierarchy; Bishop Joseph MacRory, personally appealed to de Valera to 'call away his gunmen'.[61] Devlinites had consistently opposed the IRA campaign and favoured recognition of the northern parliament. By mid-1922, the use of force was widely perceived amongst nationalists as having been both ineffective and counter-productive. The Northern Ireland government had after all survived, whilst the minority had suffered from the severity of the resulting sectarian backlash. The incipient civil war in the south lowered its morale yet further.

The death of Collins, in August, reinforced the sentiments of despair, isolation and abandonment. It accentuated the changed direction of provisional government policy; this, in turn, was reflected in Westminster's dwindling interest in the administration of justice in Northern Ireland. Under W T Cosgrave's leadership, partition ceased to be a political priority. He consciously strove to improve north-south relations and forswore the use of non-constitutional methods to achieve unity, publicly at least. The Dublin administration progressively abandoned its obstruction of the Northern Ireland government and the minority was for the first time encouraged to recognize the Belfast parliament. One peculiar legacy from Collins' involvement in the earlier physical force campaign remained. By December 1922, over 500 members of northern IRA divisions were undergoing training at the Curragh; facilities at the camp had been provided after an approach to Dublin from the volunteers.[62] It is unclear whether the southern government under its new leader valued their presence more as a safeguard against their defection to the irregulars or as an investment in the eventual resumption of the armed struggle in the six counties.

From mid-1922, the political siege eased; Northern Ireland had weathered the crisis. But it was at considerable cost to itself – in lives and in finance, in the depth and durability of its internal divisions, and in the glacial coldness of its 'cold war' relations with the Free State. Moreover, until World War II, Westminster felt only a sense of obligation to the province, but no genuine commitment, and adopted isolationist and ungenerous policies towards it.

Partition at base was not the product of self-seeking British imperialism, or of unscrupulous class manipulation by local business interests. Rather it was the institutional recognition of pre-existing and genuine divisions within Ireland. The essence of this verdict was expressed convincingly in a letter to the *Freeman's Journal* on 19 June 1916. It was submitted by the Reverend M. O'Flanaghan. C.C., then secretary of Sinn Fein, in response to the Lloyd George negotiations, during the aftermath of the Easter Rising. He wrote

> Geography has worked hard to make one nation of Ireland. History has worked against it. The island of Ireland, and the national unity of Ireland, simply do not coincide ... . The test of separate identity is the wish of the people ... . The unionists of Ulster have never given their love and allegiance to Ireland. They love the hills of Antrim and Down in the same way that we love the plains of Roscommon, but the centre of their patriotic enthusiasm is London ... as ours is Dublin. We claim the right to decide what is our nation. We refuse that same right to Orangemen... . Are we going ... to compel the Orangemen of Antrim and Down to love us by force?

References

1. *Belfast Telegraph*, 24 December 1920; *Northern Ireland Parliamentary Debates* (Commons) vol. 1, cols. 36–37, 23 June 1921 (hereafter cited as N.I. Parl. Deb (c)).
2. For background to formation of Northern Ireland, see P. Buckland, *Irish Unionism 2: Ulster Unionism and the Origins of Northern Ireland 1886–1922*, Gill & Macmillan, Dublin/New York ,1973; P. Gibbon, *The Origins of Ulster Unionism: the Formation of Popular Protestant Politics and Ideology in Nineteenth Century Ireland*, Manchester University Press, Manchester, 1975; N. Mansergh, 'The Government of Ireland Act 1920: its origins and purposes: the working of the 'official mind', in J. G. Barry (ed.), *Historical Studies, 9*, Appletree Press, Belfast, 1974; A. S. Queckett, *The Constitution of Northern Ireland*, 3 vols. HMSO, Belfast, 1928–46.
3. The problems and prospects of the Northern Ireland government, 1920–22, are discussed in P. Buckland, *The Factory of Grievances: Devolved Government in Northern Ireland 1921–39*, Gill and Macmillan, Dublin 1979, pp. 1–6, 9–77; P. Arthur, *Government and Politics of Northern Ireland*, Longmans, Essex 1980, p. 83; Professor Newark is quoted as stating that the 1920 Act was a 'legislative ruin' within seven months of its passing. Chapter 2 contains a good analysis of the 1920 Act.
4. *United Kingdom Parliamentary Debates (Commons)*, 5th series, vol. 133, 25 October 1920, col. 1504 (hereafter cited as U.K. Parl. Deb. (c)).
5. *Northern Whig*, 6 December 1920.
6. G. B. Kenna, *Facts and Figures of the Belfast Pogrom, 1920–22*, O'Connell Publishing Co.,Dublin, 1997, p. 63.
7. P. Buckland, *Irish Unionism 2*, op. cit., p. 149.
8. They sent delegations to meet de Valera in order to strengthen his bargaining position and stiffen his resolve, they passed resolutions refusing to recognize the Northern Ireland parliament and finally they pledged allegience to Dail Eireann. See records of Fermanagh and Tyrone County Councils, July–December 1921, LA4, 6 Public Record Office of Northern Ireland (PRONI).

9. Remarks by Sir Hamar Greenwood, chief secretary, *Cabinet Conclusions*, 31 August 1921, PRONI CAB4/17.

10. *Cabinet Conclusions*, 16 August 1921, PRONI CAB4/14; P. Buckland, *Factory of Grievances*, op. cit., pp. 179–185; E. Phoenix, *The Nationalist Movement in Northern Ireland, 1914–28*, PhD thesis, Queen's University, Belfast, 1984, pp. 179–185.

11. See PRONI CAB4/17, which contains the conclusions for three cabinet meetings, two held on 31 August and the other on 1 September 1921, and also an unsigned typescript headed 'History of attempts to get peace keeping forces on satisfactory footing'.

12. P. Buckland, *Factory of Grievances*, op. cit., pp. 187–192; *Cabinet Conclusions*, 1, 12 September 1921, PRONI CAB4/17, 19.

13. Philip McVicker, *'Law and Order in Northern Ireland, 1920–1936'*, (PhD thesis, University of Ulster, 1985), pp. 44–48; P. Buckland, *Factory of Grievances,* op. cit., pp. 192–4; A. Hezlet, *The B Specials; A History of the Ulster Special Constabulary*, Pan, London 1972, p. 54, 53–85 passim. Diary of Frederick Crawford, Larne gunrunner, Crawford Papers, 27 October 1921, PRONI D640/11A.

14. Ibid., 15 November 1921.

15. N. Mansergh, *The Government of Northern Ireland*, Allen & Unwin, London, 1936, pp. 119–120.

16. N.I. Parl. Deb (c), vol. 2, 14 March 1922, col. 9; P. Buckland, *James Craig*, Gill andMacmillan, Dublin, 1980, p. 70.

17. This response was actively promoted by the Sinn Fein leadership in Dublin. Eoin MacNeill stated: 'The policy should be the same whether Belfast contracts in or out of the Free State', E. Phoenix, op. cit., p. 353. See pp. 346–376 for analysis of northern nationalist attitudes to the treaty and boundary commission.

18. *Report of the Ministry of Home Affairs on Local Government Services*, Belfast, 1923, p. 9; also *Cabinet Conclusions*. 1 December 1921, PRONI CAB4/28.

19. Ibid., 10 January 1921, PRONI CAB4/29. During discussions, ministers agreed that though refusal to take part would be popular with unionists, it contained the risk of a representative being appointed to act on the province's behalf and thus of a larger area being lost. Also such a course might jeopardize residual Conservative Party sympathy and not to co-operate in implementing a settlement agreed to by Westminster, might make the unionist government seem ridiculous. Thus ministers considered nominating Carson – better terms might therefore result and, in Craig's view, some boundary change might be advantageous.

20. The most detailed cabinet consideration of priorities is in *Cabinet Conclusions*, 12 May 1922, PRONI CAB4/41.

21. Ibid., 26 January 1922, PRONI CAB4/30; also, on 11 January 1922, Craig indicated to Churchill that he was willing to meet Collins 'to ascertain clearly whether the policy of Southern Ireland is to be one of peace or whether the present method of pressure on Northern Ireland is to be continued,' M. Gilbert, *Winston Churchill*, Volume IV, 1916–22, Heinemann, London, 1975,p. 684.

22. E.Phoenix, op. cit., p. 421.

23. Ibid., p. 431.

24. T. P. Coogan, *Michael Collins*, Arrow Books, London' 1991, p. 339; also pp. 333–343 for discussion of Collins' approach to Northern Ireland.

25. Cabinet Conclusions, 14 February 1922, PRONI CAB4/32.

26. M.Gilbert, op. cit.,p. 696.

27. P.Buckland, *James Craig*, op. cit., pp. 57, 76.

28. Details of Craig's meeting with Treasury officials on 9 February 1922, in PRONI CAB9A/4/1; P. McVicker, op. cit., pp. 65–66.

29. N.I. Parl. Deb. (c), vol. 2, 14 March 1922, col. 10. During debate, R. J. Lynn stated that since 1 January 1922, eighty-three murders had taken place in Belfast and 'no-one brought to justice', ibid., col. 24; P. McVicker, op. cit., pp. 68–70; B. Barton, *The development of*

Northern Ireland government policy in relation to law and order and local government, 1921–22, M A thesis, University of Ulster, 1977, pp. 25–29.

30. *Cabinet Conclusions,* 14 February 1922, PRONI CAB4/32.

31. N.I. Parl. Deb. (c), vol. 2, 14 March 1922, col 15.

32. Comment by Otto Ernest Niemeyer, deputy controller at the Treasury, 23 January 1922, in P. McVicker, op. cit., p. 65.

33. *Memorandum* by Tom Jones and Lionel Curtis, 18 March 1922, in S. G. Tallent's papers, Public Record Office, Kew, CO 906/30 (PRO).

34. Cabinet Conclusions, 14 February 1922, PRONI CAB4/32; discussion of British policy towards Northern Ireland in P. Buckland, *Factory of Grievances,* op. cit., pp. 197–201.

35. Text in D. McCardle, *The Irish Republic,* Transworld Publishers, London 1968, pp. 894–896; detailed analysis in M. Farrell, *Arming the Protestants: The Formation of the Ulster Special Constabulary and Royal Ulster Constabulary, 1920–27,* Pluto Press, London, 1983, pp. 104–124.

36. *Cabinet Conclusions,* 18 April 1922, PRONI CAB4/40.

37. Dawson Bates regarded the committee as a 'voluntary' body and therefore refused it funding, denied it access to government reports on disturbances and responded dilatorily to its requests. It met twice (on 12 and 19 April); by early May its Catholic membership had withdrawn and it quietly lapsed. See editorial in *Irish News,* 20 April 1922, and E.Phoenix, op. cit., pp. 505–507.

38. T. P. Coogan, op. cit., p. 362.

39. Craig to Collins and Collins' reply, 25, 28 April 1922, in E. Phoenix, op. cit., pp. 509–511.

40. A. Hezlet, op. cit., pp. 62, 73. *The Departmental Committee on Police Reorganization in Northern Ireland 1922,* Cmd. 1, p. 5, recommended (though not unanimously) that one-third RUC places be reserved for Catholics; Hezlet suggests that this was ultra vires under the terms of the 1920 Act. The stipulation was not included in the bill, see N.I. Parl. Deb (c), vol 2, 24 May 1922, col. 654. Despite initial good intentions and fair selection procedures the government did little to attract Catholic recruits. Their recruitment peaked in early 1924 at 552, (19.2% of force strength), see M. Farrell, op. cit., p. 191; P. Buckland *Factory of Grievances,* op. cit., pp. 21–22. Between June–December 1922, 81.7% of RUC recruits were ex-RIC or ex-Ulster Special Constabulary, P. McVicker, op. cit., p. 101.

41. *Cabinet Conclusions,* 19 April 1922, PRONI CAB4/40.

42. *Cabinet Conclusions,* 13 March, 19 June 1922, PRONI CAB4/35, 48; A. Hezlet, op. cit., pp. 66–67, 82–88.

43. G. B. Kenna, op. cit., p. 94; P. Buckland, *Irish Unionism, 2,* op. cit., p. 169 and *Factory of Grievances,* op. cit., pp. 195–196, 320.

44. Craig told the house of internment and the proclamation order on the afternoon of 23 May 1922, N.I. Parl. Deb. (c), vol. 2, col. 599. By then 202 had been interned. The decision that certain nationalist movements should be 'immediately proclaimed' was taken by cabinet on 20 May 1922; see PRONI CAB4/43. Bates issued the relevant orders on 22 May 1922, E. Phoenix, op. cit., pp. 542–549.

45. *Cabinet Conclusions,* 23 May 1922, PRONI CAB4/44; N.I. Parl. Deb. (c), vol. 2, 23 May 1922, cols. 603–4.

46. C. Younger, *Ireland's Civil War,* Fontana, London, 1982, pp. 208–9; Tom Jones, *Whitehall Diary,* Vol. ,III Oxford University Press, Oxford, 1971, p. 204.

47. P. McVicker, op. cit., p. 87.

48. B. Jones, op. cit., p. 212.

49. Quoted in P. McVicker, op. cit., p. 91; also Jones, op. cit., p. 207.

50. P. McVicker, op. cit., p. 91.

51. *Tallent's Papers,* June, July 1922, PRO CO 906/23–30.

52. T. P. Coogan, op. cit., p. 371. The author suggests that if the extent of Collins' involvement had been revealed, it could have brought the British government down.
53. Tallents to Masterson-Smith, 4 July 1922 and *Tallent's Report*, 6 July 1922, PRO CO 906/30; Tallent's diary, PRO CO 906/24.
54. G. B. Kenna, op. cit., pp. 98, 117–8; P. Buckland, *Factory of Grievances*, op. cit., p. 197.
55. Ibid., p. 210 n; also E. Phoenix, op. cit., p. 456.
56. E. Phoenix, op. cit., p. 623. The comment was made on 2 August 1922.
57. Quoted in *Irish News*, 10 June 1922.
58. P. McVicker, op. cit., p. 97. Churchill added: 'You are fighting not only for the freedom but for the unity of Ireland'.
59. See description of memorandum entitled 'Policy in regard to the north-east', dated 9 August 1922, by Ernest Blythe, (Acting Minister of Home Affairs), in Phoenix, op. cit., pp. 625–9.
60. Ibid., p. 623.
61. MacRory interview with Tallents, in PRO CO906/26.
62. Phoenix, op. cit., p. 625.

4 Politics of North-South Relations in Post-partition Ireland

Dennis Kennedy

All this part is beautiful wild country, mostly peat bog, but freely dotted with little white farms. It is far more thickly populated than such country would be in England, because there are so many small holdings. The beautiful blue mountains of Donegal stood up on the West, cut off from us, alas, by this tragic state of civil war. It gave me a strange feeling to see a country so unnaturally and ungeographically divided – like seeing a living creature cut in two.[1]

Thus commented Lilian Spender, later Lady Spender, wife of Sir James Craig's close associate Sir Wilfrid Spender, in her diary for June 1923, while visiting west Tyrone and Fermanagh on a tour of the border country of Northern Ireland. An English lady, fiercely unionist, and with no sentimental attachment to the island of Ireland, her reaction to the physical reality of partition is a reminder of how dramatic, almost unthinkable, the division of the island was to those living in it at that time, even to those who saw partition as their only means of salvation, and devoted almost their entire energies to maintaining it.

What shocked the diarist were the trenched roads and checks on the new border; the 'civil war' she refers to was not the civil war which had ravaged the Free State, but was by then effectively over, but the longer war between republicanism and unionism which had divided the island. Also, by June 1923, the first customs sheds had appeared on the border, erected by the Free State to enforce its new import duty imposed in the spring of 1923.

Subsequently later generations of unionists have tended to emphasise the historic distinctiveness of 'Ulster', or at least of the core territory of what is now Northern Ireland, and to view partition, while artificial and arbitrary in its exact geographical detail, as essentially confirming a deep and established division, even as inevitable. In one sense, perhaps the more correct legal one, the unit which was partitioned in 1921 was the United Kingdom of Great Britain and Ireland; the departure of the twenty six counties from that United Kingdom was a much more significant and dramatic event in the wider his-

71

torical context than the creation of two administrative and political entities in the smaller island.

But this view has tended to underestimate, if not ignore, the extent to which the island of Ireland had been one administrative unit within the United Kingdom, particularly in the decades immediately preceding partition, and also the considerable extent to which the cultural, religious, social and other aspects of life in the island were organised on the basis of the island of Ireland, rather than that of the United Kingdom.

At the beginning of the nineteenth century the Act of Union had abolished the Dublin parliament and brought about legislative union. But this had not been accompanied by a unification of administration, or even government. As Nicholas Mansergh notes, Ireland was part of the United Kingdom, but not an integrated part in that there was no attempt to incorporate it administratively in the United Kingdom system.[2] Throughout the nineteenth century Ireland was governed by its own administration under the direction of the lord lieutenant, or more often the chief secretary, supported by what seemed an ever-increasing number of administrative boards. Balfour, in 1905, told the House of Commons there were forty seven such boards.[3] Redmond said he did not know how many they were, but condemned them all as permanent, centralised, nominated and stuffed full of members of the ascendancy party; they were 'omnipotent in the government of Ireland'.[4] One or other of the lord lieutenant or the chief secretary was a member of the cabinet in London, and answerable there, and in parliament, for Irish affairs. But Ireland was administered and indeed governed, as a unit, by and from Dublin Castle.

This was the context in which Irish nationalism had developed in the nineteenth century. It was essentially a territorial nationalism, firmly attached to the geographical island. When nationalists spoke of 'Ireland' and personified it as Cathleen na Houlihaun or Dark Rosaleen they thought as much, and perhaps more, of the island than they did of the people. Ireland, as a piece of geography, had a more obvious distinct and separate identity from Britain than had the mixed inhabitants of the island from their fellow citizens in the rest of the United Kingdom. Indeed much effort at the end of the nineteenth century was devoted to the re-discovery, some would say invention, of a distinct Celtic and Gaelic Irishness as a support for political nationalism. No such effort was required where geography was concerned.

To note this is not to enter a debate on the validity of the claims of Irish nationalism on the historic unity of the island, or on the rightness or wrongness of partition. The point is to remind ourselves that a whole system of government and administration in Ireland – ramshackle as it may have been – was abruptly terminated by partition. For a century or more people had looked to Dublin and the Board of Education, the Local Government Board, the Congested Districts Board and a host of other boards for the control, direction and administration of their affairs on the basis of the whole island. Suddenly, in the space of barely one year, this framework was torn apart. For the new entity of Northern Ireland this meant an entirely new administration and focus. For the emerging Free State, there was room for continuity between the old Dublin Castle administration, and that of the new political entity in the twenty six counties. But what about matters affecting both? What about Lady Spender's 'living creature cut in two?'

One of the most remarkable features of the history of the island of Ireland over the past seventy five years has been, at government level, the near totality of partition, the replacement of a long-established single administrative system by two separate administrations, who managed, or contrived, to keep all contact to a minimum, who built no new structures, however modest, to take care of common interests in practical matters, and who for many decades had no dialogue at all at political level. This despite the fact that one side of the political divide continued to hold the unity of the island as the highest principle in its creed, while the other, in many aspects of its non-political life, continued to behave as if partition had never happened.[5] The purpose of this chapter is to explore concepts of the oneness of the island, and to seek to explain why relations between the two administrations remained almost non-existent.

Part of the explanation lies in the circumstances in which a settlement was reached in 1921–22. The Articles of Agreement for a Treaty between Great Britain and Ireland signed in London on 6 December 1921 was not a calm and careful assessment of conflicting Irish and British aspirations, but an attempt, under extreme pressure of violent events, to adapt the settlement already on the statute book – the Government of Ireland Act of 1920 – which itself had emerged from at least one and arguably three decades of wrestling with the problem. The act inevitably reflected the problem as it had been perceived during those earlier years, rather than in the form it had now assumed, reshaped by the triumph of republicanism committed to full separation of Ireland from England, and by the violence of the period from the passing of the act to the signing of the treaty.

The very title of the treaty, Articles of Agreement for a Treaty between Great Britain and Ireland, indicates the rapidly changing circumstances, and the uncertainties of the situation. The Government of Ireland Act of 1920 was a statute of the United Kingdom of Great Britain and Ireland, while the treaty purported to be an agreement between two entities, Ireland and Great Britain, neither of which had any recognised legal or political existence. They were, at the time of the treaty negotiations, simply geographical terms. Nor was the treaty a final settlement of the problem. Under it an Irish Free State, of the whole island, was to be created, but then the six counties of Northern Ireland were given the right to opt out. Even then the exact boundary between Free State and Northern Ireland was provisional, to be determined finally, if necessary, by a boundary commission.

The treaty itself has very little to say about what the relationship between Northern Ireland and the rest of the island might be if Northern Ireland did indeed exercise its right to opt out of the Free State. The treaty simply, almost in an aside, says the provisions of the Government of Ireland Act (including those relating to the Council of Ireland) shall continue to be of full force and effect.[6] Yet the Council of Ireland was devised and defined in the 1920 act to govern relations between two administrative units in Ireland, both of which were to be within the United Kingdom, both returning members to Westminster, and the reunion of which was explicitly envisaged in the act.

By December 1921, however, the most likely, indeed inevitable outcome of the treaty was the totally different situation, resulting from an Ulster opt-out, of a complete political and administrative separation between north and south in Ireland, a situation not even envisaged when the Council of Ireland was written into the 1920 act.

But if the Council had not been devised to meet the position that actually emerged in 1921–22, the need for some such mechanism certainly still existed. The functions of the Council, as laid down in the original act, were to bring about

> harmonious action between the parliaments and governments of southern Ireland and Northern Ireland, and ... the promotion of mutual intercourse and uniformity in relation to matters affecting the whole of Ireland, and to (provide) for the administration of services which the two parliaments mutually agree should be administered uniformly throughout the whole of Ireland, or which, by virtue of this act, are to be so administered ...

Given the plethora of Dublin-based administrative boards pre-partition, and the 'unnatural and ungeographical' nature of partition, then the provision of some such mechanism for co-ordination and harmonisation would have seemed essential. The only specific powers assigned to the Council under the act were public services in connection with railways, fisheries, and the administration of diseases of animals acts, all of which had a clear, physical cross-border dimension. But the legislation made provision for the two parliaments on the island, by agreement, to assign other areas of responsibility to the Council,. The clear expectation in the act was that this would happen, and that expectation was presumably carried forward into the treaty. As originally envisaged, the Council was to be an institution of some weight, and was authorised in the act to employ its own staff.

Such practical considerations were not the only justification for the creation of the Council. It was set up specifically 'with a view to the establishment of a parliament for the whole of Ireland'. As the preamble declares, the act

> contemplates and affords every facility for union between north and south, and empowers the two parliaments by mutual agreement and joint action to termi-

nate partition and to set up one parliament and one government for the whole of Ireland. With a view to the establishment of a single parliament, and to bringing about harmonious actions between the two governments and parliaments, there is created a bond of union in the meantime, by means of a Council of Ireland ...[7]

The act allowed the two parliaments, by passing identical acts in each, to set up a parliament for the whole of Ireland, thereby bringing about 'Irish union', and, incidentally, ending the existence of the Council.

The motivations behind the inclusion of the Council of Ireland in the 1920 act were probably mixed. There was an obvious need to make provision for common administration of cross-border services and other matters of mutual interest. There was also a reluctance on the part of many, including those in London, to contemplate partition as anything other than a temporary and limited measure, which, after a period of calm and healing, might be found unnecessary. In June 1921, at the state opening of the new northern parliament in Belfast, King George V looked forward to the day in which the Irish people, north and south, 'under one parliament or two' would work together in common love for Ireland.[8] Finally, and more compelling, was the need to preserve the concept of Ireland as a whole – the essential unity of the island – without which it would plainly be impossible to sell any partition settlement to Irish nationalism.

It was this approach which meant the treaty of 1921 had to enshrine the formality of including Northern Ireland in an all-island Free State, then allowing it immediately to vote itself out of it. It was possible to argue that the 'essential unity' of Ireland had thereby been acknowledged in the treaty. British ministers may also have seen advantage in leaving it to the Irish themselves to partition the island, via the Ulster opt-out, rather than imposing it directly. If they did, this was a subtlety lost on succeeding generations of Irish nationalist rhetoricians.

The Council of Ireland was to consist of forty members, plus a president nominated by the lord lieutenant. Each of the two parliaments was to nominate twenty members, thirteen from commons, seven from senates. The president would have a casting vote in case of stalemate. Nominations were to be by vote of the respective chambers, thereby ensuring, one assumes, that the Council would have been equally divided between northern unionists and southern nationalists. Elections to the Council were to be the first business of both parliaments.[9]

The northern parliament duly elected its members on 23 June 1921. Despite its clearly stated role as a 'bond of union', and its mandate to promote and facilitate Irish union, the response to the Council was marginally less hostile in Belfast than it was in Dublin. No members were ever nominated by Dublin, no president was nominated, and the Council never met.

75

Carson initially welcomed it. Speaking in the House of Commons in November 1920 he described its conception as the biggest advance towards unity in Ireland, and declared himself optimistic enough to hope that there was, in the Council, the germ of a future united Ireland.[10] Southern unionists generally regarded the proposed Council as a safeguard, though they were disappointed that it would have no actual power, and it was presumably as a southern unionist that Carson was still speaking in 1920. It is worth noting that while speaking before partition had happened, he regarded Ireland as already divided, and a united Ireland as something that might be achieved in the future, no doubt within the United Kingdom.

Sir James Craig seemed to show similar modest support for the Council. Opening his campaign for the election of the new northern parliament, Craig told an audience in Banbridge in May 1921 that the first duty of the parliament would be to select a band of men for the Council of Ireland. He proposed to go himself, and if de Valera liked, he could head his quota.[11] While he did indeed put himself at the top of the delegation selected in June !921, Craig subsequently showed little enthusiasm for the Council, stating in September 1921 that it dealt only with minor matters and that 'really, the north here is very little affected whether the Council ever comes into operation or not'.[12] Indeed Craig's readiness to support the Council was directly related to the desire of northern unionists to see the Government of Ireland Act implemented, their own parliament in operation, and powers transferred to it. In May 1921 this was all in jeopardy, as the rest of Ireland was still violently rejecting the act and the settlement under it.

As we have seen, the Council of Ireland did, in theory. survive the treaty, though in somewhat altered form. While the Free State continued to have the right to select half the Council, the Council was now restricted to exercising authority in Northern Ireland only. When Craig and Michael Collins met in January 1922 they agreed that the two governments 'would endeavour to devise a more suitable system than the Council of Ireland for dealing with problems affecting all Ireland'.[13] This followed a suggestion by Craig during the meeting that the Council might be replaced by joint meetings of the two cabinets.[14]

While the two Craig-Collins pacts of 1922 collapsed, agreement between London and Dublin prior to the formal creation of the Free State and the implementation of its constitution removed any pressure for the setting up of the Council. The Irish Free State (Consequential Provisions) Act, of December 1922 enabled the parliaments in Belfast and Dublin to alter the constitution of the Council if they desired by passing identical acts, and pushed back the deadline for the transfer from London to the Council of powers regarding Northern Ireland for a further five years.[15]

Effectively that was the end of the Council. London tried to revive it in the course of the discussions on the boundary question in 1924, when J H Thomas, colonial secretary, suggested replacing it with a north-south legislative body to administer joint services. Dublin replied that this would offer little more than the Council of Ireland, and might also give the northern parliament a veto over Free State legislation.[16] The Council was finally buried by the British-Irish agreement of 1925, which stated that the powers in relation to Northern Ireland assigned to the Council of Ireland in the Government of Ireland Act 'shall be and are hereby transferred to and shall become powers of the parliament and the government of Northern Ireland'.[17] The same article then continued: 'and the governments of the Irish Free State and of Northern Ireland shall meet together as and when necessary for the purpose of considering matters of common interest arising out of or connected with the exercise and administration of the said powers'.[18] The legislation embodying that decision laid down the date for the transfer of those powers as 1 April 1926, when the Council of Ireland was formally buried.[19] Its replacement, meetings between the two governments as a when necessary, simply never happened.

The story of the Council is illustrative of the key aspects of relations between the two parts of Ireland post-partition. At one level it was an eminently sensible idea, given the degree of administrative integration that existed pre-partition, and the continued need to work together in a variety of sectors affecting the whole island. There seems to have been an acceptance by both north and south that some mechanism to handle these matters was needed. As early as 1922 the lack of the Council led to the appointment of an imperial secretary in Belfast to handle the matters assigned to it under the 1920 act.

From a nationalist point of view, the Council might have been expected to be the symbolic embodiment of a united island, an institutional expression of that essential unity which was so important to the treaty negotiators.[20] It was clearly seen as such, by the British side, from the earliest days of drafting the Government of Ireland bill. Moreover, it was inserted not just as a mechanism for practical co-operation in Ireland, but specifically as a means of promoting unity, and as a vehicle for enabling an all-Ireland parliament to be brought into being.

Nationalists were, not surprisingly, dissatisfied with the limited functions and powers actually given to the Council in the legislation. In May 1920 the remaining nationalist members at Westminster dismissed the proposed Council as a powerless sham.[21] The unionists, on the other hand, Carson and Craig among them, fought vigorously to reduce the functions of the Council to a minimum. In the treaty negotiations little, if any time seems to have been devoted to the Council, and as we have seen there is only a parenthetic reference to it in the treaty itself. From the Sinn Fein point of view it was irrelevant, given their determination to prevent partition, and their insistence on the supremacy of an all-Ireland parliament, even if devolution was granted to the north. As late as 22 November 1921, the Irish reply to the latest British proposals made no provision at all for a situation where Ulster refused to accept an all-Ireland parliament. Griffith and Collins were persuaded, or persuaded themselves, that their primary goal of preserving the essential unity of Ireland would be met by the boundary commission, even if Ulster did exercise its right to opt out of the Free State. (In November 1921, when Craig was being pressed by Lloyd George for his response to points raised in the negotiations by Sinn Fein, particularly as regards the essential unity of the island, he responded that as for unification, the Council of Ireland constituted a mechanism for creation of an all-Ireland parliament whenever both parts of the country wanted it).

Hopes pinned on the Boundary Commission were a key factor in Dublin attitudes towards Northern Ireland right up to 1925, and were one important reason why neither the provisional government, nor the first Free State government paid much attention to the Council of Ireland. A second, and perhaps more important consideration was ideological. To bring the Council into existence, by selecting the southern members of it, would, from the nationalist viewpoint, have amounted to formal recognition of the government of Northern Ireland. And central to policy, at least until the death of Collins in August 1922, was non-recognition.

It could be argued that Collins' meetings and formal pacts with Craig in January and March 1922 amounted to such recognition – the nationalist *Irish News* in Belfast certainly thought so[22] – but clearly even the pro-treaty leadership was not prepared to contemplate such a formal act of recognition as would be involved in bringing the Council of Ireland into existence. There was also the problem of the make-up of the Council, with its equality of membership from north and south. As Erskine Childers stated in a draft paper prepared during the treaty negotiations, there could be 'no question of equal representation' for the north in 'any national body taking the place of the Council of Ireland'.[23] That the composition of the Council was not an issue in the treaty negotiations is more a confirmation of the Sinn Fein view that it was irrelevant and would never be needed, than any indication that its composition was acceptable.

This was not just a case of misplaced hopes in the Boundary Commission; the Sinn Fein treaty negotiators, and the subsequent provisional and Free State governments saw themselves as representatives of a sovereign and independent government of the whole island of Ireland. Thus whatever compromises might have been forced upon them to take account of the realities of unionist resistance, they could neither grant any formal recognition to the northern government, nor seem to accord any status to it comparable to a sovereign government of the whole island. The Free State Interpretation Act of 1923, for example, defines 'Northern Ireland' as being 'such part of Ireland as the powers of the parliament and government of Saorstaat Eireann shall, for the time being, not extend to'[24] and this formula was to find much wider coinage in de Valera's 1937 constitution.

Clare O'Halleran, in *Partition and the Limits of Irish Nationalism* has convincingly documented what she calls this 'tortuous nationalist rhetoric designed to cloud the reality of partition and preserve the aspiration to unity'.[25] The fate of the Council of Ireland, potentially of practical value and of symbolic worth in preserving 'the essential unity' of the island, was an early victim of that phenomenon. Eamon Phoenix, in his comprehensive account of northern nationalism, describes the abolition of the Council – 'the last formal bridge between north and south' – as 'an unmitigated disaster' from a nationalist standpoint. Such a body, though its powers were limited, he comments, might have at least offered the prospect of all-Ireland co-operation and understanding in the future. He quotes the Fermanagh nationalist, Cahir Healy as telling a meeting in Omagh that with the passing of the Council of Ireland disappeared 'the last hope of unity in our time'.[26]

Phoenix, and others,[27] see the abolition of the Council as a victory for unionist diplomacy, and for Craig in particular. Craig had no great enthusiasm for the Council, and certainly not for its ascribed role as a facilitator of Irish unity under a single Irish parliament, and he had suggested scrapping it as early as 1922, but unlike Dublin he had actually taken the first crucial step towards its coming into being by selecting the northern representatives to it, including himself. It was Irish nationalism's addiction to rhetorical purity, more than unionist machination, which killed off the Council.

Council or no Council, there were matters to be resolved between the two new administrations in Ireland. As we have seen, the opening of an imperial office in Belfast in 1922 was found necessary to deal with routine matters. At a higher political level, the meetings convened in London in January and March 1922 between Craig and Collins, and the formal agreements resulting from them, stemmed from the critical situation in the north, and the need for some communication and understanding between the two regimes. Apart from the extremely vital matter of the Boundary Commission, the meetings were essentially about issues inside Northern Ireland – the trade boycott of Belfast and other northern towns, and its enforcement by the IRA, the question of catholics expelled from workplaces in the shipyards and other Belfast plants, refugees, unemployment relief, and policing and the court system.

In some of these, apart from the obvious issue of the boundary, Collins and the new provisional government had direct involvement. The Belfast boycott was organised and financed by the Dublin government; that government was responsible for the IRA, and refugees had fled both north and south across the new border. But other issues, notably policing and the courts, were questions internal to Northern Ireland, for which Dublin had no responsibility. However, as the arrangements made under the second agreement clearly showed, Collins was present to defend, and in a sense represent, the interests of the catholic minority in Northern Ireland.

Two key decisions between Craig and Collins in March 1922 involved the setting up of committees; one was a police advisory committee made up of local catholics who would recommend co-religionists suitable for recruitment into the police, and the other was a joint conciliation committee to investigate outrages and work to restore some degree of calm in Belfast. It was to be made up of equal numbers of catholics and protestants. The responsibility for nominating the catholic members of these two committees was given to Michael Collins, the head of the provisional government of the Irish Free State.

The arrangements under the Craig-Collins pacts soon broke down, overtaken by more violence in Belfast, and by events in Dublin and the approaching civil war. But the English civil servant appointed to inquire into the breakdown was highly critical of 'the present system by which the Belfast Catholics appeal direct to Mr Collins, who then passes on their complaints to London'. In his confidential report to government, S.G.Tallents continued:

> I venture to doubt whether it will be found in future wise to allow Mr Collins to act as their (the Belfast catholics) representative, even to the extent to which he so acted in the agreement of March 30th.[28]

This comment was made in the context of a discussion of the possibility of Belfast catholics recognising the northern government, and dealing directly with it. This, Tallents suggested, would be the ideal course.

It is this background which helps explain why Collins was prepared to meet Craig, and enter into public pacts with him, while at the same time refusing to accord any formal recognition to the northern government. Dealing with Craig on practical issues was no more than acceptance of the actual situation which had been forced on the provisional government, it was not giving formal agreement to partition. Moreover, insofar as the basis of the pacts was seemingly Collins' right to represent the catholics of Belfast, not least vis á *vis* the government in London, they could be seen as undermining, not confirming, the legitimacy of the northern government.

This also presumably helps explain why Collins was ready, in the first meeting with Craig, to agree that the two governments would 'endeavour to devise a more suitable system than the Council of Ireland for dealing with problems affecting all Ireland' and seemingly to accept Craig's suggestion to replace it with joint meetings of the two cabinets. While at this remove this may seem like giving up a formal symbol of the unity of the island, and a proper mechanism for dealing with all-island matters, in return for a vague undertaking to seek another way, it did leave Collins as the acknowledged representative of northern catholics, and avoided setting up a body which, from Collins point of view, symbolised the division of the island, and implied a similarity, if not equality of status between the two governments.

What is harder to explain is why the agreement in 1925 that the two governments would 'meet together as and when necessary for the purpose of considering matters of common interest' was allowed to lapse. Relations between Belfast and Dublin reached a high point of cordiality in 1926. As the *Belfast Telegraph* noted on 11 January 1926, there was no reason why the relations of Ulster with the Free State 'should not be of the best'. Mutual goodwill and a spirit of co-operation between the Free State and the imperial parliament, as well as with Ulster, were within the sphere of practicality.

In January the two agriculture ministers met informally in Dublin,[29] and in April Cosgrave's parliamentary secretary, Eamonn Duggan T.D., visited Belfast and observed the northern parliament from the distinguished strangers' gallery. He was reportedly in Belfast to discuss matters related to the Free State budget.[30] Possibly as a result of that contact, in July 1926 the governor general, Tim Healy, wrote to Craig inviting him and Lady Craig to be his guests in the vice-regal lodge for the Dublin Horse Show in August. Craig replied in courteous vein, but suggested it might be wise to postpone such a visit 'for perhaps another year'.[31] It never happened, and it would seem the invitation was never repeated.

Just how significant the Healy invitation to Craig was is hard to assess. Certainly the presence of Sir James and Lady Craig in the governor general's box at the Royal Dublin Society show in August would have appeared to many a very public recognition of Sir James and his government. It is highly improbable that the invitation was issued without the approval of the Free State government, but it is also normal practice to issue such invitations only after first ascertaining that they will be accepted.

It is clear from other sources, however, that by 1926 the Free State government had little enthusiasm for developing relations with Northern Ireland. Clare O'Halloran recounts how the secretary of the north east boundary bureau, E M Stephens, was rebuffed when he lobbied for a new appointment as co-ordinator of policy towards Northern Ireland, following the signing of the 1925 treaty and the abolition of the bureau. Ernest Blythe, minister for finance, saw no need for any such appointment. Cosgrave told the Dail in June 1926 'nothing is being done' as regards dealing with the north, and gave as his opinion that nothing should be said or done, in order to allow bitter feeling between north and south to subside. As O'Halloran notes, Blythe's reply to Stephens' suggestion that a new post was needed to help honour the government's commitment to 'an active policy of friendly co-operation' with Northern Ireland, summed up the government's apathy if not hostility to such co-operation, and was in marked contrast to Blythe's own memorandum of 1922, when he had advocated recognition of Northern Ireland, and opposed both armed action and economic boycott against it.[32] The gulf between north and south that was to characterise the next forty years was already opening by 1926.

The Cosgrave government had been attacked, by some of its own supporters, among others, for the degree of formal recognition of Northern Ireland implied in the 1925 treaty, and indeed made explicit by the clause defining 'Northern Ireland' as the territory set out in the Government of Ireland Act. De Valera had emerged from defeat in the civil war, and from prison, to enter the politics of the new state with his announcement of the setting up of Fianna Fail in April 1926, with a united independent Ireland as its first objective. His shadow was to hang heavily over Cumann na nGaedheal governments until he finally drove them from power in 1932, having effectively served notice on them by winning 44 seats in the 1927 election to Cumann na nGaedheal's 47. There was little room in Free State politics for any opening towards the north.

As O'Halloran summarises it

> For successive governments after 1925 ... nationalist rhetoric became a substitute for any major policy initiatives, while day to day policy continued to be ad hoc, pragmatic, and defensive.[33]

And the triumph of this approach was confirmed in what she calls 'the comforting formula' of articles 2 and 3 of the 1937 constitution. Article 2, by defining the national territory as the whole island, states the claim and preserves the rhetoric, article 3, by conceding that the laws of Eire will not apply in Northern Ireland, acknowledges the reality of partition. It is the classic recipe for, at the one time, denouncing partition and living with it.

Inside Northern Ireland Sir James Craig had, by 1925, already shown his readiness to use border politics to help cement his rather fractious unionist support by dissolving the northern parliament and calling an election for April of that year on the boundary question. Every election he fought in the course of his long career, he did on the preservation of the Union, and the threat to it from the southern state. Close co-operation and overtly friendly relations were no more politically useful in the north than they were in the south. Except where direct contact was unavoidable, the northern government adhered rigidly to the constitutional rectitude that external relations were matters reserved to London, and that its own authority did not extend to dealings with Dublin. In 1937, when the new Irish constitution and its claim to the territory of Northern Ireland was raised at Stormont, the speaker ruled the matter out of order, belonging to Westminster.

It is some indication of the gap that had opened between north and south that in 1938 a group of notables, in both parts of the island, came together to form 'an Irish Association' (later to become the Irish Association for Cultural, Economic and Social Relations) among the aims of which were promoting business and commercial relations between the two parts of the island, working for co-operation in matters of general social interest and promoting more social intercourse. They were motivated by concern at sectarian animosity inside Northern Ireland, and by the psychological and other barriers they saw increasing the division between northerners and southerners, something surely remarkable in a small island which had been part of one state, and administered as one unit within that state less than two decades earlier.[34] For four decades low level ad hoc co-operation in a very limited number of essential areas continued alongside the absence of any formal mechanism, and in contrast to well-publicised arguments over matters of theory and rhetoric. The change in the royal title in 1926, is illustrative. The events of 1921 and 1922 had left King George, 'by the Grace of God', king 'of the United Kingdom of Great Britain and Ireland'. This was both inaccurate, given that the United Kingdom, so defined, no longer existed, and distasteful to the Free State. At the 1926 imperial conference, the Free State proposed changing the title to king '...of the United Kingdom of Great Britain, and of Canada, Australia, New Zealand, South Africa and the Irish Free State...', a rather transparent attempt to ignore the existence of Northern Ireland, while at the same time clearly detaching the Free State from Great Britain in terms of the function of the crown.

The Irish wording was not accepted in full, but Irish concerns were reflected in the new title, which made George V king 'of Great Britain, Ireland and of the British dominions beyond the seas...'.[35] (The comma inserted between 'Great Britain' and 'Ireland', instead of 'and' is the famous 'O'Higgins comma'.) The omission of any reference to the United Kingdom, and to Northern Ireland, caused anger in Belfast, which took this as an implication that Ireland was one political unit under the crown.[36] Such was no doubt O'Higgins' intention, and he appears to have believed that the preservation of the royal title over the whole island did indeed preserve its 'essential unity', and that this would one day facilitate Irish unification as a separate monarchy under its king of Ireland, who would also be king of Great Britain.[37]

This concern to preserve the 'essential unity' of the island at a theoretical level persisted alongside a determination to demolish all remnants of the 1921–22 settlement which in any way bound the Irish state to the United Kingdom. But in demolishing links with London, Dublin was also widening the gulf between south and north. The unilateral abolition of the right of appeal from Irish courts to the judicial committee of the privy council in 1933, perceived threats to the British citizenship of residents of the Free State, the removal of the governor general and the deletion of the crown from the constitution, the progressive 'catholicisation' of southern society in the 1930s, all contributed to a deepening of partition, culminating in Irish neutrality in World War II. In 1949 the Irish Free State formally became a republic and left the Commonwealth. By way of response, in the Ireland Act of 1949, Westminster gave a new guarantee to the constitutional position of Northern Ireland within the United Kingdom. In that same year Sir Basil Brooke was seeking to have the 'Ireland' removed from Northern Ireland, and the name of the region formally changed to 'Ulster'. (The southern state insisted upon general usage of the term 'Ireland' as the name of the state, not Republic of Ireland, or Irish Republic.) In 1947 the border had been reinforced in a significant and unusual fashion by the passing of the Safeguarding of Employment Act, under which residents of southern Ireland required work permits to take jobs in Northern Ireland.

Ironically it was soon after this series of divisive moves that significant progress was made on formal cross-border co-operation in specific sectors. The 1950 agreement on the Erne, enshrined in legislation in both jurisdictions, facilitated a major drainage scheme in Northern Ireland, and the construction of the Ballyshannon hydro-electric station in Donegal. The two governments acted together to set up the Foyle Fisheries Commission in 1952, and later the Great Northern Railway Board. This increase in cross-border co-operation at governmental level coincided initially with John A. Costello's first inter-party, or coalition, government in Dublin (1948–1951) when the Irish state moved out from under the shadow of de Valera for the first time for a decade and a half.

It is worth noting that in all three cases practical circumstances forced the co-operation, not any desire in principle or pursuit of a political point. The Foyle Fisheries example is the most complex and most interesting, and the inter-governmental action arose out of specific demands from the owners of the cross-border fishery, the Honourable the Irish Society, to the two administrations to act together to ensure the survival of the fishery, then seriously threatened by unrestricted exploitation, arising out of disputed rights, and the difficulties of enforcing restrictions in two jurisdictions.[38]

Moreover it came well before Sean Lemass succeeded de Valera as leader of Fianna Fail, and as Taoiseach, in 1959, though Lemass is generally credited with instituting a new era in north-south relations by his overt promotion of practical co-operation to the top of his agenda. In a major speech to the Dail at the outset of his premiership he suggested a new trade committee between Belfast and Dublin, hinted at southern tariff reductions for northern goods, and said he saw no reason why 'people in the north should refuse to consider[...]possibilities of concerting activities for the practical advantages that may result'.[39]

In 1961 both the United Kingdom and Ireland lodged formal applications for membership of the European Economic Community, foreshadowing radically closer relations between north and south in Ireland on a range of economic and other matters. It was to be the next decade before membership became a reality, but meanwhile, in 1965, Lemass signed the Anglo-Irish free trade area agreement with London, thereby considerably liberalising commercial relations between north and south. The pragmatic approach to relations with Northern Ireland was given dramatic expression by Lemass's formal visit to Terence O'Neill at Stormont on 17 January 1965. A short time later O'Neill returned the visit, travelling to Dublin on 9 February. It was almost exactly forty years since their two predecessors in 1925 had solemnly signed up to the two governments meeting 'as and when necessary' to discuss matters of mutual interest.

The initiative undoubtedly came from Dublin, though O'Neill was ready enough to respond to it. Lemass arrived in Belfast with what his most recent biographer calls a shopping list – 'the abolition of barriers to tourism; the facilitation of educational exchanges; sharing health facilities where urgent and necessary; trade matters; the joint development of nuclear power where this proves economic; joint agricultural research projects; reciprocal practising rights for lawyers; and the joint administration of certain charities'.[40] The visits, and the subsequent exchange in December 1967 and January 1968 between Lemass's successor, Jack Lynch, and O'Neill, certainly encouraged practical co-operation at departmental level, though they scarcely constituted an implementation of the 1925 agreement. A senior departmental official in Dublin described the new situation to the current writer in 1965 by opening a drawer in his filing cabinet and pulling out a folder marked 'Northern Ireland', explaining that every subject he handled now had to have a sub-section covering any Northern aspect it might have. The folder was empty.

Whatever it might have been, the potential for developing north-south relations after the initial Lemass-O'Neill visits on a more formal or even constitutional level was rapidly submerged in more dramatic events. Sectarian conflict in the north had re-emerged in 1964, and the temperature rose with the fiftieth anniversary of the Easter Rising in 1966. By 1968 nationalist energies in the north had been channelled into a civil rights campaign, and by 1969 the slide down through communal antagonism to violence and the sustained terrorism of the 'troubles' had begun.

Lemass's forthright advocacy of practical co-operation with Northern Ireland constituted a change of approach from that of his predecessor, as did his partial jettisoning of nationalist rhetorical baggage, as in his readiness to use the term 'Northern Ireland' instead of the formulaic 'six counties'. But he repeatedly insisted that he was not abandoning the fundamental nationalist position – that partition was unjust and unjustified, and the island rightly should be united. Rather he advocated his policy of co-operation as the best means of achieving that end.

His dramatic visit to O'Neill in Stormont – the very building which had become a nationalist synonym of unionist rule and misrule – had, to many, all the appearance of an act of formal recognition of the northern government and of Northern Ireland. Four years later Terence O'Neill, in his own defence, was to tell the Stormont parliament that when Lemass's car drove through the gates of Stormont, the 'grandiose and empty claims of Eire's constitution were exposed for the vanity they are'.[41] Yet it could also be argued that by his visit Lemass was simply continuing the very policy embodied in articles 2 and 3 – acceptance of the reality of the existence of the northern government, alongside refusal to give theoretical recognition to its historical or moral legitimacy.

Nevertheless a policy of unity by consent or persuasion accompanied by increasing friendly co-operation sat uneasily beside the harsh wording of the Irish constitution. In 1966 Lemass set up an all-party committee to review the constitution, mainly to take account of changes in Irish society, notably on attitudes towards marriage and religion, but in the course of its work the committee also looked at articles 2 and 3. In an interim report of 1967 – which turned out to be its only report – the committee recommended replacing article 3, which asserts the right of the Dublin parliament and government to exercise jurisdiction over the whole island but effectively limits that jurisdiction to the twenty six counties, 'pending the re-integration of the national territory', with a new clause saying 'the Irish nation hereby proclaims its firm will that its territory be reunited in harmony and brotherly affection among all Irishmen'.

This early flirting with the idea of replacing article 3 with an aspiration came to nothing, as neither the political parties nor the government were enamoured of the committee's recommendations, and they went largely unheeded. The committee made no recommendation as regards article 2, which defines the whole island as the national territory, and effectively makes the territorial claim. That the rather timid suggestion of the committee was widely regarded in the Republic as generous towards unionists, even dangerously radical, to the point of unacceptability from a nationalist perspective, is perhaps an indication of how limited had been the evolution of southern thinking on the north over the Lemass decade.

In 1972, when a second all party committee was set up in Dublin specifically 'to make recommendations on the steps now required to create conditions conducive to a united Ireland', no progress was made and it became clear that the southern political establishment would contemplate changes in articles 2 and 3 only in the context of a deal with unionists on the form Irish unity – or some new arrangement for the whole island – might take.

By 1972 the violence in Northern Ireland had already intensified to the point where others were anxiously seeking a political solution, and the possibilities of movement were being explored elsewhere than in articles 2 and 3. Since then the pursuit of a political accommodation on the island has concentrated primarily on modifications in the constitutional arrangements for governing Northern Ireland within the United Kingdom, and on possible linking mechanisms with the Republic, leaving the southern constitutional claim as something to be bargained against satisfactory progress on these other matters. In this regard successive United Kingdom governments have been remarkably understanding of Dublin's reluctance, or refusal, to drop the territorial claim.

The purpose of this chapter is to consider concepts of unity and institutional arrangements between north and south designed to implement those concepts, not to relate the whole history of the Anglo-Irish approach to a settlement from 1973 onwards. It is sufficient therefore to note that London's original contention, stated at the outset of the 'troubles' in the Downing Street declaration of August 1969, that 'responsibility for affairs in Northern Ireland is entirely a matter of domestic jurisdiction' had been sufficiently modified two years later to allow Edward Heath to bring Jack Lynch and Brian Faulkner, the new northern prime minister, together at Chequers to discuss the crisis.[42]

By late 1973 this 'Irish dimension' had grown enough to allow the Dublin government to be a full partner in the Sunningdale Agreement on the future of Northern Ireland. From that point on the context in which institutional arrangements between north and south in Ireland would be considered was significantly altered in several regards. Institutional links, such as a council of Ireland, were now enthusiastically demanded by Dublin; the historic fear that such links would cement partition by according formal recognition to the legitimacy of Northern Ireland – the basic reason for southern lack of enthusiasm for the Council in the 1920s – gave way to a policy based on the belief that these links would be the best available means of promoting unification, or at least of arriving at some compromise which would satisfy nationalism by moving in that direction.

This was in line with the Lemass approach of maintaining the historic pursuit of unification, but seeking to achieve it by consent, through persuasion and demonstration of the mutual benefits of practical co-operation. At Sunningdale the government of the Republic 'fully accepted and solemnly declared' that there could be no change in the status of Northern Ireland without majority consent, while at the same time affirming its belief in Irish unification. As subsequent debate, in the courts and elsewhere, made clear, there was, in nationalist eyes, no contradiction between the position stated in articles 2 and 3, and recognition of the practicality that that position could be implemented only by consent. Jack Lynch summed it up by stating that while he agreed that unification could come about only with agreement of a majority in the north, he could never accept that any section of the people had a right to detach itself from the nation. In other words the Henry Ford principle applied – unionists could have any solution they were prepared to agree to, so long as it was unification.

Sunningdale also saw the United Kingdom government reverting explicitly to the position embodied in the Government of Ireland Act and the Treaty, of readiness to support Irish unity, if a majority in Northern Ireland should so wish. The rapid turnaround in the British position can have a number of explanations; the level of violence in Northern Ireland demanded a radical solution over and above internal guarantees of civil rights for all; the involvement of the Dublin government, as the 'second guarantor' representing the northern minority was deemed essential, and it is not unlikely that there was a growing realisation in London that the Republic of Ireland, at governmental and at general public level, was rapidly losing interest in actual unification of the island, and would happily settle for any new arrangement which paid some respect to nationalist ideals, gave adequate guarantees to the minority in the north, and left London paying most of the bills.

The key to this was the Council of Ireland, agreed at Sunningdale, but, like its predecessor, destined never to come into existence. The joint statement issued by the two governments at Sunningdale was largely devoted to a lengthy outline of the institutions and functions of the Council. It was to have a council of ministers and a consultative assembly; it was to have a secretariat with a secretary general and a permanent headquarters. The ministerial council was to have executive and harmonising functions, the assembly advisory and review functions. A list of subject areas for potential executive action by the council included development of natural resources, conservation, agriculture, forestry, fisheries, co-operative ventures in trade and industry, electricity, tourism, roads and transport, public health advisory services, sport, culture and the arts.

It was an enormously ambitious proposal, which would undoubtedly have been cumbersome and extremely expensive to operate. Remarkably, the joint statement made no attempt to justify the creation of such an apparatus, apart from three sentences suggesting 'objectives to be borne in mind' as the best utilisation of scarce skills, expertise and resources, the avoidance of duplication, and complementary rather than competitive effort where this would be to the advantage of agriculture, commerce and industry.

These modest objectives could presumably have been achieved by routine inter-departmental co-operation, such as that favoured at the time of the Lemass-O'Neill meetings. The Council of Ireland foundered on unionist outrage, and when it went down, effectively the power-sharing executive went with it. At the time there was much anger at unionist rejection of it, and even some surprise that unionists should reject a council which would act only by unanimity, and on which therefore, they would exercise a veto. This was to misunderstand the fundamental unionist position, which saw only political motivation and no practical justification for such a council, and was therefore little interested in how it would function.

The very name 'Council of Ireland' evoked memories of the earlier council, which had been set up as a 'bond of union' between the two parts of Ireland, in part to facilitate the termination of partition and the creation of an all-Ireland parliament. Even if unionists had missed the point, the SDLP was quick to remind them that their interest in an all-Ireland institution was to produce 'a dynamic that could lead ultimately to an agreed single state for Ireland'. According to Paddy Devlin this meant that 'SDLP representatives would concentrate on their entire efforts on building up a set of tangible executive powers for the Council which, in the fullness of time, would create and sustain an evolutionary process'.[43] The SDLP had, in 1972, declared itself in favour of joint British-Irish sovereignty over Northern Ireland as an interim stage towards an independent united Ireland, an eventuality in favour of which the SDLP wished the British government to declare itself.[44] The Council of Ireland, Brian Faulkner later admitted, was the price paid to keep the SDLP on board at Sunningdale.[45]

In fact that 1972 SDLP document, *Towards a New Ireland*, contained the germs of ideas that have dominated the Anglo-Irish governmental approach to the problem of Northern Ireland ever since. It argued that Northern Ireland as a political unit lacked legitimacy both because of the way it had been created, and because of the way it had been governed. Nationalists could give their support to institutions in Northern Ireland, even on an interim basis, only if there were also institutions created whereby nationalists could find expression for their loyalty to the Irish state. Accordingly in 1972 the SDLP proposed the setting up of a national senate of Ireland to plan the harmonisation of 'structures, laws and services' in both parts of Ireland, and to agree on a constitution for a 'new Ireland' and its relationship with Great Britain. The Council of Ireland agreed at Sunningdale a year later clearly went some way towards satisfying this approach.

After the collapse of the power-sharing executive in 1974, all-Ireland institutions were off the agenda, but not for very long. In December 1980 Margaret Thatcher and Charles Haughey agreed to give 'special consideration to the totality of relationships within these islands', and a year later Mrs Thatcher and Mr Haughey's successor, Dr FitzGerald, formally established the Anglo-Irish Intergovernmental Council to give 'institutional expression' to the unique relationship between their two countries. Four years later the Anglo-Irish Agreement took this approach a significant step further by creating the intergovernmental conference, backed by a secretariat, according a treaty-based right to the Dublin government to a broad consultative role in the administration of Northern Ireland. While the agreement was 'Anglo-Irish', the focus was Northern Ireland, and Dublin's involvement in it.

The agreement of 1985 was not primarily concerned with the creation of a north-south link along the lines of a council of Ireland, but with a more fundamental reassertion of the 'essential unity' of the island based on the historic nationalist case, which had just been restated in some detail by the New Ireland Forum of nationalist parties in the island in 1984. In particular there was now insistence upon the right of northern nationalists to 'political expression of their Irish identity', which, it was asserted, could be guaranteed only under some form of unity, or at least of joint Irish-British authority over Northern Ireland.[46]

The forum, called by the Dublin government, was asked to report on possible new structures and processes through which lasting peace might be achieved in a 'new Ireland'. In terms of the formulation of a nationalist position in the light of continued violence in Northern Ireland, it was highly significant. The conclusion of the forum was that the new Ireland it sought to provide would best be found in a sovereign, independent Ireland united by consent. Its preferred form of Irish unity was a unitary state embracing the whole island, though it did also suggest alternatives in the form of a federal/ confederal Irish state, or joint Irish-British authority over Northern Ireland, giving London and Dublin equal responsibility for all aspects of the government of the province.

In fact during the negotiation of the Anglo-Irish Agreement, Dublin argued strongly for joint-authority, with a Dublin minister sharing in executive power in a Belfast administration. Garret FitzGerald had maintained that this would not require majority assent in Northern Ireland, under the consent principle, as it would not effect the sovereignty of the United Kingdom over Northern Ireland. Joint authority, he tried to argue, was not at all the same as joint sovereignty, rather the implementation of joint authority could be the way in which London could chose to exercise its sovereignty over Northern Ireland. As Garret FitzGerald records, London informed Dublin that joint sovereignty was not on, joint authority could be contemplated, but joint responsibility would be preferable. At that point FitzGerald's negotiating tactics, he tells us, were to indicate a possibility of movement on articles 2 and 3 in return 'for a major package involving movement in the direction of joint authority'.[47] In the end he had to settle at Hillsborough for some movement in the direction of joint authority. The controversial agreement which resulted was indeed denounced by many of its critics as a limited form of joint authority, though Dublin's role remained no more than advisory.

Ten years after that, with the majority in Northern Ireland still refusing to accept the Anglo-Irish Agreement and the institutions created under it, the United Kingdom and Irish governments produced the *Frameworks Documents* of 1995, proposing arrangements and institutions bearing an uncanny resemblance to the Sunningdale Council of Ireland. Unlike Sunningdale, however, the *Frameworks* do go to some length to explain the motivation behind them. Paragraph 5 of a *New Framework for Agreement* says a vital element of any new arrangement in the island of Ireland will be 'new institutions and structures to take account of the totality of relationships and to enable the people of Ireland to work together in all areas of common interest while fully respecting their diversity'. Paragraph 7 talks of a '...fair and honourable accommodation ... which would enable people to work constructively for their mutual benefit, without compromising the essential principles of the long-term aspirations or interests of either tradition or of either community'.

Paragraph 13(b) envisages north/south institutions with functions very similar to the Sunningdale Council of Ireland '... to serve to acknowledge and reconcile the rights, identities and aspirations of the two major traditions'. This and the above quotations constitute a frank admission that the main, if not the sole, purpose of the new cross-border institutions will be political.

They are to be the mechanism by which the Irish government can be involved in the affairs of Northern Ireland, thereby enabling nationalists living in Northern Ireland to ascribe a measure of legitimacy to Northern Ireland and its institutions. This is spelled out even more clearly in paragraph 19.

> They (the governments) agree that future arrangements relating to Northern Ireland, and Northern Ireland's wider relationships, should respect the full and equal legitimacy and worth of the identity, sense of allegiance, aspiration and ethos of both unionist and nationalist communities there. Consequently, both governments commit themselves to the principle that institutions and arrangements in Northern Ireland, and north/south institutions, should afford both communities secure and satisfactory political, administrative and symbolic expression and protection.

This paragraph is stating that in its dealings with the outside world, with the European Union (EU) for example, Northern Ireland must respect the 'full and equal legitimacy' of the nationalist identity and sense of allegiance, and that the two governments are committed to institutions or arrangements which afford 'satisfactory political, administrative and symbolic expression and protection' to the nationalist identity and sense of allegiance. This is clearly an attempt to meet one of the key points of the New Ireland Forum, that nationalists in Northern Ireland have a right to 'political expression of their Irish identity'.

The dilemma facing the two governments in all their negotiations on Northern Ireland has been that none of the three Forum options has been available, given the precondition of the consent of a majority in the north to constitutional change. In particular the British government has found itself pledged to satisfy the aspirations of Irish nationalism to 'parity of esteem' and to political expression of an Irish identity, when nationalists, in the Forum, have already indicated that the only means of achieving these ends is some form of Irish unity, or at the very least, joint authority.

This is a dilemma not just for London, but for Dublin and all nationalists who affirm their support for the principle of consent. One response has been to seek a solution through the innovative mechanisms and institutions of the European Union (EU). As early as its 1972 document the SDLP had cited European integration as the example to follow. In the Brooke-Mayhew interparty talks of 1991–92, the party returned repeatedly to the European dimension, and in a paper submitted in September 1992 it included this passage:

> The context in which the aim for Irish unity is now expressed is in many respects radically different to what it was seventy years ago. Today, both parts of Ireland share membership of the European Community which is uniting people in an unprecedented experiment in continental democracy. To achieve its aims the European Community is overcoming barriers of history, geography, language,

91

nationality and religion. The people of Ireland, North and South, are making a significant contribution to this process in ways which cannot fail to impact positively on relationships within the island itself. The SDLP believes, therefore, that as we plan new structures for future relationships between the people of Ireland, we should be conscious of the principles and experiences of the European Community.

A paper from the Irish government in June-July 1992, had also suggested that radical lessons might be learned from Europe:

> We are living through times of unprecedented change in human society and political structures alike. The development of the European Union promises to transform our political and economic environment. Issues of sovereignty and borders no longer mean what they meant in the days of Lloyd George. The European Community offers new points of reference, new possibilities free of the connotations of the past. These could be invaluable assets, if we chose to use them, in the process of agreeing our relationships in this island we are destined to share.

The thrust of these two interventions is to try to take the issue of constitutional change in Ireland out of the context of nationalism and the traditional claims of the Irish 'nation', and move it into the new world of European integration, where national sovereignty has little relevance, and where old suspicions must no longer be allowed to block innovative solutions to old problems. In this brave new world of shared sovereignty and respect for difference, both communities in a new Ireland could enjoy full expression of their identities.

The SDLP's proposal for an arrangement based on the institutions of the EU, including a nominee from Brussels on an executive commission to administer Northern Ireland, received little support. The contention that the European experience and the EU provide relevant models for a solution to the Northern Ireland problem was denied in the talks, and has been criticised elsewhere.[48] But it is possible to see what was in the SDLP's mind when it talked of the aim of Irish unity being expressed in a radically different context. For instance the party proposed the establishment of a north-south council in Ireland as an expression of 'relationships between the people of the whole island' and which would have responsibility for European Community issues with implications for the whole island. Thus, in regard to some aspects of European Community membership, a limited form of Irish unity would be achieved.

The device of expressing a degree of unity through giving the Irish state and its government in Dublin a role in handling the external relations of the whole island has long appealed to some. Garret FitzGerald, in 1972, suggested that within the European Community, one of the powers as regards Northern Ireland that might possibly be transferable from London to Dublin was foreign affairs.[49] Dr FitzGerald and others have linked this approach to the assertion that Northern Ireland's interests within the EU are more closely aligned to those of the Republic than they are to those of the UK generally, and that therefore the government of the Republic might more appropriately and efficiently represent Northern Ireland in Brussels. The Institute of European Affairs in Dublin recently considered the policy options for Dublin regarding Northern Ireland and the EU in a situation where the United Kingdom continued to resist further European integration, and extended its (then) practice of opting out of major policy areas, and made the following suggestion:

> Northern Ireland could be designated as a special region of the Union entitled to choose whatever Community policies suited its regional interests from among the policy packages applying separately to the Republic and to the UK. This idea has been already advanced on the grounds that economic growth could be enhanced by allowing the Northern Ireland economy to dine á la carte off the EU policy menu.[50]

Another publication, in 1996, from the same Institute, based on a project headed by Dr FitzGerald, argued that northern unionist politicians might find it opportune to support this idea of 'sovereignty sharing by (sic) the Irish state in a key area of external policy'.[51] In 1997 Michael O'Kennedy, one of the Republic's most experienced politicians who has served as foreign minister, and as European commissioner said it could be argued that the 1937 constitution imposed on Dublin 'a de jure if not de facto obligation to provide non-discriminatory representation at international level' for all the people on the island. He suggested that representatives of Northern Ireland should be accorded formal access to Irish delegations at the Council of Ministers in the European Union.[52] While such proposals are invariably presented by their advocates as practical, sensible and possible, given enough imagination, they are based on an assumed level of integration in Europe far beyond anything already achieved or likely in the foreseeable future. Many of them, even if they were acceptable to all the parties concerned, would require far-reaching changes in the basic treaties of the EU. They would also raise fundamental questions of democratic representation and accountability.

In the later stages of the inter-party talks which resulted in the new agreement of April 1998 the key issue dividing unionists and nationalists was again the nature of formal north-south structures on the island of Ireland. For a long time it seemed the one question most likely to prevent any agreement, and the one on which the worth of that agreement would be judged by rank and file unionism and nationalism. In a discussion paper, presented to the talks in January 1998, the United Kingdom and Irish governments posed a list of questions which they hoped would stimulate systematic and detailed debate on the establishment of north-south institutions. At the top of the list, the first question asked; 'what broad purpose or purposes should formal north/south structures serve?' In reality it is the answer to that question which still lies at the heart of the dispute over north/south structures. Under the 1998 Belfast Agreement as it emerged, pro-agreement unionists claimed that the degree of control they had secured for a northern assembly over the proposed north-south council, and the seemingly limited functions to be accorded initially to that council, meant that it was essentially a vehicle for practical co-operation, and of little constitutional significance. Nationalists, on the other hand, could argue that the very existence of such a council, and unionist acceptance of it, indicated acknowledgement of the essential unity of the island, and constituted a step on the way to Irish unity.

Conclusion

This chapter began with a comment on the near completeness of partition after 1921, and the rapid abandonment of the Council of Ireland, that 'bond of union' between north and south enshrined in the Government of Ireland Act. This was followed by the broadening gulf between the two parts of the island up to the end of the second world war. But at the same time a non-political unity of sorts was preserved by people away from politics and government. In 1925 the Belfast unionist newspaper, *The Northern Whig*, commented in an editorial that at partition 'Ulster did not surrender its title as part of Ireland, nor renounce its share in those Irish traditions in art, in learning, in arms, in song, in sport and in science that were worth preserving in a united form'.[53] To that list could be added all the churches, trade unions, and many specific organisations and learned and professional bodies.

These pockets of non-political unity survived as the two political entities on the island moved further apart, and most citizens north and south knew and thought increasingly little about each other. From the 1950s on, however, developing commercial contacts and vastly improved personal mobility for tourism and travel, began to open new paths for many across the north/south divide, a trend crudely interrupted by the worst of the 'troubles', but resumed with renewed vigour over the past several years.[54] In many ways, therefore, conditions are more appropriate now than they ever have been since 1925 for the creation of formal links between north and south which could serve practical purposes to benefit both, and which could symbolise the non-political unity of the island. But Irish nationalism still appears to cling to cross-border bodies as symbols of, and possibly gateways to, political unity. This in turn makes it easier for unionists to ignore the non-political unity of the island, recognition of which, by both sides, would provide the only sure foundation for new structures of mutual practical benefit.

References

1. Lady Spender's Diaries. PRONI D 1633.
2. N.Mansergh, *The Unresolved Question*, Yale University Press, New Haven and London, 1991, p. 14.
3. H C Debates, vol. clxxiv, col. 104, 1905.
4. N.Mansergh, op. cit., p. 17.
5. See D. Kennedy, *The Widening Gulf*, Blackstaff Press, Belfast, 1988.
6. *Articles of Agreement*, Article 12.
7. Quoted in T. Hennessy, *A History of Northern Ireland 1920–96*, Gill & Macmillan, Dublin, 1997, p 10.
8. Quoted in St John Ervine, *Craigavon, Ulsterman*, George Allen & Unwin. London, 1949, p. 422.
9. The detailed provisions of the Government of Ireland Act on the Council of Ireland are in Sir Arthur Quekett. *The Constitution of Northern Ireland*, HMSO, Belfast, 1933, part ii, Appendix B.
10. HC Debates, vol. 134 , col. 925–7, Nov. 1920. Quoted in T. Hennessy, op. cit., p. 10.
11. *Belfast News Letter*, 3 May 1921.
12. *Belfast News Letter*, 21 September, 1921.
13. Text of first Craig-Collins Agreement, SPO S1801/A. Quoted in E. Phoenix, *Northern Nationalism*, Ulster Historical Foundation, Belfast, 1994, p. 171.
14. E.Phoenix, op. cit. p 170.
15. Sir Arthur Quekett, op. cit., part 2, pp. 223–224.
16. E.Phoenix, op. cit., p. 299.
17. The text of the Agreement is given in the *Schedule to The Ireland (Confirmation of Agreement) Act*, 1925.
18. Ibid., p. 232.
19. Michael Collins used the phrase. See F. Gallagher, *The Anglo-Irish Treaty*, Hutchinson, London, 1965, p.157.
20. E.Phoenix, op. cit., p. 83.
21. J.M.Curran, *The Birth of the Irish Free State 1921–23*, University of Alabama Press, Alabama, 1980, p. 101.
22. E.Phoenix, op. cit., p 173, quotes the *Irish News'* view that the most important aspect of the January 21 Pact was that the two Irish governments had recognised each other.
23. J.Bowman, *De Valera and the Irish Question 1917–1973*, Clarendon Press, Oxford, 1982, p. 59.
24. Interpretation Act, 1923 (no. 46 of 1923), quoted in D. Barrington, 'The Council of Ireland in the constitutional context', *Administration*, vol. 20, no 4, 1973, p.28.
25. C. O'Halloran, *Partition and the Limits of Irish Nationalism*, Gill & Macmillan, Dublin, 1987, p. 96.
26. E.Phoenix, op. cit., p. 332–333.
27. E.Phoenix, op cit., p. 332. See also J.M. Curran, op. cit., p. 263.
28. *Tallents Report*, PRO. CO.906.30, 4 July 1922.
29. *Irish Times*, 22 January 1926.
30. *Belfast Weekly Telegraph*, 24 April 1926.
31. Craig to Healy, PRONI CAB 9R4. 24 July 1926.
32. C. O'Halloran, op. cit., pp. 119–120.
33. Ibid., p. 96.
34. An account of the origins of the Irish Association is given in P. Bew et al., *Passion and Prejudice*, Institute of Irish Studies, Queen's University, Belfast. 1993.

35. PRO Cmd. 2768, 1926. P. 14. For an account of this matter, see D. Harkness, *The Restless Dominion,* New York University Press, New York, 1970, pp. 101–106.
36. *Northern Whig,* 22 January 1927.
37. D. Harkness, op. cit. p. 106.
38. For a brief account of the Foyle Fisheries Commission see E. O'Kelly, 'Foyle Fisheries Commission', *Administration,* vol. 7, No 3, 1959.
39. Dail Debates, vol. 176, col. 1576, 21 July 1959. Quoted in J. Horgan, *Sean Lemass, The Enigmatic Patriot,* Gill & Macmillan, Dublin, 1997, p. 257.
40. J.Horgan, op. cit., p.279.
41. NI House of Commons Debates, vol. 71, col. 413, 29 January 1969.
42. Joint Declaration of United Kingdom and Northern Ireland governments, 19 August 1969, quoted in M.Wallace, *Northern Ireland: 50 Years of Self Government,* David & Charles, Newtown Abbot, 1971, p. 168.
43. P.Devlin, *The Fall of the Northern Ireland Executive,* Belfast 1975, p. 32. Quoted in T. Hennessy, op. cit., p. 223.
44. *Towards a New Ireland,* SDLP policy document, Belfast, 1972.
45. T. Hennessey, op. cit., p. 223.
46. *New Ireland Forum Report,* Stationery Office, Dublin., 1984, p. 9.
47. G.FitzGerald, *All in a Life,* Gill and Macmillan, 1991, Dublin, p. 498.
48. D. Kennedy, 'The European Union and the Northern Ireland Question', in B. Barton and P.J. Roche (eds), *The Northern Ireland Question: Perspectives and Policies,* Avebury, Aldershot, 1994.
49. G. FitzGerald, *Towards a New Ireland,* Charles Knight, London, 1972, p. 108.
50. *1996 Intergovernmental Conference, Issues, Options, Implications,* Institute of European Affairs, Dublin, 1996, Ch 26.
51. P.Gillespie (ed), *Britain's European Question; The Issues for Ireland,* Institute of European Affairs, Dublin, 1996, p. 60.
52. M. O'Kennedy, *Address to the Magill Summer School,* 15 August 1997.
53. *The Northern Whig,* 18 August 1925.
54. For a discussion of surviving north-south links see J. Whyte, 'The Permeability of the United Kingdom-Irish Border: A Preliminary Reconnaissance', *Administration,* vol. 31, no.3, 1983.

5 Discrimination in Housing and Employment under the Stormont Administration

Graham Gudgin

Introduction

Accusations of discrimination against Catholics by unionist governments in Northern Ireland from 1921–72 played an important role in the politics of the time. This was particularly true in the 1960s and it has remained true of much of the subsequent period as nationalists sought to discredit past unionist administrations and by association current unionist politicians. The importance of the allegations to current politics lies in the fact that, almost uniquely in the western world, Northern Ireland Protestants are not trusted to form a government in circumstances in which they gain a clear majority of votes in democratic elections.

This lack of trust has underpinned all constitutional talks over the last 30 years and has resulted not only in a power-sharing government in the new Northern Ireland assembly, but also in a strong form of power-sharing unknown elsewhere in the western world. One of the important but unremarked aspects of the 1998 Agreement has been the justification it provides for the view that all previous forms of regional government in Northern Ireland were unacceptable.

A belief in the importance of past discrimination is not the only factor underpinning the inevitability of power-sharing government. The need to accommodate a large permanent minority and to bring an end to the violence has led to a search for unconventional political arrangements, but the form of these arrangements is heavily coloured by an ethos of victims and oppressors. Without this ethos the outcome might have been different and we might note that situations in which violence is difficult to eradicate have led neither the Spanish or Italian authorities to adopt the power-sharing 'solution' of Northern Ireland.

All of the many histories of the Stormont period 1921–72 tell the sequential story of the civil rights protests against discrimination and the subsequent descent into violence from which Northern Ireland is yet to fully recover. The sequence of events and their frequent repetition have led the causes of the troubles to become closely linked in many people's minds with discrimination. This is almost axiomatic among the nationalist community in Ireland and their supporters elsewhere, and the violence of the last 30 years is widely interpreted as having at least some justification in the behaviour of the unionist people and government of the 'failed political entity' of Northern Ireland. It is also increasingly common in middle and professional class circles within the unionist community where a sense of guilt or at least embarrassment is an important element underlying political development.

One result of years of largely undefended allegations is that Northern Ireland Protestants are frequently described in terms usually reserved for the world's least savoury political cultures. Consider the following from Bowyer Bell, professor of history at Columbia University and author of several major books on Northern Ireland

> Many Protestants, who were mostly plain, often poor children of their own history, were also prejudiced practically from birth, decent folk but fearful of the alien. The system began by teaching toddlers differences, superiority and privilege. Thus most were bigots, some simple and gentle, others nasty and if need be brutal.[1]

To the celebrated Irish historian, Professor Joe Lee of University College Cork, the northern Protestants have a 'herronvolk' mentality.[2] Political scientists Brendan O'Leary and John McGarry take a similar view in stating that, 'the UUP could rely on ingrained ethnic prejudices to sustain discrimination'.[3] More political writers have been even less restrained. For instance, Michael Farrell (1976) and Eamonn McCann (1974), the latter currently a columnist for the *Belfast Telegraph*, depicted discrimination as being so pervasive as to be the foundation of the state.[4] Paul Foot, *Daily Mirror* columnist and nephew of a former British Labour Party leader, wrote, 'nowhere in the world was bigotry taken to such extravagant lengths as it was in Northern Ireland'.[5] Perhaps most influential was the report of the New Ireland Forum, established by the government of the Republic of Ireland, in 1983, that northern Catholics were 'deprived of the means of social and economic development'.[6]

Perhaps not many would follow Foot in assessing discrimination in Northern Ireland as being worse than in apartheid South Africa or in the pre-integration southern states of the USA, but the tide of rhetoric on this issue has been so strong that many people are willing to view the Stormont regime as having strong similarities with these odious regimes. This is the case despite a growing tendency for histories of Northern Ireland written in the 1990's to take a more objective or even overtly pro-unionist view.[7]

Accusations of discrimination, and more general abuse of civil rights, have formed the backbone of sympathy for the nationalist cause among neutral observers and of antagonism to the unionist cause. Even though unionists have had minimal power in Northern Ireland for a quarter of a century, the accusations are regularly repeated and renewed. There are essentially four charges:

(a) Discrimination in housing
(b) Discrimination in jobs – especially in the public sector
(c) Gerrymandering of electoral boundaries
(d) Abuses of civil power, in the use of legislation (the Special Powers Act of 1922) backed by a sectarian auxiliary police force (the B Specials).

This chapter deals with allegations of discrimination in housing and employment since the focus here is on how power was used rather than on how power was achieved. In the following chapter Sidney Elliot takes up the issue of biases in electoral arrangements. Finally, allegations of abuse of civil power are usually related to the pre-war era or to subsequent periods of violence, and as such can be seen as much as a consequence of the rejection of the Stormont government by nationalists as a cause of that rejection. Since it is the latter which is of concern here, neither this chapter nor the next deals with allegations of abuse of civil power.

The most comprehensive and rigorous existing evaluation of the extent of discrimination under the Stormont regime was undertaken by the late Professor Whyte.[8] There are three reasons for revisiting this issue and attempting to add to Whyte's scholarly assessment. Firstly, Whyte's article was largely a literature review, albeit the most wide-ranging available, making limited use of census material to give an overview. Since the available literature inevitably focuses on problems rather than normality, attempts to provide a complete census-based picture are important. Secondly, recent research, especially in the area of labour economics, was unavailable to Whyte and this affected what was perhaps the weakest part of his review, namely job discrimination within the private sector. Finally, it is clear from living in Northern Ireland that Whyte's balanced assessment has had a limited impact on public perceptions, even among the most highly educated. My own discussions, for instance with European officials addressing current social problems in Northern Ireland, suggest that the abuses of the past are greatly exaggerated. Much of current nationalist politics is built around an equality agenda aimed at removing the consequences of past injustice, and it is clear that the past must be continually revisited as a guide to the present.

As a test of the extent and importance of discrimination, this chapter and the next will ask whether the allocation of housing and employment is very different after the reforms of the 1970's and 1980's, and whether reformed electoral arrangements have made much difference to the outcome of elections. Finally, some reasons are suggested for the failure of much of the academic literature to make an accurate assessment of the level of discrimination.

Discrimination in housing

Accusations of discrimination in housing have been among the most important criticisms of the Stormont regime. This is not only because of the intrinsic importance of housing – a roof over one's head is after all among the most basic of necessities – but because the civil rights movement and hence the 'troubles' themselves began around the issues of housing allocation. However there has been much exaggeration. Professor Wilson states that,

> the charge of discrimination [in housing] directed against unionist policy has been repeated so often and with such total assurance that its validity now appears to be widely accepted without evidence, as though it had been fully substantiated as to have made any further presentation of the evidence no longer necessary.[9]

Allegations of discrimination in housing have a long history in Northern Ireland but they first came to more than local prominence in the civil rights campaign in the 1960s. The civil rights movement began with a campaign against the mis-allocation of housing by Dungannon rural district council – an area of 25,000 people. The campaign had begun with a campaign led by Conn McCluskey and his wife, two local doctors who formed the Campaign for Social Justice in 1964 in the Wellington Park Hotel in Belfast.

The campaign was later advanced by Austin Currie and others who organised the squatting in two council houses in Caledon, county Tyrone, by two Catholic families waiting to be re-housed. One family, the McKenna's, was evicted and the house allocated to Miss Emily Beattie, a single Protestant, 19 years old, and secretary to the local unionist councillor, who was also a unionist parliamentary candidate.

As Austin Currie said, 'if we had waited a thousand years we would not have got a better example', hence indicating that it was unusual.[10] In fact, Miss Beattie was engaged to be married, and married a few weeks later. Her fiancee was from Monaghan and hence ineligible to register for the house in his own name. She came from an over-crowded home and her brother, an RUC officer involved in the eviction, came to live with her and her husband. However, as Lord Cameron said in the report of the Cameron Commission, 'by no stretch of the imagination could Miss Beattie be regarded as a priority tenant'.

This incident was widely reported internationally and came to symbolise the abuse of civil rights by unionist authorities in Northern Ireland. Of course, the incident could not have attracted so much sympathy, were it not for a large number of accusations of discrimination in housing over a number of years.

The accusations largely concerned a number of small local authority districts west of the Bann, especially Dungannon and in Fermanagh. Figures from the McCluskey's and from similar reports in Fermanagh are repeated in all histories of the 'troubles'. These instances are usually taken uncritically as examples of discrimination in Northern Ireland as a whole, although the figures for the rest of Northern Ireland are never included in these accounts. In particular, Belfast is never mentioned.

The strength of the accusations have, if anything, grown over the years, and become all embracing: Let us return again to Bowyer Bell writing in 1993

> The construction of small council houses for the poor caused most resentment. The state controlled houses for the poor. And houses, like all else, went to unionists. Many Catholics felt that if houses did not go to Protestants they simply would not be built. Without a house the Catholics would go away. With a house the Catholics would stay and put the gerrymandered districts to threat. So there were few houses for Catholics.[11]

The picture painted here is clear, and is widely believed, including by a significant number of Protestants. It is, however, untrue, as can be clearly seen in the 1971 census of population taken in the dying months of the 50 year unionist rule from Stormont.

In that year there were 148,000 local authority dwellings in Northern Ireland, of which between 45,000 and 55,000 were occupied by Catholic families (depending on what is assumed about the religion of those who declined to answer the religion question in the population census of that year). We can see immediately that the idea that there were few houses for Catholics is completely wrong. In fact, Catholics had a disproportionately large share of local authority housing. Catholics comprised 26.1% of households, but occupied 30.7% of local authority households (see Table 5.1). To put the figures another way, 4 out of every 10 Catholic families were in local authority houses compared with just over 3 out of every 10 Protestants.

We might ask how it can be that it is widely believed that the unionist authorities built few houses for Catholics, when in fact the statistics show that they provided proportionately more for Catholics than for Protestants. The first thing to say is that even with the figures in Table 5.1, it may have been that unionist authorities were still not responding fully and fairly to the need of Catholics. There are three obvious ways to measure needs: firstly, relative to income; secondly, relative to family size; and thirdly in light of the existing housing conditions.

By luck there is some good quality evidence on these issues. A major survey was undertaken in 1968 by an American professor based in Glasgow, Richard Rose. This was published in his famous book on Northern Ireland, *Governing Without Consensus*. The survey covered a very wide range of political and social issues and provides an invaluable benchmark of conditions and attitudes in the last years of the Stormont regime and immediately prior to the 'troubles'.

Table 5.1 Distribution of local authority housing by religion in Northern Ireland in 1971

	Percentage of households	
	All households	Households in local authority dwellings
Catholic	26.1	30.7
Other Denominations	65.2	60.8
Not Known	8.7	8.5
Total	100.0	100.0

Source: Northern Ireland Census of Population, 1971.

The survey included a section on housing conditions, and Professor Rose discovered what was later confirmed by the 1971 census, that is, that Catholics had a disproportionately large share of local authority houses. The advantage to Catholics was very marked in Belfast, which had a unionist council (19% of Catholics were in local authority houses compared with 9% of Protestants), and in areas with nationalist councils (39% of Catholics compared with 15% of Protestants). Elsewhere, Catholics and Protestants got an equal share of local authority houses. Professor Rose's conclusion was that there was:

> ... no evidence of systematic discrimination against Catholics. The greatest bias appears to favour Catholics in areas controlled by Catholic councillors.[12]

Professor Rose controlled for the possibility of differing needs for local authority housing, firstly, by taking into account the incomes of families. He examined the allocation of local authority houses between Catholics and Protestants within six separate income groups. In five out of the six income categories the proportion of Catholics in local authority housing was higher than for Protestants. In other words, Catholics did not get more local authority houses only because they were poorer. At any given level of income Catholics fared distinctly better than Protestants.

The reason for this advantage is likely to be the larger family size of Catholics – in most housing allocation systems in the UK larger families receive priority – a practice formalised within the Northern Ireland Housing Executive (NIHE) from its inception in 1971. Prior to the establishment of the NIHE, it is possible that large Catholic families did not receive as much priority as the (much less common) large Protestant families. For families with six plus children (78% of which were Roman Catholic) Rose reported that there

102

were 12% more Protestants than Catholics in local authority housing. Rose does not provide figures for other family sizes.

The end of 50 years of housing policy in Northern Ireland, largely under unionist control, left Protestants over-represented in privately rented housing – usually thought of as poorer in quality to either local authority or owner-occupied housing, although much owner-occupied property in rural areas may have been of very low quality.

By 1971, the census of population showed that 30% of homes in Northern Ireland still lacked exclusive use of basic amenities including hot water, a fixed bath and indoor toilet. The figures for homes lacking amenities also show that Catholics were worse off than Protestants, although poor housing conditions were widespread in both communities. Thirty-six per cent of Catholic homes lacked these basic amenities, compared with 31% for Church of Ireland members and 27% for Presbyterians. The reasons for these differences are unclear and may reflect a range of influences including patterns of urban and rural home ownership.

All denominations clearly suffered poverty and poor housing, and differences between religions were not huge. Slum conditions were well known to both communities. A Building Design Partnership study of Belfast in 1969 found 'gross deficient' standards in most houses in both Catholic Cromac Street and Protestant Sandy Row. The unionist regime may be criticised for not raising standards for all. However, its resources were limited through much of its history. A significant housing problem had built up during the financially difficult inter-war years when only 50,000 new houses were built, a level only proportionately half as large as that in the rest of the UK.[13] In the post-war years up to 1970 a total of 178,000 houses were built, of which 120,000 were built by the public sector, a major achievement. However it was not until 1985 when a further 150,000 houses had been built that the housing shortage can be said to have finally disappeared.

The thorny issue of differences between Catholics and Protestants in family size is important in understanding the housing issue. This issue here, which is almost never raised in discussions on the allocation of housing in conditions of shortage (or indeed in respect of unemployment or public spending), is how can housing be allocated on a fair basis when one community has consistently higher birth rates than the other.

In fact, one recent book does describe the difficulties in an open way. This is the autobiography of Maurice Hayes, formerly town clerk in Downpatrick and later permanent secretary in the Department of Health and Social Services (DHSS) and ombudsman for Northern Ireland. Dr. Hayes' account of the difficulties faced by the nationalist council in Downpatrick are worth repeating.

Down council attempted a fair allocation of local authority housing in the 1960s and was in Dr. Hayes' view one of the first councils to introduce a points system. This system favoured larger families and hence Catholics received most houses. To avoid this over-representation the council subsequently introduced two separate lists, one for Catholics and one for Protestants. This in turn had the undesirable consequence that single Protestants were allocated houses while large Catholic families remained on the waiting list. This in turn was viewed as unacceptable and the council reverted to its earlier points system.[14] Similar problems may have been responsible for large disproportion in the allocation of council houses in Newry in 1963 where all but 22 of the 765 houses were allocated to Catholics.[15]

Here we have a conundrum. When a unionist council in Dungannon gave a house to a single Protestant in preference to a Catholic family, the result was the civil rights movement leading eventually onto the 'troubles'. When a nationalist council did exactly the same, for the best of motives, it attracted no attention whatsoever, either then or since. Despite the fact that Catholics did best in local authority housing, unionist councils as a whole became tarred with the brush of discrimination. Despite Rose's view that the clearest evidence was of nationalist councils discriminating against Protestants, nationalists attracted little opprobrium.

One point to make is that much of the argument on housing took place between 1964 and 1969 when the Northern Ireland Housing Executive (NIHE) was announced (although it was not set up until 1971). Few systematic figures on the allocation of housing between Roman Catholics and Protestants were available until Professor Rose's book *Governing Without Consensus* was published in 1971 and until the religion tables of 1971 census were published in 1975. By then the civil rights argument on housing had been won by nationalists.

Even so, we might reasonably ask why have the facts not subsequently been corrected or at least acknowledged by historians and other analysts of the Northern Ireland problem? One answer is that historians are ill-equipped to answer such questions, too rarely examining statistical sources. To be fair to them they usually see their task as reporting significant events (such as the origins of the civil rights movement in Northern Ireland), and repeat what contemporary activists said or thought about the events. Because the accusations of discrimination in housing were not countered at the time, some historians were content to report contemporary opinion. Historians might also argue that what people thought at the time was a more important influence on events than what was true.

Some historians have however gone further, and give the clear impression that the allegations of discrimination were true. In this respect, they go beyond their competence in an unself-critical way. Some might also be accused of, at best, a lack of professionalism. Professor Bowyer Bell, for instance, refers in his forward to his 'friend' Professor Rose. He has, however, ignored his friend's evidence on the allocation of housing. Professor Bell is one particularly stark example. Other historians appear to follow each other. Dungannon and the McCluskey's appear again and again, but the census figures quoted above are almost wholly absent.

The McCluskey evidence appears to be widely regarded. Bardon for instance calls it 'an impressive dossier'.[16] Although its contemporary political importance cannot be doubted, as a survey of discrimination and especially of housing conditions it leaves much to be desired. The authors confuse disadvantage with discrimination, and make sweeping assertions where the evidence is purely circumstantial. The main section on housing consists of five short paragraphs and is largely concerned not with housing conditions but with the location of housing for purposes of gerrymandering. The housing figures for Dungannon are incomplete and difficult to assess. The only complete figures are for Omagh and Armagh. In both of theses cases the allocation of houses between Catholics and Protestants is close to their respective shares in the local population. What the McCluskey pamphlet does show for Dungannon, Omagh and Armagh (but nowhere else) is that the local unionist councils built few houses for Catholics. Instead houses for Catholics in these areas were mostly built by the Housing Trust, which controlled around 40% of state owned housing in Northern Ireland. As we argue below no assessment of housing standards in Northern Ireland can be made without taking into account the role of the Housing Trust.

What happened in housing is relatively clear at least for the 1960s. A number of small local authorities in Fermanagh and Tyrone built very few houses for Catholics either within their boundaries or in areas where doing so would upset the electoral balance. This was made clear at the time in a series of exhaustive articles on Fermanagh by the then young *Belfast Telegraph* reporter Dennis Kennedy, later to become deputy editor of the *Irish Times* and EC representative in Belfast.

Dennis Kennedy's articles showed clearly that the unionist council in Enniskillen built houses for Catholics only in the one ward which returned a nationalist electoral majority. This was an open practice. No one attempted to deny it. The councillors were acutely concerned about where these would be built. In the Enniskillen case, many of the houses for Catholics were built not by the council itself, but by the Northern Ireland Housing Trust operating with a subsidy from Enniskillen council. Other houses for Catholics were built just outside the town boundary in anticipation of future boundary changes.

All of this is very unsatisfactory. It certainly amounts to malpractice to maintain unionist control. It does not however amount to an attempt to deprive Catholics of housing equal in standard to that allocated to Protestants. What these councils established was not necessarily a discriminatory regime in the availability of housing, but certainly a segregated housing pattern.[17] Whether this made much difference in practice is harder to say. Dr. Hayes describes ruefully how his attempts to integrate local authority housing in Downpatrick failed due to the location of churches and schools (in some cases due to the absence of co-operation from education authorities). Some of the most segregated estates in Downpatrick remain sectarian black spots.

Perhaps the best summary of the housing issue was made by Charles Brett, the first chairman of the Northern Ireland Housing Executive

> It is my view that the majority of councils did not consciously or deliberately engage in any kind of discrimination; but a minority did so and thereby discredited the whole.[18]

Many councils, notably including Belfast, had in Oliver's view a blameless record in housing and most 'struggled manfully to maintain standards and to do the right thing'.[19] Even the Cameron Commission in commenting on the four councils most affected by disturbances concluded that houses were allocated in rough proportion to numbers of Catholics and Protestants. Cameron's criticism in these areas was again one of using housing to maintain electoral control.[20] It should also be noted that no legal challenge was ever mounted to the many Northern Ireland housing acts, all of which required and got royal assent. Moreover when a British based ombudsman and commissioner for complaints were installed in 1968 they received few complaints, and in his first report in 1971 the ombudsman praised the quality of administration in Northern Ireland ministries.[21]

Almost all allegations of discrimination in housing ceased when the Northern Ireland Housing Executive was set up in 1972 to take responsibility from both the local authorities and the Housing Trust. It should be said immediately that the Stormont regime's delay in responding to the indefensible behaviour in a few councils west of the Bann was not excusable and played no small part in its downfall. With 68 local authorities for a population of only 1.5 million, many were tiny. The pool of talent among elected officials must have been greatly stretched, and the temptation to misallocate housing in councils which built only a handful of units each year would always have been considerable. Local control of housing is always open to abuse in one party administrations and it is only the unusual circumstances of Northern Ireland west of the Bann which made the problem so much worse than in similar one party situations in Scotland, south Wales or north east England. It was however typical of unionist politics to ignore the need for institutional change. Whereas Ulster conservatism contributes much to aspects of social stability in Northern Ireland, unionist conservatism in delaying the reform of badly performing institutions was the Achilles heel of a government faced with, admittedly daunting problems. Oliver, a permanent secretary during this period, takes the view that behaviour of the small local authorities close to the border was wrong, but understandable in the context of continuous and often violent opposition to the state. He says, 'our failure to deal with those attitudes and practices was one of our most serious failures overall, for while the practical effect was small their psychological and political effect was great'.[22]

Table 5.2   Distribution of local authority housing by religion in Northern Ireland in 1991

Percentage of households

	All households	Households in local authority dwellings
Catholic	32.8	38.3
Other Denominations	60.1	54.5
Religion Not Known	7.1	7.2
Total	100.0	100.0

Source: Northern Ireland Census of Population, 1991.

More than a quarter century after the formation of the Housing Executive little has however changed in the distribution of houses between Catholics and Protestants. Table 5.2 shows that Catholics are over-represented relative to their numbers by almost exactly the same amount as they were at the end of the Stormont years. Moreover the degree of physical segregation, about which the McCluskeys complained most bitterly is much worse after 30 years of terrorist violence. In aggregate little has changed except the overt use of housing location for electoral advantage in a few local authorities. While protesters were correct to complain about the abuses which did occur prior to 1972, the civil rights movement did not raise the cases of discrimination against Protestants in nationalist controlled councils, and it is clear that housing was used as a stick with which to beat unionism. In this it was spectacularly successful. In any other society the demand would have been to reform housing allocation in the small number of offending councils. In Northern Ireland the issue helped to initiate 30 years of violent conflict. This over-reaction to a serious but limited problem has been legitimised by its treatment in academic and journalistic accounts of the period. Michael Farrell's self consciously partisan account, for instance, highlights only one area (Fermanagh), confuses general housing shortage with misallocation and fails to mention any instance of nationalist discrimination against Protestants.[23]

107

Discrimination in employment

Allegations of discrimination in employment, like those in housing go back to the first days of the Stormont regime and before. Catholic workers had been violently expelled from the Belfast shipyards several times during the nineteenth century. Those Catholics who had obtained jobs in engineering while Protestants were fighting in the 1914–18 war, were expelled from the Harland and Wolff shipyard and other large engineering firms during the 1920 sectarian unrest which preceded partition.[24] Although there were clear examples of segregation and discrimination in employment in the Stormont years these did not play a large role in the civil rights movement despite featuring strongly in the McCluskey's memorandum. Unlike housing the issue of job discrimination has remained alive up to the present day[25] and frequently features in Sinn Fein criticisms of the administration of Northern Ireland. Despite the passing of two fair employment acts, in 1976 and 1990, and the setting up of a Fair Employment Commission and the Standing Advisory Commission on Human Rights (SACHR), belief in job discrimination appears almost as strong today as it was 30 years ago. In 1998 further strengthening of the fair employment act was undertaken.

Central government

Throughout the Stormont period there appears to have been some bias towards employing Protestants in senior levels of the civil service. Catholics were certainly greatly under-represented at senior levels within the civil service. The Campaign For Social Justice recorded that between the rank of deputy principal and permanent secretary in the civil service Catholics occupied only 7.4% of posts. On the other hand, autobiographical accounts now exist from at least four former civil servants who reached the highest rank of permanent secretary, two of whom are Catholic and two Protestant.[26] All of these paint a convincing picture of a fair and efficient civil service.

Both Shea, a Catholic, and Oliver, a Protestant, refer directly to the issue of under-representation of Catholics among the most senior jobs, around 50 in all, which needed the approval of cabinet ministers who were of course almost invariably unionist. Shea records that he had good reason to believe that his promotion to the second highest grade (assistant secretary) was delayed for perhaps a decade, although he makes no comparison of qualifications and experience and makes too little of the fact that as a non-graduate he faced tough competition from the stream of Oxbridge graduates entering the Northern Ireland civil service through national UK competitions. Bloomfield, who eventually became head of the civil service in the 1980s, asserts that he never encountered religion or politics in almost 40 years experience on selection and promotion committees. It does however seem likely that some

108

of the partition generation of unionist politicians were unwilling to promote Catholics to the top policy making positions, although Bonaparte Wyse, a Dublin Catholic, was permanent secretary in education from 1927–39. Once the next generation of unionists gained power in the person of Terence O'Neill there was a relaxation and this may be associated with the fact that Shea was promoted to assistant secretary. At the end of the Stormont period Shea eventually got the top job of permanent secretary in the department of education, despite not being a graduate. Indeed until 1992 he was the only holder of this post not to have been at either Trinity College Dublin or at Oxbridge. We might note as a curiosity that from partition until 1998 no Ulster Protestant ever rose to the rank of permanent secretary in the department of education.[27]

None of this should suggest that there was an ethos of personal hostility to Catholics. Shea comments

> The cabinet ministers with whom I came into contact were, almost without exception, kind to me, conscientious in their attitude to the public services, anxious to manage their departments efficiently. In private conversation many of them showed a liberality of mind pleasantly at variance with the accepted image of unionist politicians.[28]

The unionist ministers preferred senior civil servants who were in their eyes 'loyal', and saw little purpose in employing in senior positions those who were or might be dedicated to the overthrow of the state. It is possible to have some understanding with this view and many of those who easily decry this behaviour come from jurisdictions were the problem does not arise. Oliver for instance defends the principle that ministers should have in their small private offices those they prefer to work with.[29] The real charges against unionist ministers were that they indiscriminately treated all Catholics as *ipso facto* disloyal, including cases like Shea's where there was no evidence of disloyalty. They also carried these attitudes on for too long after partition. As Shea says: 'a little magnanimity would have gone a long way'.[30] Finally, ministers, in Shea's view, far too often appeared to bend to the wishes of the Orange Order against their own better judgement.

At the same time there were too few Catholic applicants to challenge these prejudices. Shea suggests that too many Catholics preferred second class citizenship to working for the government. Even in the 1970s as permanent secretary in the department of education Shea, as someone who had 'gone over to the other side', was rarely invited to Catholic schools in Belfast. Oliver adds that Catholic hostility in the 1920s and 1930s towards working for the Northern Ireland state inevitably meant that 'there could be few rising to the highest ranks in the 1940s, 1950s and 1960s'.[31] Entrance to the Northern Ireland civil service was open to high fliers to apply through the London first division competition from 1929 onwards, but it was not until the mid-1960s that the first Catholic succeeded in entering through this path despite the complete absence of any taint of discrimination or influence from unionists.

Whether or not this made much difference to all but those few like Shea who were directly affected is difficult to say. Of the eight permanent secretaries in the 1960s, three were from the British mainland recruited through national competitions. A pro-rata share for Northern Ireland Catholics at this rank might have thus been two if suitable candidates had been available. There may have been some justification in unionist ministers preferring officials with a reasonably similar outlook, as is normal in the USA. However in the circumstances of Northern Ireland it was surely important to publicly demonstrate that Catholics could and should rise to the highest administrative positions and indeed were willing to do so. Once again unionists acted unintelligently either because of their own predilections or due to pressure from their supporters. In the latter case the lack of an active intellectual strand in unionism meant that these pressures were too rarely questioned or countered.

Whether unionist administrations had a deliberate policy of job discrimination 'with a view to maintaining the population balance between the two communities', as suggested by Boyle and Haddon[32] and O'Malley[33] is open to much more doubt. Neither Boyle and Haddon nor O'Malley provide evidence for this strong proposition, the former instead referring readers to the 1987 SACHR report 'for a general review of issues and statistics on discrimination in employment', and the latter referring to studies of Catholic disadvantage rather than discrimination.

Local authorities

Perhaps the clearest examples of job discrimination came among the non-manual employees of local authorities. By 1971 total employment in local authorities had grown to 5,700 of which an estimated 1,600 or 28% were Catholic.[34] Hence the under-representation of Catholics in the overall employment of local authorities was slight, a matter of perhaps 300 jobs in total. However there was a strong tendency in smaller, rural and western areas for councils, both unionist and nationalist to discriminate in favour of their own supporters. Local imbalances were often large even if the aggregate employment balance was more reasonable. The local imbalances in gerrymandered areas of Fermanagh, Dungannon, Omagh and Armagh caused particular resentment since few Catholics were employed, especially in the better paid non-manual posts, despite local Catholic majorities among the population at large.[35]

Equally large imbalances within nationalist controlled councils, for instance Newry urban district council where only 3 out of 161 employees were

110

Protestant, attracted little if any public attention.[36] Cameron for instance appeared to excuse officials in Newry on the grounds that 'in Newry there are relatively few Protestants', that Protestant unemployment was low and that in recent years Newry council had introduced a competitive examination system in local authority appointments.[37] In fact Protestants comprised 25% of the population of Newry and its immediate environs, and were thus heavily under-represented. Cameron's reference to unemployment betrays a limited understanding of how labour markets work. It seems likely that the refusal of many unionists to co-operate with the Cameron Commission may have led their case to be understated.

These imbalances (but not those in favour of Catholics in nationalist controlled councils) were highlighted by the McCluskeys and before them by Frank Gallagher in his book *The Indivisible Island*.[38] Gallagher pointed out that in 1951 while Catholics comprised 31.5% of local authority employees (slightly more than their share of the population of working age), they held only 12% of the 1095 non-manual jobs in Northern Ireland's local authorities. Some of the latter imbalance may have reflected differences in educational attainment, but many may have been due to discrimination, at a direct cost of around 200 jobs to the Catholic community. Bardon argues that favouritism and patronage in appointments had long been endemic throughout Ireland and were entrenched by the 1898 local government act.[39] Once again the unionist government's failure to modernise and reform practices which were no longer widely accepted, except under severe pressure, was both inexcusable and ultimately self-defeating.

Although the instances of discrimination against Catholics in the public sector were of both political and individual importance the numbers involved were very small, amounting to less than 400 jobs foregone by a Catholic population of economically active adults of around 250,000. To assess the claim of the Irish government's *New Ireland Forum Report* in 1984 that northern Catholics were 'deprived of the means of social and economic development' we must turn to the private sector which, during the Stormont years, employed three out every four of those working in Northern Ireland.

The private sector

There are two ways in which Catholics have claimed to be discriminated against in the Northern Ireland private sector. One is in the location of workplaces, the other is through an employer's preference for Protestants in recruitment, retention or promotion. In the former case nationalists claimed that inward investment projects coming into Northern Ireland were steered to the east and away from the more predominantly Catholic areas west of the Bann. There is no evidence to support Catholic suspicions that unionists attempted to influence incoming firms to locate in predominantly Protestant areas and these were described by Oliver as 'nonsense'.[40] Oliver lists an impressive range of multinational companies who were induced to locate in the west, along with the major infrastructural developments undertaken to assist large international chemical companies such as Du Pont to locate in county Londonderry. One personal experience comes from the head of the British Enkalon company which moved to Antrim in 1957 to eventually to employ 3,000 people who attests that his firm, one of the single largest inward investors, was left completely free to locate where-ever best suited the company. The normal higher rate of grant was available to locate west of the Bann , but the company's best interests were served by a location close to the east coast ports and the airport, and thus it chose Antrim 15 miles from Belfast.

Bradley, Hewitt and Jefferson in a 1986 study for the Fair Employment Commission found that jobs in in-moving firms were distributed across Northern Ireland in approximate proportion to the population of working age.[41] This was particularly the case after 1963 when UK regional policy was stepped up following Labour's accession to power in Great Britain. Incoming firms did not however choose locations fully in proportion to the distribution of the unemployed who were proportionately most numerous in western areas. Since high unemployment was the main criterion for giving assistance to incoming firms within Great Britain this might be viewed as evidence of bias by the Stormont government.

Any attempt at bias is unlikely since the Stormont government paid a higher rate of grant to attract firms to locate west of the Bann. Grant levels for firms locating in the west were high and any attempt to widen the difference between east and west in the value of grants is likely to have involved lower grant levels in the east. This could have deterred some firms like British Enkalon which although locating in the east attracted recruits from all parts of Northern Ireland. We might also note that during the same period most firms moving into the Republic of Ireland chose east coast locations. In both north and south this was to prove a disadvantage for these eastern areas in the economically difficult 1970's and 1980's when many companies closed their Irish branches.

The main allegations of discrimination within the private sector were focused on the major engineering companies in Belfast. These companies, the Harland and Wolff shipyard, the Shorts aircraft factories, and Mackies textile machinery works employed relatively few Catholics despite the proximity of Catholic residential areas. Although more than one thousand Catholics worked in these companies at the end of the Stormont period there can be little doubt that Catholics had, and continued to have, strong difficulties in getting and keeping jobs in these firms. Paddy Devlin, in his autobiography *Straight Left*, describes how as a young man in the 1930s he obtained a job at Mackies where his fellow workers threw nuts and bolts as well as abuse at him, and he left after a few days and there is little reason to think that these conditions had fully disappeared by the 1960s.[42] Protestant workers had similar experiences in Catholic dominated firms and a pattern of job segregation was also common in many areas.

R. G. Cooper, later to become chairman of the Fair Employment Commission, worked in management in the engineering industry in the 1960s and asserts that Catholic job applicants were weeded out at an early stage. Much of the problem seems to have stemmed from shop-floor antagonisms between Catholic and Protestant manual workers. These antagonisms have a long history, including sporadic outbreaks of violence, which were soon to erupt again in the 'troubles' from 1969 to the present. The exclusion of many Catholics from these firms can be seen as an aspect of the perennial constitutional dispute and as a kind of cold war. Both management and government made little concerted effort to change this state of affairs and can be blamed in this respect. The difficulties they faced must not be underestimated however. When changes in the balance of advantage between the Catholic and Protestant working classes began to occur in the late 1960s the cold war quickly turned hot.

The pattern of job segregation in parts of the private sector was well established by the 1960s but it played little part in the civil rights movement or in the report of the Cameron Commission. This may have been because it was an accepted part of life for many, or because a rapid flow of new firms was coming into Northern Ireland with unbiased hiring policies. The problem of job discrimination may also not have been as widespread as is often assumed. The entire mechanical and transport engineering sector in Northern Ireland employed under 5% of all those at work in 1971. Nor should it be assumed that active discrimination accounted for all, or even most, of the under-representation of Catholics in these firms. Over a quarter of a century later, following two fair employment acts and many reforms in personnel practice within these companies, the Catholic share of jobs remains under 11%. Active discrimination is no longer an issue but these firms nevertheless retain a predominantly Protestant workforce for a range of other reasons.

The pattern of under and over representation across all sectors at the end of the Stormont period is shown in Table 5.3. The figures represent the percentage excess or deficit of Catholic employment in each sector, relative to the percentage of Catholics among the economically active in each year. The greatest degree of over-representation in 1971 among the sectors separately identified in Table 5.3 occurred in the hotel, pubs and clubs industry. In this sector the percentage of Catholics employed was 29% higher than the percentage of Catholics among the economically active in 1971 (34%). This degree of over-representation of Catholics was even greater than their under-representation in the shipbuilding and aircraft engineering or the security services. Catholics were also considerably over represented in construction. Catholic under-rep-

113

resentation was greatest in shipbuilding and aircraft engineering, the security services, public utilities and in financial and business services.

The fact that Catholic over-representation in some sectors did not become a political issue may reflect the small-scale organisation of the drink and construction industries which were dominated by small family businesses. It is sometimes argued that the drink and construction industries, which included a number of lower paid jobs, acted as a kind of sink for Catholics excluded from other sectors. Although a common argument, it is almost never thought through and is more complex that it looks. It underestimates the value of such jobs, and ignores the large numbers of Protestants who were in low paid occupations or who were unemployed. We might also note that the Irish in England were also at that time concentrated in construction without any suggestion of discrimination. It is true that even within each sector Catholics tended to be in less well paid occupations.[43] However this again does not prove discrimination and could well have been due to social class, educational attainment or other factors. Catholics in Northern Ireland were for instance much better off in this respect than the children of manual workers in Britain where there was also no issue of discrimination – for the British case see J. H. Goldthorpe, *Social Mobility and Class Structure in Modern Britain*.[44]

What is striking about the overall level of Catholic under-representation is that it has got worse, not better, since the fall of the unionist government in 1972. Almost 20 years later, after a period in which unionists had minimal political influence, much of industry came under state or external control, the public sector doubled in size, and two fair employment acts were passed, the level of Catholic under-representation had grown from 2.7% in 1971 to 4.4% in 1991. There was also little change in the level of over- or under-representation in several of the most imbalanced sectors. In manufacturing, construction and the public utilities the percentages in 1991 remained much as they had been 20 years earlier. The same is true of shipbuilding and aircraft engineering where Catholic under-representation increased from 23% in 1971 to 27% in 1991. Although the share of jobs in this sector going to Catholics increased over the period, the rise was less than among the wider economically active Catholic population.

What this tells us is that patterns of under-representation in employment are complex and cannot be simply equated with discrimination as has so often been done in Northern Ireland. Employment practices today are tightly controlled and widely viewed as fair and yet imbalances have grown since the days of unionist government. What many observers fail to take into account is that labour forces are continually in flux. If Catholics gain more jobs in a situation of rapid growth and a consequent persistent oversupply of labour, one common result is to increase the number of economically active Catholics.[45] As a result the level of imbalance remains the same or even grows.

Table 5.3   Percentage of under/over-representation in employment

Private Sectors	1971	1991
Agriculture	-2.7	-4.4
Mining & Quarrying	+2.3	-6.7
Manufacturing	-11.3	-9.1
of which: transport engineering	-26.2	-27.4
Construction	+9.3	+8.2
Gas, Electricity, Water	-15.1	-16.4
Transport & Communications	-1.8	-1.8
Distribution	-4.2	-7.0
Financial & Business Services	-12.3	-7.8
Legal Services	0.0	na
Other Professional Services	-7.7	na
Hotels, Pubs, Clubs etc.	+29.4	+8.9
Public Sector		
Education	-0.9	+3.8
Medical	-6.7	+2.1
Government, Administration	-7.1	-4.7
RUC, Army, Fire	-18.6	-29.5
All Sectors	-2.7	-4.4

Source of data: Northern Ireland Census of Population 1971,1991, Religion Tables.

Note: Representation of Catholics is measured as the percentage of Catholics employed in each sector less the percentage of Catholics among the economically active in Northern Ireland in each year; i.e. 34% in 1971 and 38.2% in 1991. Of those not stating a religion 55% are allocated to the Catholic figures in 1971 and 38% in 1991. In the transport engineering sector it is the Catholic percentage of those stating a religion which is used.

The same issues affect the interpretation of differences between Catholics and Protestants in rates of unemployment. The fact that Catholic unemployment was twice as high as Protestant unemployment has stimulated many to conclude that the reason must be discrimination.[46] The major study commissioned from the Policy Studies Institute (PSI) in 1989 by SACHR suggested that around half of the unemployment differential must be due to discrimination because all other influences had been eliminated. President Clinton writing in 1992 similarly assumed that high Catholic unemployment must reflect discrimination in writing that, 'the British government must do more to oppose the job discrimination that has created unemployment rates two and a half times higher for Catholic workers than Protestant workers'.[47]

In fact the PSI deduction was insupportable, as Wilson and others have observed.[48] The PSI study followed a standard approach in taking a wide (but hardly exhaustive) set of personal characteristics for both Catholics and Protestants at a single point in time. These characteristics included such things as age and educational qualifications. Having measured the impact of these factors on Catholic and Protestant unemployment, the study implies that any remaining differences are likely to be due to discrimination. However this approach by its very nature was unable to take any account of important factors which unfold over time (rather than being personal characteristics at any one point in time). These include the faster rate of population growth among Catholics and differences between Catholics and Protestants in the response of migration to levels of unemployment.

It is possible to combine these 'dynamic' factors with the personal characteristics included in the PSI study and in similar analyses. Gudgin and Breen[49] did this using a simple simulation model and claim to show these dynamic factors can interact with the personal characteristics to produce a Catholic unemployment rate double that of Protestants without any need to invoke discrimination. This report provoked strong opposition mainly over technical issues connected with such things as the modelling of migration behaviour.[50] What these criticisms overlook however is that it is only necessary to demonstrate a single plausible mechanism by which unemployment rates can diverge considerably between Catholics and Protestants to show that such divergence need not necessarily imply the presence of discrimination. Gudgin and Breen pointed out that this does not of course disprove the existence of discrimination, either now or in the past, but it does invalidate the tendency for people to argue that high Catholic unemployment must indicate discrimination both today and *a fortiori* in previous years. Those who believe that discrimination is or was an issue can no longer rely on the circumstantial evidence of unemployment, but must find more direct evidence.

There are now in essence two competing hypotheses to explain the large gap between Catholic and Protestant unemployment. One view is that discrimination is responsible. The other view is that the more rapid growth of population in the Catholic community has caused a chronic oversupply of labour which required out-migration to prevent a continuously rising rate of unemployment. The extent to which this problem causes unemployment chiefly in the Catholic community depends on the level of turnover and hence availability of jobs and the level of job creation, on each community's competitiveness in the labour market, and on the sensitivity of each community's migration to its rate of unemployment. They argue that although the rate of migration has been higher for Catholics than for Protestants, Catholic migration has been less responsive to high unemployment than has been the case for Protestants. As a result Catholic unemployment rates rise above those of Protestants, not only at a province-wide scale, but also in all areas where there are Catholic majorities, despite the generally superior record of job creation in these areas.

There is evidence to show that unemployment rates do differ in circumstances where discrimination is not an issue. Unemployment rates for Church of Ireland Protestants are for instance 45% higher than for Presbyterians in Northern Ireland, and differences in personal characteristics are unable to account for all of this gap, yet no-one has suggested that discrimination occurs between Protestant denominations. Similarly, unemployment rates for the Catholic majority in the Republic of Ireland are 70% higher than for the Protestant minority in the Republic.[51] The unemployment gap between Catholics and Protestants living in the southern border counties is larger than in the adjoining counties in Northern Ireland. Again personal differences between Catholics and Protestants cannot account for all of the gap in unemployment rates.

Because religion tables from Northern Ireland censuses were not published until 1975, the size of the unemployment gap between Catholics and Protestants in Northern Ireland was not recognised until after the fall of the Stormont government. As a result unemployment differences did not play an explicit role in the civil rights protests. Instead the later discovery that Catholic unemployment rates in 1971 were double those of Protestants has been subsequently used to reinforce the presumption that widespread discrimination was occurring. The persistence of the unemployment gap has led many, including the present Secretary of State, to conclude that discrimination still remains a problem, thus reinforcing the presumption that it is likely also to have been a problem in the past.

As with housing our conclusion is that despite the fall of the Stormont regime and many subsequent reforms, remarkably little has changed in the religious balance of employment and unemployment. The Catholic share of jobs and population has continued to grow but Catholics remain more underrepresented in employment than in 1971 and the unemployment gap is as large as ever. If the degree of imbalance today is not regarded as indicative of discrimination, at least by most practitioners in the field of fair employment, then it would be illogical to regard a similar degree of imbalance 30 years ago as likely in itself to indicate discrimination. This is not to deny the existence of some discrimination as recorded by Devlin, Cooper and others, nor to diminish the impact of discrimination on those individuals who were directly affected. It would however undermine the unsubstantiated judgement made by the 1986 New Ireland Forum and quoted above, that Catholics were deprived of the means of economic development.

This subject remains controversial and more research would be valuable. The working of labour markets containing two communities with different birth-rates remains poorly understood. In Northern Ireland further understanding is too often resisted with many preferring to fall back on the simple deduction that higher Catholic than Protestant unemployment must in part at least reflect both ongoing and past discrimination. One of the ironies of Northern Ireland is that under conditions of fair employment, high Catholic birth rates will displace Protestants from jobs that they would have otherwise been likely to gain. It is a little known fact that all of the net increase in jobs between the 1971 and 1991 censuses went to Roman Catholics while the number of Protestants in jobs declined. Fair Employment Commission data shows that this tendency for the Catholic community to gain most of the net addition to the total of jobs has continued into the 1990s despite an acceleration in job creation.

Conclusion

Having undertaken this review of the evidence it is difficult to disagree with the conclusion of Oliver that

> those of us who served in the [Stormont] administration are convinced both from our own experiences and from those totally impartial judgements, [i.e. the ombudsman, commissioner for complaints, and the royal commission on the constitution, 1973] that the so-called grievances and complaints that have been publicised all over the world have been hugely exaggerated.[52]

Oliver notes that the grievances began before the Stormont regime had made any decisions and have continued long after its demise. In his view the faults, mistakes and shortcomings of the regime were used by nationalists to denigrate the state and to try to pull it down.

This is not to deny the clear abuse of local powers by a limited number of local authorities mainly in border areas, or the atmosphere of communal hostility with which some private employers had to contend. Lord Cameron, writing in the report of the Cameron Commission, had some sympathy for the position in which unionists found themselves particularly in western local authorities

> It is in a sense understandable that, given the political history of Northern Ireland, in certain areas in particular, local unionist groups should seek to preserve themselves in power by ensuring that local authority housing is developed and allocated in ways which will not disturb their electoral supremacy.[53]

In reference to the disturbances which we now know led on to 30 years of violence he added, 'It is however natural that most Catholics should feel that the basis of administration in such areas is radically unfair'

With the considerable benefit of hindsight it seems likely that although Lord Cameron was well aware of the political dimension to the protests again discrimination, and had information on IRA influence at protest rallies, he underestimated the extent to which civil rights protests would mutate into more direct nationalist ambitions. His hope that the reforms announced by the government in response to the civil rights movement would constitute an important step towards 'eliminating causes of division and sectarian strife ... helping to unite the people of Northern Ireland' looks naive in retrospect.[54]

It is also possible to agree with Oliver that nationalists made a blunder in not throwing in their lot with the state before 1945 as they have under different circumstances in 1998. Their decision not to put their aspiration for Irish unity 'on ice', until too late, led inevitably to a culture of grievance which at the very least made the emergence of the troubles more likely. At the same time Oliver is surely correct in his assessment that the unionists political shortfall was if anything greater, since they failed to take what opportunities they had to bring the nationalists into the political system to offer them a greater stake in the future of the province and to reform the outmoded system of local elections. The history of the 1950s and 1960s contains many examples of a hard line when greater generosity would surely have paid dividends.[55] Both unionists and nationalists were in some senses trapped by a 'turbulent history and an intricate geography' and crippled by an unnecessary constitutional uncertainty (all of which remain with us) but the quality of their struggle against these difficulties prior to 1972 left much to be desired.

Finally, writing this in the week of the tragic Omagh bombing causing the death of 29 people, including many women and children, it is poignant but easy to agree with Patrick Shea's conclusion after a lifetime in the Northern Ireland civil service

> I am totally convinced that whatever may be said about the righting of past wrongs or the maintenance of inherited power and privilege, there has been no moral justification for violence or threat of violence for political ends in Ireland at any time in the present century.[56]

References

1.   J. Bowyer Bell, *The Irish Troubles*, Gill and Macmillan, Dublin, 1993, p.10
2.   J.J. Lee, *Ireland 1912–85: Politics and Society*, Cambridge University Press, Cambridge, 1989, pp. 79, 421, 596.
3.   B. O'Leary and J. McGarry, *The Politics of Antagonism: Understanding Northern Ireland*, Athlone Press, London, p. 129.

4. See M. Farrell, *Northern Ireland: The Orange State*, Pluto Press, London, 1976 and E. McCann, *War and an Irish Town*, Harmondsworth,Penguin, London, 1974. This was Whyte's summary of Farrell and McCann's views in J. Whyte, 'How much discrimination was there under the unionist regime', in T. Gallagher and J. O'Connell (eds.), *Contemporary Irish Studies*, Manchester University Press, Manchester, 1983, p.29.
5. P. Foot, *Ireland: Why Britain Must Get Out*, Chatto Counterblasts No. 2, Chatto, London, 1989, p. 3.
6. *New Ireland Forum Report*, Dublin, 1984.
7. See A. Alcock, *Understanding Ulster*, Ulster Society, Belfast, 1994; B. Bardon, *A History of Ulster*, Blackstaff press, Belfast, 1992; T. Hennessey, *A History of Northern Ireland, 1920–96*, Gill and Macmillan, Dublin, 1997; C. Hewitt, 'The roots of violence: Catholic grievances and Irish nationalism during the civil rights period', in P.J.Roche and B.Barton (eds.), *The Northern Ireland Question: Myth and Reality*, Avebury, Aldershot, 1991 and C. Hewitt, Catholic grievances, Catholic nationalism and violence in Northern Ireland, *British Journal of Sociology*, vol. 34, no.3, 1981; J. Oliver, 'The Stormont administration' in P. J. Roche and B. Barton op. cit.
8. J. Whyte, op. cit.
9. T. Wilson, *Ulster: Conflict and Consent*, Blackwell, Oxford, 1989, p. 124.
10. *Disturbances in Northern Ireland*, Report of the Cameron Commission appointed by the Governor of Northern Ireland, Cmnd 532, HMSO, London, 1969, p. 21.
11. J. Bowyer Bell, op. cit., p.49.
12. R. Rose, *Governing without Consensus: An Irish Perspective*, Faber and Faber, London,1971, p.293.
13. T. Wilson, op. cit., p. 125.
14. See M. Hayes, *Minority Verdict: Experiences of a Catholic Public Servant*, Blackstaff Press, Belfast, 1995.
15. See D. P. Barritt and C. F. Carter, *The Northern Ireland Problem: A Study in Group Relations*, Oxford University Press, Oxford, 1962.
16. J. Bardon, op. cit., p. 638.
17. D. Kennedy, *Belfast Telegraph*, 1968.
18. C. E. B. Brett, *Housing in a Divided Community*, Dublin and Belfast, 1986.
19. J. Oliver, op. cit., p.92.
20. *Disturbances in Northern Ireland*, op. cit., para. 140.
21. *Report of the Northern Ireland Parliamentary Commission for Administration*, 1971, p. 4.
22. J. Oliver, op.cit., p.93.
23. M. Farrell, op. cit., p. 87.
24. B. Bardon, op. cit.,
25. F. O'Connor, *In Search of a State: Catholics in Northern Ireland*, Blackstaff Press, Belfast, 1993, p. 182.
26. See P. Shea, *Voices and the Sound of Drums: An Irish Autobiography*, Blackstaff Press, Belfast, 1981; M. Hayes, op. cit.; K. Bloomfield, *Stormont in Crisis: A Memoir*, Blackstaff Press, Belfast, 1994; J. Oliver, 'The Stormont administration', in P. J. Roche and B. Barton (eds.), op. cit.
27. I am grateful to Arthur Green, formerly under secretary in the department of education, for this point.
28. P. Shea, op. cit., p.196.
29. J. Oliver, op. cit., p.90.
30. P. Shea, op. cit'. p. 196.
31. J. Oliver, op. cit., p. 89.
32. K. Boyle and T. Hadden, *Northern Ireland: The Choice*, Penguin, London, 1994, p. 45.
33. P. O'Malley, *The Uncivil Wars*, Blackstaff Press, Belfast, 1983, p. 149.

34. *Census of Population*, 1971.
35. *Cameron Report; Disturbances in Northern Ireland*, Report of the Commission appointed by the Governor of Northern Ireland, Cmnd 532, HMSO, Belfast, 1969, para. 138.
36. T. Hennessey, op. cit., p. 113.
37. *Cameron Report*, op. cit., para. 138.
38. F. Gallagher, The Indivisible Island, Gollancz, London, 1957.
39. J. Bardon, op. cit., p.639.
40. J. Oliver, op. cit., p. 84.
41. J. Bradley, V. Hewitt and C. Jefferson, *Industrial Location Policy and Equality of Opportunity in Northern Ireland*, Research Paper No. 10, Fair Employment Agency, Belfast, 1986.
42. P. Devlin, *Straight Left: An Autobiography*, Blackstaff Press, Belfast, 1993.
43. E. A. Aunger, 'Religion and class: an analysis of 1971 data', in R.J. Cormack and R.D. Osborne (eds.), *Religion, Education and Employment Aspects of Equal Opportunity in Northern Ireland*, Appletree Press, Belfast, 1986.
44. J. H. Goldthorpe, *Social Mobility and Class Structure in Modern Britain*, Clarendon Press, Oxford, 1980, Table 2.2.
45. Increase in the number of economically active people can occur because out-migration is reduced, in-migration rises or the number of people seeking work expands.
46. B. O'Leary and J. McGarry, op. cit., pp. 129–30.
47. C. O'Clery, *The Greening of the White House*, Gill and Macmillan, Dublin, 1996, p.22.
48. T. Wilson, op. cit.
49. G. Gudgin and R. Breen, 'Evaluation of the Ratio of Unemployed Rates as an Indicator of Fair Employment', *Central Community Relations Unit*, Belfast, 1996.
50. A. Murphy, *Comments*, in G. Gudgin and R. Breen, op. cit. and V.K. Borooah, 'Is there a penalty to being a Catholic in Northern Ireland', forthcoming in *The European Journal of Political Economy*.
51. G. Gudgin, 'Catholic and Protestant Unemployment in Ireland, North and South', *Northern Ireland Economic Research Centre Working Paper*, No. 10, Belfast 1994.
52. J. Oliver, op. cit., p. 96.
53. *Cameron Report*, op. cit., para. 141.
54. Ibid., para. 131.
55. See for instance H. Patterson, Party versus Order: Ulster Unionism and the Flags and Emblems Act, forthcoming in Contemporary British History.
56. P. Shea, op. cit., p. 201.

6 The Northern Ireland Electoral System: A Vehicle for Disputation

Sydney Elliott

The electoral provisions of the Government of Ireland Act 1920 were the result of four home rule proposals over thirty-four years and debate about safeguards for minorities. Under the 1920 Act, so far as Northern Ireland was concerned, representation at Westminster continued but with thirteen instead of thirty members and no power to amend electoral laws relating to Westminster elections. The Northern Ireland House of Commons had fifty-two members for sixteen borough, thirty-two county and four university seats. Members were elected by single transferable vote (STV), using the Westminster constituencies, for a five-year term. The Senate was elected by the Northern Ireland House of Commons by STV for a period of eight years, with half retiring every four years. All electoral laws then applying in the United Kingdom also applied to Northern Ireland. The electoral system was guaranteed under the 1920 Act for a period of three years after which it could be altered by the Northern Ireland parliament. The local government electoral system was not mentioned by the Act; it derived from the Local Government (Ireland) Act 1898 and the Local Government (Ireland) Act 1919 which introduced STV for local elections. Finally, the 1920 Act prohibited laws which interfered with religious equality. This system represented what was considered appropriate for local needs and reflected the current debate on electoral systems in the United Kingdom.

The devolved institutions created in 1921 added a new level of elections between those for parliament and those for local authorities. During the seventy years since 1921 two different methods of election have been used. Elections to parliament at Westminster have always used the simple plurality system in single-member districts (the first-past-the-post system). Elections to the Stormont parliament in 1921 and 1925 used the single transferable vote (STV) method of proportional representation (PR) but reverted to the Westminster system from 1929 to 1969. The STV method was reintroduced for the new devolved assembly in 1973, the constitutional convention in 1975, the assembly of 1982 and the new assembly of 1998. In 1996 the Northern Ireland forum election used a unique constituency list form of PR. At local government level the experiment with PR in 1920 was reversed in 1922 and the simple majority system was restored until 1972. The restructured and reformed system of district councils after 1973 returned to STV in multi-member units. The elections to the European parliament since 1979 have used STV in a single constituency with three members. PR has survived since 1972, in part, because control of elections became a function reserved by Westminster, also because its reintroduction still awaits official evaluation and because there has been an increasing acceptance of the system by the parties. The system was continued in the new assembly elected in 1998.

The basic problem facing Northern Ireland in 1921 was to bring dissident opinion, nationalist, unionist and other, into the life of the new political entity. Enloe outlines three strategies for states lacking unity due to ethnic factors,[1] namely, allocation of resources, autonomy for border areas and use of the electoral system. In Northern Ireland, the third of these strategies had the most potential. In general, if the electoral system assisted the formation of coalitions or promoted cross-cutting cleavages it could pull groups into the political system. By giving minorities representation, PR could specifically reduce tension over electoral boundaries and the feeling of injustice where plurality methods were used.

The penalty for failure was outlined by Rabushka and Shepsle.[2] Their paradigm of politics in plural societies set out the dynamics of ethnic competition and stressed the significance of electoral machination in a progression towards violence. They stated that the temptation to manipulate was overwhelming in two types of circumstances: first, where the majority felt politically insecure due to the size of one of the minorities; and second, where there was a dominant majority and minorities were significant only in the event of splits in the majority or in the use of violence. In both these circumstances small communities were less willing to co-operate and more likely to insist on communal representation and other protections against majoritarianism.

The electoral system contains several elements capable of manipulation for partisan advantage. The first element is the retention of outdated or fancy franchises and the disfranchisement of opponents. The second is the over-representation of rural or urban constituencies by boundary neglect or, intentionally, by gerrymandering through the manipulation of electoral boundaries. The third is the manipulation of voting rules and methods of representation: dominant groups prefer majoritarianism while minorities prefer proportionalism; dominant groups prefer representation by territory but minorities prefer communal representation.

Franchise

Northern Ireland inherited the same franchise as applied throughout the United Kingdom in 1920. Under the Representation of the People Act 1918 there was universal male adult suffrage on the basis of residence. Apart from the university vote, the only other franchise retained was for occupancy of business premises worth £10 per annum. The local government franchise was granted to all owners or tenants but not to all residents. There was a residence qualification of six months in the constituency, contiguous borough or county. Servicemen had a less restrictive residence qualification, and could vote at nineteen, while conscientious objectors were disfranchised for five years. Women over thirty were enfranchised if they were local government electors or the wives of local government electors. Plural voting was permitted only on different types of qualification and no one could vote more than twice.

This franchise was used in Northern Ireland at the Westminster elections of 1922, 1923 and 1924. It was also used for Stormont elections in 1921 and 1925 and for the local government elections of 1920, 1923, 1924 – and annually or triennially thereafter. It was altered for Westminster elections by the Representation of the People (Equal Franchise) Act 1928. The Bill had two substantive provisions: the first two clauses granted the parliamentary and local government franchise on the same terms to women as to men; the fourth clause enabled women to vote on their husband's business premises qualification. The equivalent bill in Northern Ireland was the Representation of the People Act (NI) 1928. The principle of equalizing the franchise was welcomed unanimously. Opposition centred round the introduction of a three-year residence qualification, extended to seven years in 1934,[3] and a limited liability company franchise in local government elections. Both proposals were carried against nationalist and labour opposition. The main provision increased the electorate in Northern Ireland by 24.9 per cent: the male electorate increased by 3.3 per cent and the female electorate by 55.6 per cent. Women were a majority of the electorate (51.4 per cent) and were in the majority in every county borough and county except Fermanagh and Tyrone.

The franchise remained the same until the wartime preparations for peace. The Vivian Committee[4] recommendations on registration were embodied in two acts at Westminster and one at Stormont, the Parliament (Elections and Meeting) Act (NI) 1944. The speaker's conference of 1944 recommended several important changes, including a boundary commission to redistribute seats and the assimilation of the parliamentary and local government franchises. The latter became law in the Representation of the People Act 1945. However, Northern Ireland decided against assimilation and retained the ratepayer franchise in local government, making only a few adjustments to meet hardships created by wartime conditions. Finally, the Representation of the People Act 1948 abolished the business and university vote, extended postal vote facilities and abolished the residence qualification.[5] Northern Ireland did not follow the lead for Stormont elections on the business vote and university vote.

In summary, therefore, after the electoral reforms at Westminster between 1944 and 1949, the unionist government chose to retain the business vote and university vote for Stormont elections and the ratepayer suffrage and the company vote in local government. Speeches revealed that the government believed the choice provided the best possible electoral system for Northern Ireland. The question was whether the decisions had any partisan impact singly or cumulatively.[6]

The company vote

The local government company vote was the only new franchise initiated by the Northern Ireland parliament. Its introduction in 1928 was criticised by political opponents on grounds of principle and because Britain had no comparable franchise. The unionist government hoped the new franchise would give recognition and encouragement to companies for their role in developing the community and perhaps encourage businessmen to become involved in local government. Opposition parties regarded it as an attempt to increase unionist votes and to move away from the principle of the vote as an individual right to the rights of property. The company franchise was regularly criticised in formal motions in Stormont debates. With fewer than 4,000 limited liability companies the maximum number of company nominees was 24,000. Despite incomplete records, it is clear that the company franchise did not fulfil its expectations. The numbers claimed ranged from 785 in 1936 to 3,894 in 1964 and comprised 0.1 and 0.6 per cent of the electorate in these two years. Analysis of their distribution shows the dominance of the two main urban areas, Belfast and Londonderry. Belfast normally had 60 per cent, with up to 35 per cent in West Belfast, and Londonderry 14 to 30 per cent. By the 1960s the numbers claimed in Belfast had fallen radically with 16.7 per cent in 1964 and 6.9 per cent in 1967. Londonderry, in contrast, increased its percentage from 20.7 in 1937 to 30.3 in 1964. Opposition parties claimed that the company vote favoured unionists but there is no evidence that it was ever responsible for winning control of any seat. In addition, where figures exist for areas of political rivalry the picture is not one sided. In Dungannon in 1967 there were 113 company votes, 55 were held by Catholics and 58 by Protestants. In the end it was the fact that Britain had no such franchise which was fatal to it in 1968 rather than the fact that it had not been a successful innovation. If it was intended to recognise the role of companies it was never appreciated and used to any extent.

The Stormont business vote

Although it survived until the Electoral Law (NI) Act 1968 it was not subject to the same level of criticism as the ratepayer franchise or company vote. It was mentioned in a motion in 1951 and an unsuccessful attempt was made to remove it in 1961 legislation. The Stormont prime minister, Terence O'Neill, promised in 1966 to remove it before the next election. Figures published in 1974 revealed the small number of business votes – in 1968 there were 12,954, comprising 1.4 per cent of the electorate. They were heavily concentrated in Belfast and West Belfast in particular with around 70 and 35 per cent respectively. Three Stormont constituencies had higher concentrations of business votes – Central, St Annes and Windsor with 20, 7 and 6 per cent respectively. Central was always won by an anti-unionist candidate, including Joe Devlin, T. J Campbell, F. Hanna and J J Brennan and unionists only bothered to contest it on three occasions. The business vote was never responsible for the result in any Stormont constituency. Unionists probably had a majority of business votes in the Belfast area but in Londonderry the nationalist registration association claimed two thirds of the 400 in the city in 1967. The number of business votes, their distribution meant they were of little importance – a view expressed by Gerry Fitt at the time:

The abolition of the business vote meant nothing ... why the government held on to it for so long I fail to understand because they did not win any particular seats by its institution.[7]

Residence qualification

The Representation of the People (NI) Act 1928 introduced a three year residence qualification for Northern Ireland elections. During the debates concern had been expressed about the summer 'swallow' phenomenon by which agricultural workers from the Irish Free State took up casual summer employment and, if resident for three months, qualified for the franchise in Northern Ireland elections. Border unionists were especially concerned. Joe Devlin, the nationalist leader, said the proposal was provocative, insulting and would probably affect no more than 100 votes. The measure was not regarded as effective and in 1934 the period of residence was extended to seven years. The nationalist opposition regarded it as unnecessarily increasing the distinction between north and south.

The ratepayer franchise

The retention of the ratepayer suffrage after 1946 in Northern Ireland meant that by 1961 only 73.8 per cent of the adult population had the local government vote. In 1967 this meant that some 220,000 Westminster electors in Northern Ireland could not vote in local government elections. In addition, by refusing assimilation of the parliamentary and local government franchises and creating some exceptions for servicemen and those affected by wartime housing shortages, there were seven different categories of voter on the local government register. Nationalists argued constantly after 1946 that the ratepayer suffrage affected them adversely, that it was responsible for unionist control of Tyrone and Fermanagh and that the Dail had assimilated the parliamentary and local franchise in 1935. The literature to the present time assumes that it was a significant disadvantage to nationalists.

Some scattered but specific local evidence suggests that this may not have been correct. For example, in Armagh in 1964, 71.5 per cent of Protestant adults could vote in local government elections and 72.5 per cent of Catholics.[8] Consider also Table 6.1. The evenness in the distribution of local government electors had little direct connection with the percentage of the Roman Catholic population. The lower figures for Tyrone and Fermanagh appeared only between 1951 and 1961. Most of the adults without the vote were from areas with a proportionally large non-Catholic population. Belfast was the largest single unit and had 28.9 per cent of all adults without the vote in 1961. Finally, the lower figures for Tyrone and Fermanagh may have been a factor of the more rural nature of the population, because Londonderry county borough, 67.1 per cent of whose population was Roman Catholic, had 75.3 per cent of its adults on the register, and was ranked second only to county Antrim.

Table 6.1   Adults, local government electors and religion, 1961

Area	Adult Population	Electorate as % adult population	Roman Catholic as % adult population
Belfast	264,686	75.0	27.5
Antrim	167,629	75.4	24.4
Armagh	70,627	73.7	47.3
Down	67,592	74.9	28.6
Fermanagh	31,075	67.6	53.2
Londonderry	94,316	71.1	50.6
Tyrone	78,184	69.9	54.8
Total	874,109	73.8	34.9

Source: Northern Ireland Census of Population, 1951 and 1961.
Ulster Year Book 1950 and 1960–62.

The stable party situation in local government, the frequent annual and triennial elections and the secrecy about unofficial party registration figures, make it difficult to be more precise. However, there are other means of getting closer to an answer. First, it is possible to examine the increase in the electorate, 1967 and 1970 after the principle of assimilation was accepted in the Electoral Law Act

(NI) 1969. The figures are complicated by population movement, natural increase, and the decision to lower the voting age from twenty-one to eighteen, but some generalisations can be made. In local authorities with a Roman Catholic majority of adults in 1971 the electorate increased by 5–10 per cent more than other areas in the same locality. However, there were some urban areas with Protestant majorities where the increase far exceeded that in Roman Catholic areas.

Second, the effect of the franchise change might be deduced from the change in party control in the 1973 local government elections. The elections were for a new system of district councils and new electoral areas impartially determined, with a new method of election favourable to minorities, STV, and the new franchise. These changes were expected to alter completely the party control of local authorities: the SDLP expected to win at least six of the twenty-six district councils. However, with a turnout of 68 per cent, the results showed that unionists had a majority in twelve districts and loyalists controlled one; unionists constituted the largest party in nine other districts and the SDLP the largest in three, including Londonderry, with one in which no party was predominant.[9] The face of local government had changed but not the party face. It is possible that the reason was that unionists gained significantly from the franchise change in the east; in the west, where political competition was intense, the effect was much more evenly balanced than hitherto believed.

Under the Northern Ireland Constitution Act 1973 control of electoral and franchise matters was reserved to Westminster and the secretary of state. Over time two broad trends were apparent. First, the legislation for special local needs continued. This included the single transferable vote and the almost universal availability of postal voting to counter the effects of intimidation and significant population movement between 1973–5. The postal vote provisions were gradually restored to normal. However, action to counter premonition in the Election (NI) 1985 Act required the production of a specified document before a ballot paper could be issued. Second, despite the separate legislative bases, the Representation of the People Acts in Britain and the Electoral Law Acts in Northern Ireland, there were moves to make the procedures uniform. This was especially so after the comprehensive Representation of the People Act 1983. Northern Ireland voters were enabled to qualify for the vote at more than one residence and citizens were allowed to qualify even though they had resided abroad for up to 20 years. The elections for the new Northern Ireland assembly were governed initially by the Election (NI) Act 1998 and thereafter by the Northern Ireland Act 1998.

Electoral boundaries and vote counting

When the Government of Ireland Act was passed in 1920 the idea of an independent body responsible either for the conduct of elections or the supervision of electoral boundaries did not exist. The Northern Ireland parliament had power to regulate its own elections; but it could not increase the number of members and in any redistribution it was bound to pay due regard to the population of constituencies. For local government elections, county boroughs and boroughs could recommend their own ward structure. The county council electoral divisions had to be as nearly equal in population as convenient, with regard to changes since the last census and the pursuits of the urban and rural population. The Local Government Act (NI) 1922 added rateable valuation to the factors to be considered. In addition, the redistribution of parliamentary seats in 1917 provided a recent body of practical guidance on procedure.

The adequacy of these provisions was tested throughout the period. Disputes over electoral boundaries were the main feature of the electoral debate between the unionist government and opposition parties. They emphasised the different expectations over territorial versus communal representation. The detailed nature of the disputes precludes anything other than a cursory review of the main types and periods of dispute.

The single-member Stormont constituencies formed in 1929

When it became clear that the unionist government would abolish PR before the end of the second parliament, opposition parties demanded a commission to redistribute seats. Nationalists feared that the opportunity would be taken to reduce their members from ten to six; Labour members asserted that failure to establish a commission would be proof of an intent to gerrymander. However, the request was rejected in 1927 and when the bill was introduced in 1929 the prime minister, Viscount Craigavon (James Craig) stressed his personal responsibility for it.

During the debate there were some claims for communal rather than territorial representation; some nationalists were willing to accept the termination of PR in return for the guarantee of sixteen seats or representation on the basis of religion. Nationalists claimed that the redistribution scheme gerrymandered Antrim and Fermanagh by taking away a seat from them in Antrim and giving unionists two seats in Fermanagh. Craigavon replied that it was impossible to create a nationalist seat of sufficient size in Antrim and that the joint representation of Fermanagh and Tyrone would continue the same as under two PR elections in 1921 and 1925.[10]

Nationalist fears were not realised in the 1929 election, and they increased their number of seats to eleven. During the third reading Joseph Devlin, leader of the Nationalist Party, had stated that it was the duty of the government to ensure that the minority would not be worse off under the new scheme. In effect this had been accomplished with some rough justice in Fermanagh and

Antrim. If there was gerrymandering in 1929 it was of an honest variety. From a technical point of view, no constituency lay outside the normal range of plus or minus one-third of the population quota for the forty-eight territorial constituencies or the range within the multi-member constituency from which they were derived. Only two technical issues seem to have occurred – whether to give Fermanagh two or three seats and the West Belfast area four or five seats. Both issues were resolved by favouring the easier course and retaining intact the registration areas of 1920.

The redistribution of county and rural district council areas, 1923–4

The abolition of PR for local government elections in 1922 meant that the electoral areas had to be reconsidered. In the urban areas the multi-member units of 1920 could have been retained or they could revert to the electoral areas in existence before PR was introduced in 1919. The areas reverted to the previous units despite nationalist protests. In the urban elections of 1923 using simple plurality nationalists retained all the councils won under PR, except Londonderry where the five ward division replaced the disputed four wards of 1920. The county and rural areas had no choice but to return to single member districts. However, these electoral units originated 80 years before in the structures created with the poor law boards and were grossly unequal. When the ministry of home affairs decided to redistribute and create new electoral areas after seeking local schemes in sensitive areas through the offices of judge Leech K.C. there was a nationalist uproar and blanket allegations of gerrymandering even before the elections were held in 1924. The elections in 1924 were boycotted by nationalists so the immediate effect of the changes in electoral areas could not be assessed. Successive triennial elections were also affected to varying degrees by boycott.

Over the period until 1939 it is possible to construct a 'normal' pattern of representation to overcome the effect of boycott in Fermanagh and Tyrone. In 1920 nationalists had won both counties by margins of 11 seats to 9 but from 1924 the 'normal' score was 13 unionist seats to 7 nationalist seats in Fermanagh and 16 unionist seats to 11 nationalist seats in Tyrone. The changes were the product of several factors – new boundaries, the simple plurality method of election and the relative state of party organisation – hence the precise effect of any one change cannot be determined. Since there were significant changes also to the control of a number of rural district councils in the two counties it adds to suspicion.

The purpose of any deliberate gerrymander scheme must be to ensure that one's own electoral areas are close to the mean and that ones opponents are dispersed especially to the larger end of the scale. The standard deviation scores for electoral areas normally won by nationalists 1924–9 were higher in

Fermanagh county council, the rural district councils of Omagh and Dungannon and all three changed hands to unionist control. Unionists had higher standard deviations in Tyrone county council and the rural district of Clogher and managed to win the county council. On the other hand nationalists had higher scores in Newry No 1, Ballycastle and Downpatrick without any change of control, as did unionists in Newry No 2 and Kilkeel. Hence the use of standard deviation scores can draw attention to potential malpractice but it might only be highlighting the relative distribution of religious denominations in Tyrone and Fermanagh. In Omagh rural district, however, the nationalist controlled council published the unionist and nationalist composition for each new ward. The standard deviation for nationalist wards was 256 and 75 for unionist wards. The result was that unionists turned a 26 to 13 deficit in 1920 into a 21 to 18 majority from 1924 and dissipated an estimated 5,000 nationalist electoral majority. The effect of this change may have been enough to have decisively influenced the composition of the county council.

Changes in Omagh, Londonderry and Armagh

In the mid-1930s inquiries were held in Omagh urban district council and Londonderry county borough as a result of ratepayers' associations seeking improved representation. The ratepayers' associations were thinly disguised and were in effect unionist. Although their ward plans were rejected in both instances, the effect of subsequent ministry action favoured the spirit of the proposals. The proposals for Omagh resulted in a change of party control to unionist and in Londonderry the three-ward structure ensured a permanent unionist majority when it would have disappeared in a few years under the five-ward system.[11] In addition, Armagh urban district council was dissolved for maladministration in 1934, and when it was returned to council control it was with a boundary extension and a new five-ward structure which reflected the new unionist majority in the city.

The failure to establish Stormont boundary commissions after 1945

After the second world war, Northern Ireland did not follow Britain in making provision for periodic boundary commissions for Stormont parliamentary constituencies. Indeed, the nationalist gerrymander motion became a hardy annual at Stormont. Allegations against Stormont constituencies gradually faded as the smallest constituencies became occupied by opposition party candidates while huge unionist constituencies built up on the fringes of Belfast. Labour members and some of the unionists with large constituencies began to demand a commission early in the 1960s. The principle was accepted in 1966 and an interim boundary commission was created in 1968 to create four new territorial seats to replace the university seats. The Electoral Law Act 1968 created a permanent boundary commission for parliamentary seats but it had not reported before direct rule in 1972.

Despite the replacement of the Londonderry corporation by a commission in 1968, allegations against local authority electoral areas persisted. The demand for 'one vote, one value' was part of the civil rights demands enshrined in the shorthand slogan 'one man, one vote.' These claims were given weight by the Cameron Commission.[12] Boundaries for the new system of district councils, recommended by the Macrory Report of 1970,[13] and the electoral areas within them, were determined by an independent commission. These single-member units were subsequently grouped into multi-member units when PR was reintroduced in 1973. The Local Government Act (NI) 1972 provided for a local government boundary commission to report every ten years (a local government boundary commission was not set up in England and Wales until 1993).

To summarise, the number and intensity of disputes over electoral boundaries made it the main area of electoral grievance. Part of the problem concerned the absence of independent procedures but the main period of dispute occurred before the second world war when independent bodies did not exist in the rest of the United Kingdom. Although there were allegations of widespread gerrymandering, research enables attention to be directed to specific areas: Londonderry county borough, Omagh urban district council, Omagh rural district council and county Fermanagh. The two Omagh decisions may have produced wider consequences for control of the county council. However, claims about electoral boundaries are difficult to disentangle, especially in the context where official records of election results do not exist for the period and where there was an expectation that territorial representation should produce what only communal representation was capable of achieving. The experience of Fermanagh after 1973 is a cautionary tale. There, despite all the changes, unionists disputed control in the 1970s, lost it in the early 1980s but regained control in 1989 with a one-seat majority over eleven nationalists and retained it in 1993. In 1997 balance was held by a socialist councillor.

The method of election

The Government of Ireland Act 1920 extended the use of STV in multi-member constituencies from local government elections, under the 1919 Act, to elections for the Northern Ireland parliament. In the debates it was described as one of the safeguards for minorities and the unionist minority in the south and west of Ireland seemed to be uppermost in debate. However, northern unionists opposed the method and wanted to retain the same system as in

Britain. James Craig had opposed PR in evidence to the royal commission on systems of election in 1910; and during the debates on the Government of Ireland bill unionists had opposed PR and committed the party to abolishing it at the first opportunity. On the other hand, nationalists favoured the principle but they had only six members at Westminster and their attention was directed against the principle of two legislatures in Ireland rather than their composition and elections.

The method of election to the Northern Ireland parliament was guaranteed for a period of three years. However, the 1920 Act did not mention local government and on 31 May 1922 the Local Government (NI) Bill was introduced in the Stormont parliament to abolish PR in local government elections and return to the previous method and electoral units. The six nationalist and six Sinn Fein members elected in 1921 were pursuing an abstention policy so that the only opposition to the bill was from a Unionist Labour member, Thompson Donald. Nationalist-controlled councils issued a resolution of protest but the bill passed its third reading on 5 July. The royal assent, however, was withheld until 11 September.

Various government statements had encouraged the belief that PR would be abolished for Stormont elections as soon as the three-year statutory prohibition ended in June 1924. However, no action was taken and the 1925 election was also fought using PR. After the election, the prime minister came under pressure from the Unionist Party to abolish PR and the party had lost seats to the Labour Party and other candidates.

The principle of PR was extensively debated in 1927 on a Labour Party motion. Labour regarded abolition of PR as aimed at all minorities, while nationalists considered that they were the prime targets. In a lengthy and detailed speech the prime minister said that he believed in the two-party system and the old method of elections would produce 'men who are for the Union on the one hand or are against it and want to go into a Dublin parliament on the other.'[14] The debate hinged less on the merits of PR than on a disposition to treat the minority well through seat redistribution.

PR was abolished by the House of Commons (Method of Voting and Redistribution of Seats) Act (NI) 1929. During the debates the opposition parties expressed diverse views about whom the bill was directed against. There was less debate on the merits of PR than in 1927 and a greater concern about the consequences of redistributing the seats from the multi-member constituencies. The bill became law on 16 April 1929 and the 'X' vote for single-member districts was restored for the forty-eight territorial seats. In the 1929 Northern Ireland parliament elections thirty-seven unionists, eleven nationalists, three independent unionists and one Northern Ireland Labour Party member were elected. All the parties previously represented retained representation: Unionists and nationalists gained over the 1925 results and Labour lost two seats. Apart from an increase in the number of unopposed returns in

1929 there seemed little to choose between the two methods of election. However, the steady increase in the number of independent and unofficial unionist candidates during the 1930s, culminating in 1938 when more than a quarter of the candidates came from that section, meant that the abolition of PR was aimed at divisions within unionism over social and economic policy and administrative performance. The effect of the change to the simple-majority system and single-member constituencies from 1929 to 1969 can be briefly summarised. The two largest parties, the unionists and nationalists, both benefited in their share of contested seats and unopposed returns. The Northern Ireland Labour Party and splinter unionist candidates were consistently underrepresented. Anti-partition Labour candidates consistently benefited from the system after 1938, but this may have been due to the size of the constituencies contested. All other groups were underrepresented in proportion to their share of the votes.

In the post-war period there were motions for the reintroduction of PR in 1947 and 1951. During the Electoral Law Bill debates of 1962 nationalists sought PR but without success. It was only after 'one man, one vote' had been conceded in the Electoral Law (No 2) Bill 1969 that the call for PR was seriously renewed, to the discomfiture of the Stormont government. Every opportunity was taken to press for PR and the issue was debated in March 1971. However, the withdrawal of the SDLP and nationalists from Stormont in July 1971 and the suspension of the Northern Ireland parliament and government on 30 March 1972 terminated the parliamentary debate.

The principle was conceded by the secretary of state, William Whitelaw, as the means to gain SDLP participation in the district council and assembly elections of 1973.[15] The secretary of state never gave any substantial reason for the change except to say that it was the method that most parties mentioned to him. Several years later he stated that there were expectations that it might enable voters to build up the centre ground in politics. Against a background of party fragmentation the only expected outcome was that the parties would win representation in proportion to their votes and entrench the new divisions.

The method of election and the parties in the first three of four regional elections, in 1973,1975,1982, using the STV method in multi-member Westminster constituencies, the nationalist minority parties retained similar representation. The SDLP was the exclusive representative in 1973 and 1975 with nineteen seats (24.4 per cent) and seventeen seats (21.8 per cent), respectively, out of seventy-eight; in 1982 the SDLP won fourteen seats (18.0 per cent) and Sinn Fein 5 seats (6.4 per cent). With a larger assembly, with half as many seats again as in the old Stormont House of Commons, and PR, minorities ought to have benefited more but their share of the seats remained relatively stable. The active mobilisation of republican voters helped improve nationalist representation in the 1998 assembly election when 24 SDLP members (22.2 per cent) and Sinn Fein 18 (16.7 per cent) were elected from the 108 members.

The experience of two different methods of election, simple plurality and PR(STV), in Northern Ireland provided the basis for a unique comparison. Comparison of the two methods usually focuses on the relationship between the party share of the votes polled and the seats won; this is usually referred to as 'proportionality' or 'distortion.' Electoral distortion is the product of several interactive factors: some arise from the rules of the electoral system, the method of election and constituency size; others result from the political environment in which the system operates. But it is the area into which the most empirical research has been conducted. In his comparative study Rae presented a number of propositions concerning electoral systems in general and some which distinguish plurality from proportional systems. Rae found that the average deviation of vote and seat percentages in thirty-nine plurality elections was 3.96 per cent and 1.63 per cent in seventy-one PR elections.[16] In Northern Ireland the average deviation of vote and seat percentages in ten plurality elections was 4.9 per cent. In five STV elections the average deviation was 1.65 per cent; this was close to Rae's average of 1.63 per cent for PR elections. Hence, there was a marked difference in distortion for the STV elections of 1921, 1925, 1973,1975 and 1982 and the plurality elections of other years. Rae also found that the largest party gained disproportionately from electoral systems: in proportional systems there was a benefit of 1.24 per cent but in plurality systems a benefit of 8.12 per cent. In Northern Ireland the average bonus to the largest party in five PR elections was 2.5 per cent; in 1975 there was a negative score of − 1.0 per cent; the bonus in ten plurality elections was 12.7 per cent.

Rae also calculated that the two largest parties gained by 2.9 per cent in all PR elections and in plurality elections by 5.46 per cent. In Northern Ireland the two largest parties benefited by 12.0 per cent in ten plurality elections but in four STV elections the average was − 0.1 per cent. The Unionist Party was invariably the largest single party in votes and seats but the second largest varied and frequently the second largest party in terms of votes was not the second largest in seats. The second largest party in seat share was nnationalist but in 1921 it shared that position with Sinn Fein and in 1973 was replaced by the Social Democratic and Labour Party. However, in terms of vote share the nationalists were the second party only in 1925 and 1949; frequently, the second largest share of the vote was won by independent unionists or the Northern Ireland Labour Party, but in 1973 the emergence of SDLP regularised the position.

Northern Ireland has a multi-party system operating within a division, formed in the home rule struggles from 1886, on the constitutional link with the United Kingdom. Between 1921 and 1969 parties with forty different labels contested elections and twenty-two were successful. The outbreak of the 'troubles' caused further fragmentation. In the 1973 election to the new assembly fifteen parties were in competition and eight were successful; in 1975 twelve parties contested and nine were successful; in the 1982 assembly ten parties contested the seventy-eight seats and seven won representation. In 1998, 23 different party labels sought election and nine won representation. In district council elections it is not unusual for thirty different party descriptions to be used. This variety of opinion pre-dated the reintroduction of PR but gained from it.

Table 6.2   **Distortion in seats/votes relationship in Northern Ireland elections, 1973–98**

Election Year	Parliament United Kingdom	Northern Ireland	Stormont Assembly	District Councils
1973			7.6	12.6
1974	19.1	40.6		
1974	18.3	29.1		
1975			7.4	
1977				6.7
1979	14.9	31.5		
1981				5.1
1982			11.6	
1983	23.5	28.5		
1985				4.9
1987	19.7	24.4		
1989				5.5
1992	17.0	26.3		
1993				5.4
1996			7.8	
1997	20.4	26.8		7.3
1998			5.6	
Average	19.0	29.6	8.0	6.8

Source: Sydney Elliott and W.D. Fleckes, Northern Ireland Political Directory, 5th edition, forthcoming in 1999.

The variety of forms of election in Northern Ireland enables some reflection on the effects of the different methods used. The simple plurality system using single member districts employed for parliamentary elections showed an average distortion of 19.0 per cent: for the Northern Ireland seats alone the distortion was greater with an average of 29.6. These same constituencies were used for the Stormont assembly/convention/forum elections as multi-member seats for STV. The average distortion fell sharply to 8 per cent and gave a reflection of the effect of the proportional method of election. The boundaries were completely different for the district council elections with much smaller units – 26 district councils and 101 electoral areas – but the average distortion was only 6.8 per cent. However, the European parliamentary elections since 1979 used STV in a single constituency with three elected and the distortion figures averaged 21.5 per cent. Since a broad range of candidates fought each type of election the increased distortion may have been influenced by the number of members to be elected, namely three. The European elections displayed almost as much distortion as the UK parliamentary average.

In examining Northern Ireland experience of elections it is clear that an enormous amount of time was spent considering electoral activities. Electoral competition was very salient in group relations. The abolition of PR, the retention of outdated franchises, and the control over electoral boundaries by the government produced an active series of causes for minorities. Finally, the one man, one vote' issue, taken over by the Northern Ireland civil rights association from the Northern Ireland Labour Party and the unions, provided the occasion for a bid for power by the only means available in a majority-dominant system. Retrospectively, several of the grievances seem to have had less significance than was believed at the time. Cumulatively, they were believed to be significant and that was sufficient in a situation of tension to produce a spark. After 1972 it was not surprising that power over electoral matters was reserved to Westminster. One of the under-estimated reforms, provided for by Stormont legislation, was the creation of the office of chief electoral officer forNorthern Ireland. The office is responsible for the electoral register and the conduct of elections. It took electoral administration out of public controversy and into the hands of an independent official.

References

1. C. H. Enloe, *Ethnic Conflict and Political Development*, Little, Brown, Boston, 1973, pp. 85–8.
2. A. Rabushka, and K.A. Shepsle, *Politics in Plural Societies: A Theory of Democratic Instability*, Merrill, Columbus, Ohio, 1972, pp. 7–92.
3. *The Representation of the People Act (NI) 1934*.
4. Vivian Committee, *Report of the Committee on Electoral Machinery*, Cmd. 6408, HMSO, London, 1942.
5. The Representation of the People Act 1949, which permitted citizens of the Republic of Ireland to vote in UK elections, meant that there developed a difference between the register for Stormont and local elections, on the one hand, and Westminster elections, on the other. This was evident when the Stormont equivalent legislation, the Electoral Law Act of 1962, retained the residence qualification.

6. S. Elliott, *The Electoral System in Northern Ireland since 1920*, unpublished PhD thesis, Queen's University, Belfast, 1971, pp. 757–70,787–94.
7. HC Deb. (NI) 65 (13 December 1966) 129.
8. *The Armagh Observer*, 16 May 1964.
9. R. J. Lawrence, S. Elliott, and M.J. Laver, *The Northern Ireland General Elections of 1973*, (Cmnd. 5851), HMSO, London, 1975, p. 37 para 80.
10. The new single-member constituencies in 1929 returned three nationalists and two unionists in Tyrone and two unionists and one nationalist in Fermanagh. The eight member Fermanagh-Tyrone constituency in 1921 and 1925 elected four unionists and four nationalists using PR. See also R. D. Osborne, 'The Northern Ireland Parliamentary Electoral System: the 1929 reapportionment.' *Irish Geography*, vol. 12, 1998, pp 42–56.
11. This provided a *cause celebre* for campaigns such as the Mansion House campaign at the end of the 1940s and the Northern Ireland Civil Rights Association campaign of 1967–9. The figures used showed one unionist vote to have the same value as two nationalist votes. They ignored the deprivation of Labour representation.
12. The Cameron Report, *Disturbances in Northern Ireland*. Cmd., 532, HMSO, Belfast, 1969, ch. 12.
13. P. Macrory, *The Review Body on Local Government in Northern Ireland*, Cmd. 546, HMSO, Belfast, 1970.
14. HC Debs (NI), vol. 8, 25 October 1927, cols. 2275–6.
15. R. J. Lawrence, S. Elliott and M. J. Laver, op. cit., pp. 18–20.
16. D. W. Rae, *The Political Consequences of Electoral Laws*, Yale University Press, New Haven, Connecticut, 1971, pp. 70,87–103.

7   The Economics of Unionism and Nationalism

J. Esmond Birnie

Introduction

In 1988 the Anglo-American historian Paul Kennedy caused something of a stir with his book, *The Rise and Fall of the Great Powers*. His thesis was both powerful and simple. The flux in the international balance of military and diplomatic power since 1500 can be explained by the waxing and waning of the economic strength of successive great powers.[1]

Some commentators have implied that the last decade has seen a quite dramatic change in the balance of economic power within this island. As early as 1988 Rowthorn and Wayne[2] claimed that in some respects the Republic of Ireland was outperforming Northern Ireland. Kennedy[3] has argued that there has been a historic reversal of fortunes since the Republic is now, for the first time, more highly industrialised and apparently economically stronger than Northern Ireland. So, is there now a 'tiger economy' south of the border, and is it operating alongside a decrepit and subsidy-ridden Northern Ireland? Would all this imply, possibly for the first time, that the economic case for nationalism and a united Ireland is better than that for unionism?

Table 7.1 illustrates that in the mid 1990s there was not much to choose between the two Irish economies with respect to unemployment rates (international comparisons of these are always difficult), and both were poor performers in a European context, though Northern Ireland may have had a small advantage. Between 1995 and the start of 1998 unemployment in Northern Ireland appeared to fall rapidly and rate of unemployment may have dropped below the European Union (EU) average for the first time (it was unclear how far this represented a real improvement in labour market performance or simply an adjustment to greater rigour in benefit claimant procedures.[4]

With respect to income per head and especially gross domestic product (GDP) per capita, the evidence that the Republic has become a 'celtic tiger' seems to be a bit stronger. Table 7.1 shows that in 1994 both Irish economies

Table 7.1 Unemployment and GDP per capita in Northern Ireland and the Republic of Ireland compared to the rest of the European Union, 1994-5

	Standardised unemployment rate (%), 1995*	Long term unemployment as % of total unemployment, 1995*	GDP per head, using purchasing power parities, 1994 (EU15= 100)#
EU 15 average	10.7	n.a.	100
Belgium average	9.4	61.8	114
Belgium lowest region	6.9	46.7	91
Belgium highest region	13.3	81.5	183
Denmark average**	7.1	28.2	114
Finland average	18.1	29.9	91
Finland lowest region	6.2	n.a.	91
Finland highest region	18.2	30.0	126
France average	11.2	42.6	108
France lowest region	8.7	40.5	87
France highest region	15.3	53.7	161
Germany average***	8.2	47.8	110
Germany lowest region	4.9	39.6	196
Germany highest region	16.7	56.2	57
Greece average	9.1	50.9	65
Greece lowest region	4.5	50.7	57
Greece highest region	11.0	50.2	73
Republic of Ireland average**	14.3	51.1	88
Italy average	12.0	61.5	102
Italy lowest region	6.0	43.8	131
Italy highest region	25.9	72.8	68
Luxembourg average**	2.7	24.0	169
Netherlands average	7.3	44.4	105
Netherlands lowest region	6.9	46.4	101
Netherlands highest region	8.9	47.4	102
Portugal average	7.1	48.7	67
Portugal lowest region	4.6	67.2	48
Portugal highest region	7.8	60.0	68
Spain average	22.7	54.4	76
Spain lowest region	18.5	63.0	64
Spain highest region	7.8	60.0	58
Sweden average**	9.1	n.a.	98

140

UK average	8.8	43.1	99
UK lowest region	6.7	35.2	117
Northern Ireland			
(i.e. UK highest region)	13.0	51.6	80

Note: * Unemployment defined according to a standardised economic activity classification. Long term unemployed being those out of work for more than one year. (The regional long term unemployment data correspond to whichever regions had the lowest or highest rates of *total* unemployment.)

GDP is a measure of the total value of goods and services produced during each year. Although GDP is often used in international comparisons, peculiarities of the Republic of Ireland economy imply that it is an inappropriate indicator of living standards (see below). The purchasing power parity based calculations make allowance for variations in the cost of living.

** No sub-national regional breakdown was available.

*** Including the former East Germany.

Source: Regional Trends, Office for National Statistics, London, 1997.[5]

were still lagging quite far behind the EU average (by between 12 and 20 per cent). However, from about 1988 onwards there may have been something of a break in what had been the trend in the Republic's comparative performance since independence. Up to the late 1980s GDP per capita had been stuck at no more than one-half/two thirds of the United Kingdom (UK) average during a period when the UK itself had been overtaken by much of the rest of western Europe.[6] Since then a very rapid closing of the gap is indicated and by implication the Republic had caught up with and overtaken Northern Ireland.

In fact the speed of the Republic's national income growth, and by implication the pace of convergence with the UK and the rest of the EU, has been questioned by statisticians[7] and economists such as Birnie and Hitchens.[8] The growth rates of consumption have been much more modest than those for national income (the volume of GDP at market prices grew by 30 per cent during 1988–94 but the volume of retail sales by only 18 per cent) and this has led some commentators to suggest that much of the indicated increase in GDP is artificial and attributable to transfer pricing activities (see below) by multinationals.[9] For accounting reasons (that is, to take advantage of the relatively low rate of tax on profits) multinationals are imputing some value-added to their plants in the Republic which relates to activities such as research and development or marketing which occurred elsewhere within the global operations of the company.

It is certainly true that gross national product (GNP), a much more realistic measure of living standards in the Irish context given that it allows for the sizeable net outflow of resources to pay interest on international debt and to repatriate profits to foreign companies, has remained at least one-eighth

Table 7.2   Gross domestic product (GDP) per head of the population in Northern Ireland and the Republic of Ireland compared to the UK (purchasing power parity calculations, as a per cent of the UK level)

	Northern Ireland/UK (UK = 100)	Republic of Ireland/UK (UK = 100)
1926	61 (1924)	51
1947	71	46
1960	63	47
1973	73	54
1986	79	60
1990	78	70
1991	82	77
1992	82	80
1993	82	80
1994	82	86
1995	83	91

Note: See Note to Table 7.1 on GDP per capita comparisons and purchasing power parity.

Source: Johnson,[10] Kennedy, Giblin and McHugh,[11] Commission of the European Communities,[12] SOEC,[13] Office for National Statistics.[14]

lower than GDP throughout the period since 1986 and in 1995 the gap was wider than this; GNP is indicated to have been only 86.7 per cent of GDP.[15] Table 7.3 presents a more realistic indication of the comparative income per head performance of the Republic's economy relative to the UK and the EU.

Table 7.3 compares the Republic's performance in terms of GNP per head of the population to other EU member states and especially some of the other areas subject to special structural fund assistance. Against this perspective, the Republic's recent record no longer appears as that of a miracle economy. During the post-second world war period those western economies which started off with relatively low levels of income per head have generally grown more rapidly than those such as the UK, USA, Switzerland and the Scandinavian countries which were the richest countries in the 1950s. The recent performance of the Republic falls into this pattern and has, for example, been broadly similar to that of Spain; another comparatively 'late starter' to industrialisation/economic modernisation.

Even the GNP data may not be free from exaggeration given the likelihood that a substantial measure of transfer pricing is artificially inflating the measured output of the sizeable transnational corporate sector in the Republic

Table 7.3 Republic of Ireland average income per head compared to other EU (all figures shown as a percentage of the average for the pre-1995 12 members of the EU and based on purchasing power parity standards)

	1986 GDP per capita	1986 GNP per capita	1990 GDP per capita	1990 GNP per capita*	1995 GDP per capita	1995 GNP per capita*
Republic of Ireland	63	56	71	62	90	c.79
N.Ireland	78	n.a.	77	n.a.	81 1994	n.a.
UK	102	104	101	103	99	c.101
Greece	61	56	57	n.a.	63	n.a.
Spain	70	72	74	n.a.	76	n.a.
Portugal	54	51	59	n.a.	67	n.a.

Note: n.a. Not available. There were, for example, no official estimates of net property income from abroad for Northern Ireland as a regional economy within the UK.
* Comparative GNP per capita estimates were not readily available for 1990 or 1995. However, Republic of Ireland GNP per capita in 1990 has been estimate to have been 60 per cent of the UK level and 62 per cent of the EC12 average. The GNP per capita figures for 1995 were estimated from SOEC calculations of relative GDP per capita in purchasing power party terms combined with the GDP/GNP ratio shown in the Republic of Ireland national accounts.

Source: As in Table 7.2 and for GNP in 1986: NESC.[16] For GNP in 1990 see Kennedy[17] and SOEC.[18] Northern Ireland from PPRU.[19]

of Ireland.[20] In this context it is important to remember that, in the long run, in the absence of large scale transfer of funds from other parts of the world or the exploitation of a natural resources bounty, the comparative income per head of any country is mostly determined by its relative level of labour productivity which is output per worker.[21] Consideration of comparative productivity in the Republic does cast some doubt on the scale of post-1988 super-growth as well as the probability that it will continue far into the next century.[22]

These figures indicate that in those sectors where transfer pricing is unlikely to be occurring the Republic has remained a low productivity economy. Indeed, given that in many cases, at least until the 1980s, UK productivity levels were lower than those in, say, west Germany, France and the Netherlands, the Republic of Ireland shortfall compared to best practice in the EU has been even greater. The very high productivity levels implied for the Republic's manufacturing since 1985 in previous studies[23] are conspicuous as an exception to this general rule. The immediate explanation for these being the

Table 7.4 Republic of Ireland comparative labour productivity since the 1930s (compared using output price levels; net output per head as a per cent of the level in the UK) Republic of Ireland/UK (UK = 100)

	1968	1935	1985	1990*	early-mid1990s*
Agriculture[a]	55	61	77	81	85 [1993]
Construction	66 [b]	n.a.	91 [c]	63	71 [1992]
Mining and quarrying	132	65	57	53 [d]	59 [1994]
Utilities	47	54	27 [e]	39 [d]	29 [1994]
Transport	62 [f]	n.a.	n.a.	54 [g]	n.a.
Telecommunications	n.a.	n.a.	n.a.	54 [h]	n.a.
Postal services	n.a.	n.a.	n.a.	62 [i]	n.a.

Note: * Indices of the change in the volume of net output during 1985-90 and of the change in the level of employment were used to update the 1985 benchmark comparisons. Volume indices were then used again to up-date as far beyond 1990 as was possible (deflated series of total sectoral gross value added (GVA) were used for construction; SOEC, 1989, 1994).

a: Fishing and forestry were *not* included in these comparisons.

b: Using the comparative output price level of the building products industry to proxy for the comparative output price level of the building and construction sector.

c: GVA per head using the unit value ratio for the building products industry as a proxy for construction output prices.

d: Comparison for 1989.

e: Or 45, and 58 in 1989, when gas extraction was excluded from the comparisons.

f: Weighted average of physical productivity ratios for railways, buses and road freight.

g: Weighted average of physical productivity ratios for railways, buses, road freight, ports, airports and airlines (a range of years, 1986-1989).

h: Telecommunications revenues per head in 1987 compared using an appropriate purchasing power parity.

i: Physical productivity of postal services in 1987 (items carried).

Source: Birnie.[24]

activities of the internationally owned companies; especially in the computing, pharmaceuticals and soft drinks sectors. However, such levels of performance are incredible and therefore indicate a large measure of transfer pricing.[25] It cannot be true, as some of figures would imply that productivity levels really exceed those in the USA and Japan which are usually regarded as world leaders. This provides very strong evidence that transfer pricing is taking place.

Thus, the apparently very remarkable GDP growth of the Republic over the last decade has occurred notwithstanding a supply side basis which in terms of comparative productivity remains fundamentally weak. Previous analyses of the rapid growth since 1988 have acknowledged that at least part of it is due to once and for all benefits which will probably have been exhausted by the end of the next decade.[26] For example, the standard process of catch up on the more advanced economies may now be working itself to an end, the upgrading in public education from the mid 1960s onwards (which was roughly two decades behind much of western Europe) is now bringing large but probably mainly once off gains to output growth, the collapse in the Republic's birth rate in the 1980s has in the medium term produced an age structure (few young or old dependants) which is more favourable than in the rest of the EU, and there has been the largesse from the EU structural funds.

From 1999 onwards the Republic is likely to be subjected to at least three shocks which will have some negative impact on GDP growth. First, EU enlargement to include Poland, Czech Republic and Hungary will increase the likelihood that foreign direct investment will be located towards these comparative cheap labour cost and often well skilled economies.[27] Second, alongside enlargement is likely to come a redistribution of EU regional and agricultural spending away from the western European periphery. Net transfers from Brussels were equivalent to 6–10 per cent of the Republic's GDP in 1980–1991.[28] Third, the probable membership of the European Monetary Union (EMU) from 1999 onwards, whilst the UK is likely to opt-out, could well disrupt the Republic's exports.[29] Notwithstanding a trend decline since the 1960s, the UK still represents the largest destination for exports and takes about one-quarter of the total.

Assuming that the Republic can successfully adjust to these structural challenges and the squalls which will inevitably accompany the introduction of the single currency, then the most likely scenario is that current super-growth will begin to decelerate so that GNP per capita levels stabilise at levels roughly similar to those in the UK and the EU (these two levels being roughly the same) in 2005–2010. Once one makes allowance for the relatively higher public spending levels in Northern Ireland, as well as the lower levels of taxation, living standards in Northern Ireland were about one-fifth higher than in the Republic of Ireland in the mid 1990s.[30] It is probable that the Republic will be able to continue to narrow this gap but it is unlikely to overtake in the near future and certainly not before 2005. This, then, in summary terms is the economic backdrop but what of the political economy? The rest of this chapter examines the possible economic weaknesses in unionism and nationalism.

Possible economic weaknesses in the unionist case

The pro-Union position appears to have a strong basis. The Cadogan Group[31] confirmed in 1993 that the Northern Ireland population had a positive and substantial living standards advantage relative to their southern Irish counterparts – at that time 30 per cent higher when per capita levels of private consumption and public sector expenditure in Northern Ireland and the Republic were considered. It is not simply that Northern Ireland living standards are higher but also the source of this gap relative to the Republic which is highly significant. Of great significance is the so-called subvention, the fiscal transfer within the UK's integrated tax and social spending systems from the London exchequer to Belfast, whereby levels of public spending in the province can be sustained at levels far above those warranted by locally raised tax revenues.

The implication of this position is that if there was Irish unity then, in the absence of some arrangements for very substantial support payments from other sources or continued transfers from the UK (the likelihood of either is considered later) there would be either a massive decline in northern living standards or a marked decline in those in what is now the Republic (the latter arising if the Republic decided to raise its own tax collections in order to fund a replacement for the subvention). The available opinion poll evidence suggests limited support in the electorates on either side of the border for a unity bought at the price of sizeable living standards reductions. There are, however, three flaws in the economic case for the maintenance of Northern Ireland within the Union which must be considered.

Unionist weakness (1): the 180 degree turn about in the argument

John Whyte[32] noted that, whereas in 1912–14 it was held that Ulster was too strong economically to join the rest of Ireland in home rule (and later independence),[33] by the 1970s and 1980s some unionists were resorting to the opposite argument. Northern Ireland was claimed to be too weak economically for either it or the rest of the island to sustain unification. This reversal of position, and the need to resort to an argument from weakness, might appear embarrassing to unionists and probably would be if this was the only economic argument they had. In fact, it probably is not since a plausible case (considered later) can still be made that Northern Ireland's dynamic economic prospects remain better within the UK as opposed to those within any all-Ireland arrangements. Additionally, unionists might also claim that Northern Ireland's current position of economic weakness is a temporary one, largely due to the effects of the 'troubles' and one which therefore conceivably will no longer hold good in the future. Permanent peace would certainly reduce the subvention (considered later) but is not likely to be sufficient in itself (though it might be a necessary condition) to work the supply side improvements necessary to place Northern Ireland on a growth path markedly higher than the rest of the UK.[34]

Unionist weakness (2): the end of southern Irish economic backwardness

Just as the pre-first world war unionist case relied heavily on the perceived economic strength of Northern Ireland, so the assumption of economic backwardness in the rest of Ireland was an important component to their argument. It is no longer true that Northern Ireland is the primary location of industry within the island. Nor is the Republic now an agricultural backwater. In 1960 manufacturing employment in the north and south were almost exactly the same. Thirty eight years later, these figures give the Republic a sizeable advantage (215,000 compared to roughly 105,000). The question, still arises how far these changes matter in political terms. Some think they do as suggested by McCloughan who argues that '... the view that the south cannot manage its economy, a view still held in some quarters up north, is now outmoded and downright myopic...'.[35]

Moreover, the Irish historian Joseph. J. Lee[36] has argued that unionism was of necessity an ideology relying on feelings of superiority (includings those relating to economic performance) relative to the rest of the inhabitants of the island. It is certainly true that in the mid-1990s the new Ulster unionist leader, David Trimble, did begin to employ the living standards gap between Northern Ireland and the Republic (for example, in a speech to the Institute of Directors in Dublin on 10 May 1996) as a component of the case for the Union. It was ironic that unionists began to revive this argument at the very point when the Republic's economy appeared to be growing very rapidly. However, as was pointed out in the first part of this chapter, the living standards differential was still considerable in the mid 1990s and it is unlikely that the Republic will catch up, if at all, before the later years of the next decade.

Unionist weakness (3): the subvention as a unionist figleaf

The Dublin-based economist, John Bradley[37] coined this reference to the subvention as a 'unionist figleaf' to suggest that the substantial fiscal subvention (in 1993 Northern Ireland government expenditure was about £7.5 billion and tax revenues of £4 billion which implied a subvention of £3.5 billion) was not so much a problem for Irish nationalists as a liability from the point of view of the pro-Union case. From his perspective the subvention from Westminster to Northern Ireland is seen as an incontrovertible indicator of the terminal decline of a Northern Ireland economy remaining within the UK; it is said to show Northern Ireland is a dependent political entity and one which would suffer greatly when (as is argued to be likely) the subvention is reduced in the future. However, a series of unionist responses are possible to this interpretation of the subvention.

In the first place, how far is scale of the subvention a reliable indicator of Northern Ireland economic weakness? In order to render the subvention an indicator of such it would be necessary, so Simpson[38] has argued, to strip away the effects of the 'troubles' on its size and also what might be seen as Northern Ireland's share in the growth of the national public sector borrowing requirement (PSBR) during 1990–93. Such an adjusted subvention might have represented around 15 per cent of regional GDP compared to the actual level of about 25 per cent in the early to mid 1990s. In proportional terms the subvention remains sizeable though perhaps not uniquely so when compared to other UK regions; a recent Scottish Office estimate implied that the Scottish equivalent to the subvention amounted to £8 billion or 15 per cent of national GDP.[39] In other words, similar in scale to Northern Ireland's deficit (the Scottish figures do not include North Sea oil tax receipts but then this may be the correct way to estimate the underlying deficit).

The view that the relatively high levels of public spending within the province have some form of displacement or disincentive effect on private sector activity[40] cannot be entirely discounted but it is the level of spending rather than the subvention *per se* which matters in this regard. Of a subvention of £3500 million in the mid 1990s it was a relatively small part of this, say, the £400 million industry and training budget, which should probably raise the greatest concern with respect to possibly negative effects on private sector competitiveness performance.

Lastly, how vulnerable is the subvention to reduction as a deliberate act of policy in London and the treasury? The fears (or hopes, depending on one's political standpoint) that this could happen are not groundless. Indeed, during 1993–94 sections of the London press seemed to be implying that the subvention should be treated as weapon against terrorism or even so-called political intransigence. That is, if the paramilitary groups refused to join normal democratic politics then cuts in public spending should be used as a sort of stick. Similarly, pressure would be placed on the constitutional parties to come to some agreement.[41] One could doubt the wisdom of such advice as fiscal policy represents a rather blunt instrument of constitutional policy. There is the probability of what the American military strategists call 'collateral damage', that is, the people hurt by such spending cuts would not be the paramilitaries.

In any case, is the size of the subvention something which is directly controlled by the central government? Probably not. For many years it has been accepted that both taxation and spending are governed by parity principles across the UK. This may, of course, be changed by the implementation of devolution in Scotland and Wales but that remains to be seen – for example, as of February 1998, the secretary of state for Scotland was not permitting the making of social security law to be devolved to Edinburgh. This implies that the subvention occurs as the residual. The subvention as such does not make

Northern Ireland vulnerable though its existence may enable elements within the Labour Party to paint the unionists as reactionary spongers. Moreover, the subvention indirectly shields the unionist parties from having to adopt more realistic social and economic policies. The absence of such policies has probably deterred young people and professionals from participation in unionist politics. What is significant is that the ratio of public spending to regional GDP is very high, and much higher than in the rest of the UK (60 per cent compared to about 40 per cent). Given that rates of growth of public spending across the UK are likely to be relatively low during the rest of the 1990s this will inevitably constrain the rate of regional economic growth.

Notwithstanding this, most unionist politicians seem happy to be advocates for high levels of government spending. The loyalist parties, Ulster Democratic and Progressive Unionist, are quite explicitly left-wing in their socio-economic policies and in this respect there is a similarity to Sinn Fein, or at least the pre-1990s economics of Sinn Fein.[42] The Democratic Unionist Party has traditionally had a socialist tinge and opposed many of the attempts to introduce aspects of the Thatcherite agenda to Northern Ireland.[43] Robert McCartney, the UK Unionist MP and leader, made no secret of the fact that on socio-economic grounds he welcomed the Labour victory in May 1997. Even the Ulster Unionist Party may have somewhat shed its legacy of being the party of the 'big house and boss', and its interventionist view of economic policy[44] lies somewhere in the range between Harold Macmillan's social toryism and social democratic 'old' Labour.

There are some ironies to this situation. First, almost all unionist politicians opposed the introduction of privatisation to Northern Ireland in the 1980s – possibly the ill-fated integrationist Conservative Party members were the only exception within the province and some of these even called for the poll tax to be applied in Northern Ireland. However, it could be argued that to the extent that privatisation did occur this has made the political and administrative integration of the two Irish economies more difficult. Second, when Professor Tom Wilson provided[45] what is perhaps the best recent intellectual defence of the Union he did so from the classical and conservative tradition of political economy which many unionist politicians would find uncongenial and Roche and Birnie[46] in their 'economic lessons' for Irish nationalists similarly relied on market based economic argument. To some degree the unionist parties have endorsed high levels of public spending because they have little incentive to do otherwise since they have so far had little responsibility over the raising of tax revenues (Gibson,[47] amongst others, has suggested this should be changed). It could be argued that unionism, at various times in its history, has embraced planning and industrial policy because unionism has been defined in terms of notions of the state and in particular of allegiance to the state. But to be fair to the unionist representatives, the public pronouncements of the nationalist and republican parties, the main churches, the business organisations and Northern Ireland's voluntary sector have all contributed to the hegemony of pro-socialistic and anti-market economics ideas within Northern Ireland.

Possible economic weaknesses in the pro-united Ireland case

Having considered the possible weaknesses in the unionist case consideration must be given to what may be the main flaws in the economics of nationalism and republicanism.

Nationalist weakness (1): paying for the subvention

Coming to terms with the subvention represents perhaps the greatest economic challenge to anyone recommending a traditional united Ireland within any medium term horizon. A number of responses have been suggested. One approach is to deny that the Republic would be under any obligation to maintain Northern living standards at their current levels within any united Ireland and Bradley[48] leans in this direction. The north is to be wed to the south but most definitely will not be kept in the style to which she has been accustomed. If such arguments are presented transparently they do at least have the virtue of honesty. However, the use of this type of argument would not be likely to increase support in the north for unity not least among the majority of northern nationalists as numerous opinion polls have established.

Proponents of unity have therefore tended to suggest an alternative course whereby some external party picks up the tab for unification; the London government being the most obvious donor. Usually such proposals are posited in terms of transitional transfer arrangements whereby London would continue to provide a transfer to Belfast for some period (say 10–15 years), perhaps of a tapering amount. These schemes are even given an air of credibility by the argument (as used by Rowthorn and Wayne, 1988) that such a settlement would be 'cheap at the price' from the point of view of the UK exchequer. After all, what would be perhaps one billion per year over ten years compared to the current annual outlay of £3.5 billion? When these sorts of arguments were being aired fifteen years ago at the New Ireland Forum at least one of the expert witnesses tried to deflate them. Sir Charles Carter, then Chairman of the Northern Ireland Economic Council, pointed out the inability of any British government to bind its successors over a ten year period to make *ex gratia* payments to another sovereign state. The reaction of Charles Haughey to this was striking

> My view of the academic economist is well known … . If economics is the dismal science, politics must be the profession of hope, and I find it hard to

accept that eminent economists could not formulate for us in the Forum a prospect for an all-Ireland economic entity capable of developing its own inherent dynamic for progress provided the political structures are right.[49]

It is unclear whether this reaction from Haughey represented either his personal antipathy to economists, or a more general nationalist/republican attitude of denial in the face of unpalatable economic realities, or indeed the persistence of a nineteenth century nationalist position that economics as a discipline was just another tool of English imperialism and could therefore be dismissed (for example, the Limerick Declaration of 1868 said that, 'Ireland has had enough of political economy').[50]

The difficulty of tying in the UK government into making continued financial provision for Northern Ireland after unity is perhaps one reason why the Institute of Public Policy Research[51] recommended a formalised system of joint authority over the north whereby the two governments would each make a net contribution to Northern Ireland in proportion to the relative size of their GDPs. It does, however, seem unlikely that any London government would sign up to pay 95 per cent of the Northern Ireland subvention whilst having only a one-half influence on how this money was spent. Representation without taxation is likely to be as unacceptable as the converse.

If the maintenance of a subvention is necessary and if the UK government could not be bound to continue paying it after unification then some other source of funding would have to be found. The EU and the USA are the two obvious candidates. However, the relatively small scale of the additional money provided during 1993–95 suggests it would be foolish to rely on European or American money to make up for a reduction in that given by the UK exchequer. Indeed, there is some evidence that leading nationalist politicians have drawn entirely inappropriate comparisons. For example, Former Irish Prime Minister Albert Reynolds argued in a speech to *Ogra Fianna Fail* on 17 April 1994 that the Irish-American community could be a source of financial support for Ireland comparable to that provided by American Jews to Israel. Now, it is indeed true that continuous and large scale transfers from the United States (US) have been a major and probably crucial component of Israel's economic survival and relative prosperity since 1948. However, what Reynolds neglected was that most of this money represented US federal government assistance rather than individual donations, though the latter were considerable,[52] and that this American generosity was largely driven by the strategic imperatives of international politics and in particular by the imperatives of the cold war. It would be extremely surprising if in the post-cold war world the US Congress was to vote £2 billion annually to economically sustain a politically united Ireland within the EU and without significance in international politics.

Nationalist weakness (2): the limited economic case for cross-border executive bodies

A thirty-two county Ireland therefore appears to offer no solution to the nationalist dilemma of how to get rid of the so-called British presence whilst keeping hold of the British cash. From this perspective the beauty of the cross-border executive bodies, as proposed in the February 1995 *Frameworks Document* and the January 1998 Lancaster House proposals from the British and Irish governments, is that they would probably imply joint authority between Belfast and Dublin whilst not formally removing Northern Ireland from the UK and thus the subvention would continue to be paid from London. Ultimately, the cross-border bodies will stand or fall according to whether their creation can command a sufficient degree of consent in Northern Ireland. However, since the *Frameworks Document* did try to justify such bodies specifically according to their economic benefits (though without any attempt to say what these might be or what their size might be) it is worth examining the economics of such institutions.

In the first place, economies of scale have sometimes been appealed to as a reason for running various things on an all-Ireland basis – for example, by Mark Durkan, Social Democratic and Labour Party chairman, interviewed on BBC Radio Ulster, 27 August 1993. This does, however, beg the question whether economies of scale would be all that significant in moving from two units of 1.6 million and 3.7 million populations up to a single one with a population of 5.3 millions.

A second issue is the extent of competing interests between the north and south. If there are competing economic activities, and there obviously are some in tourism, inward investment, agriculture and transport, then this would make joint administration or policy making more difficult. Significantly, both Wilson[53] and FitzGerald[54] in their very different works of political economy stressed how the two Irish economies were more competitive than complementary in their structures. This is not to deny that an all-Ireland approach might still yield mutual benefits overall but this would demand systems for compensation to spread any gains in what was seen as an equitable manner and it is at least doubtful if such systems could be designed.

Joint arrangements are sometimes justified as permitting a more rational allocation of expensive capital equipment and infrastructure without expensive duplication on both sides of the border. This is a sometimes appealing argument and there is already some sharing of expensive items of medical equipment and sewage treatment between the west of the Province and some of the border counties of the Republic. Such arguments are weakened to the extent that there is competition of interests – for example, would Northern Ireland gain more from a joint tourist board or a joint business school than it would lose by giving up its own independent institutions?. Moreover, we should not be entirely confident that duplication would be reduced. Public choice considerations suggest the danger that the vested interests of the civil servants will ensure that the joint bodies will simply insert another layer of bureaucracy on top of the existing agencies (and if this did not happen and duplication between the two public sectors was actually reduced then, given that Catholics are disproportionately represented in many of the Northern Ireland public services, one ironic consequence of north-south harmonisation would be a worsening of the now infamous Catholic-Protestant unemployment differential).

A fourth problem encountered by cross-border bodies relates to the difficulties of harmonisation. To some extent this is simply the issue of the subvention by another name and the fact that Northern Ireland is currently integrated within the UK's tax and social welfare systems. The *Frameworks Document* envisages progressive harmonisation between the two jurisdictions and this, from the point of view of those who are committed to the *Frameworks Document*, is entirely logical because it is difficult to envisage a meaningful joint Belfast-Dublin health or education policy if there continued to be wide disparities in standards, levels of spending, systems of delivery and payments by users. A parallel might be drawn with the situation in Germany immediately after the collapse of the Berlin Wall. Most economists have argued that the economic integration of the two Germanys (a single currency, labour market, goods market, systems of laws, taxes and benefits) was unduly rushed and that this contributed to the catastrophic depression in east Germany during 1990–93.[55] As a matter of purely abstract economics the economists were probably right and yet they were also politically naive. Chancellor Kohl was probably right to judge that German unification would be meaningless unless accompanied by immediate integration of the legal and social systems. In the Irish case it remains unclear whether Northern Ireland is to harmonise to the Republic or *vice versa*. The two movements are not symmetrical given that levels of public spending are usually substantially higher in the north and Northern Ireland has the additional dilemma that harmonisation with the Republic could sometimes mean disharmony with the rest of the UK which is, after all, a much larger economic market.

Nationalist weakness (3): little by way of dynamic effects or synergies at the all-Ireland level

Perhaps in an effort to dispel pessimism as to an inability to pay for the subvention, and also to bolster the economic case for cross-border bodies, there has been some focus in recent years on the dynamic gains which it is alleged would follow from greater all-Ireland economic integration.[56] Three strands can be identified in such arguments.

First, it is argued that partition of the island in 1921 had large negative economic effects because of the dislocation of markets. There are really two distinct parts to this argument. Firstly, the creation of the border in 1921 had large negative static and dynamic effects on output and employment and, secondly, the removal (or softening) of the border in the 1990s would lead to strong effects in the opposite direction. The truth of either of these contentions is not necessarily dependent on the other. Munck[57] went so far as to argue that partition had been the greatest single impediment to the economic development of either Irish economy throughout this century. This rather remarkable claim, and similar claims by Dr. Martin Mansergh, special adviser to Albert Reynolds and now to Bertie Ahern, made in west Belfast on 7 August 1995,[58] were unsupported by any detailed evidence.

In fact, Johnson in his 1985 economic history of inter-war Northern Ireland argued that the trade effects on the border towns (for example, Londonderry, Newry and Strabane) losing their hinterlands was probably quite small. O'Malley[59] even claimed that partition was a good thing in economic terms in so far as it permitted the two Irish economies to adopt differing economic policies during the 1930s which reflected their varying interests and stages of economic development – for example,. the Irish Free State could use infant industry protectionism while Northern Ireland remained within the imperial free trade area. It is perhaps significant that dislocation caused by the border is not mentioned at all in Ó'Gráda's[60] 1994 economic history of Ireland during 1780–1939.

A second element of the dynamic effects arguments is an emphasis on supplementing the longstanding east-west and external orientation of the Irish economies with a much increased north-south, internal orientation. Once again, there is an historical and contemporary dimension to such arguments. For example, Bradley[61] argues an independent and unitary Irish state in the early nineteenth century might well have been able to ensure that the core of industrialisation in the north east (that is, Belfast and the Lagan valley) developed sufficient spin-offs and linkages to ensure that modern manufacturing would have spread into the twenty six counties as well. As it was, so it is claimed, under the Union industrial Ulster formed its strongest linkages across the Irish Sea to Liverpool, Glasgow etc. Like most such counterfactual arguments such claims (which seem to involve reading back into Irish economic history the contemporary vogue, á la Michael Porter,[62] for clustering and competitive advantage) are not capable of definitive proof or disproof. In their chapter on the economic thought of George O'Brien, Johnson and Kennedy[63] caution that '… counterfactual history extending across several centuries has such an open-ended character as to tend towards metaphysical inquiry'. Moreover, is it at all likely that any nineteenth century administration in Dublin would have been able to design an interventionist package sufficiently powerful to counteract those factors which possibly were the determinants of the contrast

154

between the economic fortunes of the north and south during the nineteenth century? And, once again, as with the debate about the effects of partition, there may in truth be an asymmetry in the argument. Even if all-Ireland arrangements could be shown as likely to have generated substantial positive external economy effects in the nineteenth century the same would not necessarily be true in the 1990s.

The leading exponent of the contemporary benefits of integration at the all-Ireland level has been Sir George Quigley who has called for the creation of 'an island economy'.[64] Not all commentators have been impressed by this concept of an island economy. Wilson,[65] for example, doubted if the idea had any substantive meaning because the island was always going to remain part of the world economy and individual agents would continue to make rational decisions as to whether to trade within the island or outside. What Sir George Quigley and also the employers organisations have argued is that in some sense the border has led to intra-island linkages (for example, trade, financial or company ownership and control) being smaller than they would otherwise have been.[66] Is this true and, if so, by how much? The evidence is not clear cut because it is not clear what would be the appropriate standard of comparison in order to demonstrate whether north-south trade is more or less than should be expected. Exports and imports are currently 3–5 per cent of the Northern Ireland or Republic of Ireland GDP and some of the trade flows between the Scandinavian economies or between Spain and Portugal are not dissimilar – for example, in 1986 Spanish exports to Portugal were 2.2 per cent of its total and in 1997 still only 5.4 per cent and Portugal's population is about three times that of the Republic and six times that of Northern Ireland. What is beyond dispute is that the initially very bullish projections by the Confederation of Irish Industry (latterly, the Irish Business Employers' Confederation) and the Confederation of British Industry as to the jobs gains from greater north-south trade have been shown subsequently to be badly flawed.[67] As MacEnroe and Poole[68] noted, in 1991, Northern Ireland sold about £120 of manufactured goods to each person in the Republic compared to sales of only £40 to Great Britain. Thus there was already stronger trade integration between the two Irish economies than there was between Northern Ireland and the rest of the national UK market.

Bradley[69] suggests that much of the dynamic gain will come through external economies at the level of the firm as Irish firms begin to transcend the political division through mergers, joint ventures and joint marketing exercises. One part of this argument is sound – the two Irish economies separately have not been very successful at producing internationally competitive medium sized and larger firms and this is especially so outside of food processing. It would be nice to think that the two economies together could at last achieve what has so far eluded them separately. In principle there are indeed agglomeration economies and these would be greater if firms ignored the border when making ownership, input, trade and financial decisions. However, as with the static economies of scale which we considered earlier, it is by no means clear that any such effects would be large enough to make any appreciable difference to aggregate economic performance. What is critically important is that there may be a range of supply side constraints on performance which are not likely to be changed by a greater all-Ireland orientation *per se*. A further point is that the market mechanism should probably be capable of generating a greater amount of firm level all-Ireland integration quite apart from any political integration. Indeed, in the absence of market failures the market and commercial decision making would probably produce a situation close to that which was socially desirable. To the response that this may be prevented by the probability that there are market failures it might be countered that the history of economic policy making in both Irish economies suggest that state failures are at least as likely, and perhaps more damaging.

I would argue that we are left with a situation where the conceivable gains from greater north-south economic integration (even at the most maximalist level) are not likely to be very large. Most of the gains which potentially exist could probably, in any case, be exploited by links forged for purely commercial reasons without any institutional structures imposed upon market-led solutions. Significantly, Rowthorn and Wayne[70] thought the specifically economic gains from greater north-south 'harmonisation' would be relatively small and similarly, Sir Charles Carter, in poetic vein, told the New Ireland Forum that '... their [economic gains from greater north-south economic 'harmonisation'] effects on unemployment would be equivalent to the products of nine bean rows on the Isle of Innisfree, when set against a requirement of new jobs in the north in the coming two decades which is in the order of 200,000 ...'.[71]

Nationalist weakness (4): southern economic miracle or mirage?

Earlier, this chapter considered whether northern unionist observers tend to be too dismissive of the Republic of Ireland's economic achievements and especially those since the early 1960s or the late 1980s. However, it is also worth considering whether there has been a parallel tendency for some pro-united Ireland observers to take a far too rosy view of the recent macroeconomic performance of the Republic. In this respect special attention should be paid to a number of the economic pronouncements of Dr. Garret FitzGerald. In an article in 1995 FitzGerald[72] heralded the Republic as being close to an economic miracle since rates of GDP growth since 1988 had been the highest in western Europe. Dr FitzGerald also claimed in his 1972 *Towards a New Ireland* that within 25 years living standards in the Republic of Ireland would have caught up with the UK average. This is what he said

... over time the economic gap between Ireland as a whole and Britain, and the much smaller gap between the Republic and Northern Ireland, will tend to close, because growth rates have been and under peaceful conditions are likely to remain higher in Ireland than Britain... . If that happened the gap between the living standards of the two islands would be bridged in about a quarter of a century.[73]

This, of course, has not happened. Some nationalists and republicans may hope that a high growth and high GDP per capita Republic of Ireland is more likely to push for unification and some unionists evidently fear that such a relationship will operate. In reality the link between the state of the Republic's economy and the extent of nationalism in its northern policy is unlikely to be straightforward. In the short to medium term the sudden increase in prosperity in the Republic could provoke more assertiveness in its foreign policy but, over time, increased material well-being may dull what are already weakening anti-partitionist sentiments amongst the Republic's electorate. Perhaps as a general rule the relationship between the level of GDP per capita and national assertiveness is neither simply positive or negative but 'hump-shaped' – that is, the rapid economic growth of an early phase of industrialisation provokes national pride and boldness which is then followed by contentedness as GDP levels stabilise at levels similar to those of former rivals. For example, Germany in 1914–18 and 1939–45 launched its two bids for mastery of the continent when its GDP per employee was only two thirds/ three quarters of the UK level. In contrast, in the period since 1950 when the German level of income per head has exceeded that of the UK, Anglo-German relations have generally been very good.

Conclusions

How then can the possible flaws in the economics of the two positions be summarised? Starting with unionism, the interpretation of the subvention, like notions of self-determination and majority consent, follows on the political premises which have been adopted in the unionist argument . A unionist, to the extent that he or she thinks about it at all, may tend to the position that the subvention is simply a residual implied by the operation of common taxation and spending policies across the UK. The fact that Northern Ireland receives such a transfer is no more significant than the probability that Liverpool or Scotland are similarly recipients of a net subsidy from the UK exchequer. Alternatively the subvention is seen as some indicator of the havoc wrecked by the IRA campaign (only partially correct) or a sort of recompense for a blood debt (that is, Northern Ireland's sacrifices in two world wars which is not an argument likely to cut much ice with the Treasury). Use of the subvention 'figleaf' to defend the continuation of the Union might become a liability to the extent that it was perceived that this indicated economic weakness. However, unionists have the option of arguing that the Union is still best for all economically to the extent that it best guarantees stable access to a national economic and monetary union of 57 million people. In contrast, all-Ireland arrangements will, at best, provide an economy of a only 5.3 million persons.

Turning then to nationalism and republicanism, the existence and scale of the subvention may pose much more of a problem for those who would argue for a united Ireland. A range of responses have been generated amongst nationalist and republican leaders and commentators the most widely used being 'don't pay it as the north has no right to it' or someone else will pay it or increased economic dynamism at an all-Ireland level might make it unnecessary. Probably, the most extreme nationalist interpretation of the subvention is to view it as some sort of colonial gratuity without which the ramshackle northern economy would collapse – comparable perhaps to the £5 billion which France was doling out annually to its Pacific dependencies in the mid 1990s. Whilst it is true that the performance of the Republic's economy has improved during the last ten years, and it is also the case that Northern Ireland continues to have some deep structural problems despite a relatively impressive economic performance in the 1990s, some of the arguments used by apologists for nationalism and republicanism suggest they have not entirely disenthralled themselves from the economic naivety which was a persistent feature of the nationalist pantheon of Wolfe Tone, Griffith, Collins and de Valera.[74] That is, the belief that constitutional change by itself involving the movement towards an all-Ireland independent republic would create the conditions for economic dynamism.

Note

A very large number of friends, colleagues and others have helped me to form the views expressed in this chapter. I am especially grateful to the editorial advice received from the two editors of this book. Paddy Roche, in particular, has been a long-standing and formidable source of assistance. Graham Brownlow clarified my thinking on the relationship between economics and politics, both in general and in Northern Ireland in particular. I wrote this chapter in a personal capacity as a professional, academic economist and it does not necessarily reflect the views of any institution with which I may be linked.

References

1. P. Kennedy, *The Rise and Fall of the Great Powers: Economic Change and Military Conflict from 1500 to 2000*, Fontana, London, 1988.
2. R.Rowthorn and N.Wayne, *Northern Ireland: The Political Economy of Conflict*, Pluto Press, London, 1988.

3. L.Kennedy, *The Modern Industrialisation of Ireland, 1940–1988*, Economic and Social History of Ireland, Dublin, 1990.
4. G. Gudgin, 'The economy: macro impact on the regional economy', *Paper to Conference: Twenty Five Years on The Impact of EU Membership on Northern Ireland*, Queen's University of Belfast, February 1988, pp. 2–3.
5. Office for National Statistics , *Regional Trends*, ONS, London, 1997.
6. K. A. Kennedy, T. Giblin, and D. McHugh, *The Economic Development of Ireland in the Twentieth Century*, Routledge, London, 1988.
7. CSO and the Irish Economic Association , *Proceedings of Conference on Measuring Economic Growth*, Central Statistical Office and IEA, Government Publications, Dublin, 1995.
8. J. E. Birnie, and D. M. W. N. Hitchens, 'Productivity and income per capita convergence in a peripheral European economy: the Irish experience', *Regional Studies*, vol. 32, no. 3 1998, pp. 223–234. A. Murphy, 'The Irish economy: celtic tiger or tortoise', *Report*, MMI Stockbrokers, Dublin, 1994.
9. A. Murphy, 'The two-faced economy', in CSO and Irish Economic Association, *Proceedings of Conference on Measuring Economic Growth*, Stationery Office, Dublin, 1996, pp. 17–32.
10. D.Johnson, *The Interwar Economy in Ireland*, Economic and Social History Society of Ireland, Dublin, 1985.
11. K. A. Kennedy, T. Giblin, and D. McHugh, *The Economic Development of Ireland in the Twentieth Century*, Routledge, London, 1988.
12. Commission of the European Communities , *Panorama of EC Industry 1992–1993 Statistical Supplement*, Office for Official Publications of the European Communities, Luxembourg, 1992.
13. SOEC , *Statistics in Focus, Economy and Finance*, Corrigendum, no. 5, Statistical Office of the European Communities, Office for Official Publications of the European Communities, Luxembourg, 1996.
14. Office for National Statistics, *Regional Trends*, ONS, London, 1997.
15. CSO , *National Income and Expenditure 1996*, Government Publications, Dublin, 1996.
16. NESC , 'Ireland in the European Community: performance, prospects and strategy', *Report*, no. 88, National Economic and Social Council, Dublin, 1989.
17. K. A. Kennedy, 'Long term trends in the Irish economy', *Irish Banking Review*, Summer, 1993, pp. 16–25.
18. SOEC, *Statistics in Focus, Economy and Finance*, Corrigendum, no. 5, Statistical Office of the European Communities, Office for Official Publications of the European Communities, Luxembourg, 1996.
19. PPRU, *Northern Ireland Annual Abstract of Statistics 1996*, Policy Planning and Research Unit, Belfast, 1996.
20. D. M. W. N. Hitchens, and J. E. Birnie, *The Competitiveness of Industry in Ireland*, Avebury, Aldershot, 1994. A. Murphy, 'The two-faced economy', in CSO and Irish Economic Association, *Proceedings of Conference on Measuring Economic Growth*, Stationery Office, Dublin, 1996, pp. 17–32.
21. I. B. Kravis, 'A survey of international comparisons of productivity', *Economic Journal*, vol. 86, 1976, pp. 1–44. A. D. Smith, D. M. W. N. Hitchens and S. W. Davies, *International Industrial Productivity*, Cambridge University Press, Cambridge, 1982.
22. J. E. Birnie and D. M. W. N. Hitchens, 'Productivity and income per capita convergence in a peripheral European economy: the Irish experience', *Regional Studies*, vol. 32, no. 3, 1998, pp. 223–234.
23. J. E. Birnie, 'Comparative productivity in Ireland: the impact of transfer pricing and foreign ownership', in K. Wagner and B. van Ark (eds.), *International Productivity Differences Measurement and Explanations*, Elsevier, Amsterdam, 1996, pp. 195–223.

24. J. E. Birnie, 'Comparative productivity in Ireland: the impact of transfer pricing and foreign ownership', in K. Wagner and B. van Ark (eds.), *International Productivity Differences Measurement and Explanations*, Elsevier, Amsterdam, 1996, pp. 195–223. A. Murphy, 'The two-faced economy', in CSO and Irish Economic Association, *Proceedings of Conference on Measuring Economic Growth*, Stationery Office, Dublin, 1996, pp. 17–32.

25. J. E. Birnie and D. M. W. N. Hitchens, 'Productivity and income per capita convergence in a peripheral European economy: the Irish experience', *Regional Studies*, vol. 32, no. 3, 1998, pp. 223–234.

26. D. Duffy, J. Fitz Gerald, I. Kearney and F. Shortall, *Medium Term Review: 1997–2003*, Economic and Social Research Institute, Dublin, 1997. A. Leddin, and B. Walsh, 'Economic stabilisation, recovery, and growth: Ireland 1979–96', *Irish Banking Review,* Summer 1997, , pp. 2–18.

27. D. M. W. N. Hitchens, K. Wagner, J.E. Birnie, J. Hamar and A. Zemplinerov·, *Competitiveness of Industry in the Czech Republic and Hungary*, Avebury, Aldershot, 1995.

28. M. Murshed, D. Noonan, R. Thanki, G. Gudgin and S. Roper, 'Growth and development in the two economies of Ireland: an overview', *Growth and Development in The Two Economies of Ireland*, Discussion Paper, no. 1, Northern Ireland Economic Research Centre and Economic and Social Research Institute, Belfast and Dublin, 1993.

29. P. Bew, H. Patterson and P. Teague, *Between War and Peace*, Lawrence and Wishart, London, 1997.

30. J. E. Birnie, *Without Profit or Prophets A Response to Businessmen and Bishops*, Ulster Review Publications, Belfast, 1997.

31. Cadogan Group, 'Northern limits: boundaries of the attainable in Northern Ireland politics', *Report*, no. 1, Cadogan Group, Belfast, 1993.

32. J. Whyte, *Interpreting Northern Ireland*, Clarendon Press, Oxford, 1990.

33. P. Wicks, *The Truth about Home Rule*, Pitman and Sons, London, 1913.

34. D. W. M. N. Hitchens and J. E. Birnie, *The Competitiveness of Industry in Ireland*, Avebury, Aldershot, 1994.

35. P. McCloughan, 'The economic consequence of the Irish peace', *Liverpool Research Group in Macroeconomics*, vol. 16, no. 1, 1995, pp. 33–40.

36. J. J. Lee, *Ireland 1912–85*, Cambridge University Press, Cambridge, 1989.

37. J. Bradley, 'Flawed logic mars economic lesson for nationalists', *Irish Times,* 11 August 1995.

38. Simpson, 'Fiscal realities: the degrees of difference', in M. D'Arcy and T. Dickson (eds.), *Border Crossings: Developing Ireland's Island Economy*, Gill and Macmillan, Dublin, 1995, pp. 85–96.

39. *Financial Times,* 'Scotland shells out 'above average tax revenue', 10 October 1995.

40. D. M.W. N. Hitchens, K. Wagner and J. E. Birnie, *Closing the Productivity Gap*, Avebury, Aldershot, 1990. R. Clulow and P. Teague, 'Governance structures and economic performance', in P. Teague (ed.), *The Economy of Northern Ireland*, Lawrence and Wishart, London, 1993.

41. *Financial Times,* 'Bombed out in Belfast' 28 October 1993. B. O'Leary, T. Lyne, T. Marshall and R. Rowthorn, *Northern Ireland Shared Authority*, Institute for Public Policy Research, London, 1993. *The Times,* 'A bomb for all bigots', 27 October 1993.

42. P.J. Roche and J. E. Birnie, *An Economic Lesson for Irish Nationalists and Republicans*, Ulster Unionist Information Institute, Belfast, 1995.

43. A. Aughey and D. Morrow, *Northern Ireland Politics*, Longman, Harlow, 1996.

44. Economic Policy Committee, *Economic Prosperity for All*, Ulster Unionist Party, Belfast, 1996.

45. T. Wilson, *Ulster: Conflict and Consent*, Blackwell, Oxford, 1989.

160

46. P.J. Roche and J.E. Birnie, *An Economic Lesson for Irish Nationalists and Republicans*, Ulster Unionist Information Institute, Belfast, 1995. J.E. Birnie, *Without Profit or Prophets A Response to Businessmen and Bishops*, Ulster Review Publications, Belfast, 1997.
47. N. Gibson, 'Northern Ireland and Westminster: fiscal decentralisation. A public economics perspective', in NIEC, 'Decentralised government and economic performance in Northern Ireland', *Occasional Paper*, no. 7, Northern Ireland Economic Council, Belfast, 1996.
48. J. Bradley, 'Exploring long-term economic and social consequences of peace and reconciliation in the island of Ireland', *Consultancy Studies*, no. 4, Forum for Peace and Reconciliation, Dublin, 1996.
49. M. Mansergh, *The Spirit of the Nation: The Speeches of Charles J Haughey*, Mercier Press, Dublin, 1986.
50. A. Murphy, *Economists and the Irish Economy*, Irish Academy Press, Dublin, 1984.
51. B. O'Leary, T. Lyne, T. Marshall and R. Rowthorn, *Northern Ireland Shared Authority*, Institute for Public Policy Research, London, 1993.
52. *Economist*, 'Will American Jewry always fly Israel's flag', 29 November 1997.
53. T. Wilson, *Northern Ireland under Home Rule*, Oxford University Press, Oxford, 1955.
54. G. FitzGerald, *Towards a New Ireland*, Charles Knight, London, 1972.
55. H. Siebert, 'German unification', *Economic Policy*, no. 13, 1991, pp. 287–340.
56. R. Munck, *The Irish Economy*, Pluto Press, London, 1993. J. Anderson and D. Hamilton, 'Why Dublin could afford unity', *Northern Ireland Brief*, Parliamentary Brief, London, Spring, 1995. J. Bradley, 'Exploring long-term economic and social consequences of peace and reconciliation in the island of Ireland', *Consultancy Studies*, no. 4, Forum for Peace and Reconciliation, Dublin, 1996.
57. R. Munck, *The Irish Economy*, Pluto Press, London, 1993.
58. *Sunday Independent*, 'Patronising inaccuracies from North', 20 August 1995.
59. E. O'Malley, 'Industrial development in the north and south of Ireland: prospects for an integrated approach', *Administration*, vol. 33, no. 1, 1985.
60. C. O'Grada, *Ireland: A New Economic History, 1780–1939*, Oxford University Press, Oxford, 1994.
61. J. Bradley, 'Flawed logic mars economic lesson for nationalists', *Irish Times*, 11 August 1995.
62. M. Porter, *The Competitive Advantage of Nations*, Macmillan, London, 1990.
63. D. Johnson and L. Kennedy, 'Nationalist historiography and the decline of the Irish economy: George O'Brien', in S. Hutton and P. Stewart (eds.), *Ireland's Histories*, Routledge, London, 1991, pp. 11–35.
64. W. G. H. Quigley, 'Ireland— An island economy', *Paper presented to the Annual Conference of the Confederation of Irish Industry*, Dublin, 28 February 1992.
65. T. Wilson, 'The conflicting aims of Irish nationalism', *Fourth Ian Gow Memorial Lecture*, Friends of the Union, London, 1994.
66. Sir George Quigley has elaborated his arguments in the following speeches: ' *The two economies of Ireland – introductory remarks*', 23 March 1955; ' Launch of *The Two Economies of Ireland*', 7 November 1995; 'The island of Ireland from a banking and investment perspective', *Tenth European Finance Convention*, 25 November 1996; 'European Union – gain or loss', *Conference, Twenty Five Years On – The Impact of EU Membership on Northern Ireland*, 2 February 1998.
67. R. Scott and M. O' Reilly, Northern Ireland Exports, Report, Northern Ireland Economic Research Centre, Belfast, 1992.
68. J. MacEnroe and W. Poole, 'Manufacturing: two plus two makes more than four', in T. Dickson and M. D'Arcy (eds.) , *Border Crossings*, Gill and Macmillan, Dublin, 1995, pp.110–112.
69. J. Bradley, 'Exploring long-term economic and social consequences of peace and reconciliation in the island of Ireland', *Consultancy Studies*, no. 4, Forum for Peace and

Reconciliation, Dublin, 1996.

70. R. Rowthorn and N. Wayne, *Northern Ireland: The Political Economy of Conflict*, Pluto Press, London, 1988.

71. The macroeconomic consequences of integrated economic policy, planning and co-ordination in Ireland, *Report*, Government Publications Office, Dublin, 1984.

72. G. FitzGerald 'Unionists urged to grasp the nettle', *News Letter,* 22 March 1995.

73. G. Fitzgerald, *Towards a New Ireland*, Charles Knight, London, 1972.

74. J. Meenan, *The Irish Economy since 1922*, Liverpool University Press, Liverpool, 1970.

8 Unionist and Nationalist Thinking in the 1990s

Michael Cunningham

Introduction

The principal aims of this chapter are twofold; to highlight and critique the language of unionism and nationalism in recent years and to examine their proposals for political progress and new constitutional structures. A supplementary objective is to examine what strategies the two principal political identities have adopted in pursuit of their aims. Two disclaimers should perhaps be posted here. First, I have deliberately chosen to employ the term 'thinking' rather than 'ideology' in the title. This is because the latter term arguably implies a more coherent and abstract set of ideas than will be examined here and also does not encompass specific or general constitutional prescriptions to be examined. Also, there is a considerable literature, particularly on unionism, discussing either the 'essence' of the ideas or normative defences which I do not wish to replicate here.[1] Second, as this literature indicates, the two broad identities of the title are not homogeneous and undifferentiated. Indeed much recent scholarship has focused upon different identities and experiences within the two blocs and the way in which, for example, class, region and gender may undermine and render too simplistic the idea of an 'essential' unionism or nationalism.[2] However, I would contend that this division remains the most politically salient in Northern Ireland and commonalties exist within the two blocs. Therefore, the chapter will be sub-divided principally along these lines. Lastly, the timeframe is indicative. It can be argued that the late 1980s marked an important period in the evolution of political thinking. In this period unionism was engaged in trying to rethink its abortive opposition to the Anglo-Irish Agreement of 1985 and the seeds of so-called 'pan nationalism' were being sown. The influence of these were to become manifest in the Brooke/Mayhew talks of 1990 onwards and subsequent governmental initiatives.

Unionism: some general observations

One could easily be a hostage to fortune in trying to provide a 'list' of ideas, assumptions or political formulations which are common to all forms of unionism. However, with the possible exception of a form of 'civic unionism' advocated by Norman Porter[3] which lacks any significant support, the following ideas are endorsed by contemporary unionism in its various political manifestations. For unionists of all complexions and in any (or no) party the need to secure the political legitimacy of Northern Ireland is paramount. This can be done in two broad ways; either by arguing that Northern Ireland is the legitimate entity within which self-determination is to be exercised or by focusing on the concept of citizenship as a basis for the defence of the Union.

To consider first the idea of self-determination. That conflicting concepts of self-determination are central to the Northern Ireland problem is both a crucial and banal observation and, as Gallagher has argued, the invocation of the concept cannot adequately secure the claims of either protagonist.[4] However some strands of unionism argue that there is a people of Northern Ireland and that the majoritarian principle should be adhered to in deciding Northern Ireland's future. This does not mean that no minority expression can be accommodated; rather that there can be no political and representational equivalence, as of right, for those opposed to the Union, as they are and as long as they remain the minority.

It must be stressed here that this formulation does not preclude structures which recognise the existence of those who do not accept the legitimacy of Northern Ireland or their right to express such dissent. Also, the rights of a majority within Northern Ireland should not be conflated with the rights of the majority, if the latter is used as a confessional or ethnic shorthand. This latter point is well illustrated by the frequent use of the term the 'the greater number' by James Molyneaux, leader of the Ulster Unionist Party (UUP) from 1979 to 1995 and is also to be found in the statements of one of the smaller unionist parties with paramilitary links, the Progressive Unionist Party (PUP).[5] One example from Molyneaux will serve as illustration.

> I have avoided use of the word 'majority' because that is too readily equated with 'the Protestant majority' or 'the unionist majority'. The greater number of which we speak embraces Protestants and Roman Catholics who think and vote as unionists with a small 'u'.[6]

The message here is clear. Unionism is not, for Molyneaux at least, to be identified with a confessional group and similar formulations can be found in the work of Aughey and the UKUP leader, Robert McCartney in *Liberty and Authority in Ireland* and *The McCartney Report on Consent.*[7]

The implications of the unionist conception of self-determination deserve further consideration. It is the view of much of unionism that because North-

164

ern Ireland is a legitimate political entity, and recognised by such as the Republic of Ireland through the Anglo-Irish Treaty of 1921 and *de facto* recognition of the boundary commission despite the claims of Articles 2 and 3 of the 1937 constitution, one can only legitimately discuss self-determination within the context of the people of the two states (or possibly one state and a region of another) found on the island of Ireland. The significance of 'people' and 'state' here is illustrated in an example from the Cadogan Group, which disseminates occasional papers in support of a liberal unionism. The important point here is that, since 1920, there has been a people of Northern Ireland which has a right to self-determination; and only people have a right to self-determination. Therefore, concepts such as 'traditions' and 'community', for example used by those arguing that the nationalist 'community' in Northern Ireland has a right to self-determination (or the people of Ireland as a whole) or that because the nationalist 'tradition' (and the unionist one to a lesser degree) transcend existing political boundaries new political structures are necessary, are logically flawed and therefore illegitimate.[8]

It could be maintained that this position does not cover unionism in its entirety. This leads us to the second formulation which constructs a defence of unionism employing the concepts of state and citizenship, rather than self-determination, and is exemplified by the work of Aughey.[9] He argues that unionism is (or should be) concerned with the idea of the state, since there is no British nation, and with the maintenance of the rights and equal treatment of British citizens within it. Invoking self-determination is unhelpful because it belongs to the lexicon of nationalism and unionists need not fight their battles on terms laid down by others; by contrast the concepts of state and citizen more easily provide a defence of unionism which has no ethnic or religious implications or overtones. The union is a multi-cultural polity which can accommodate a plurality of cultures, religions and identities.

Although these two broad schools may differ in their terminology, I think both utilise a conception of rights that is broadly individually-based in its construction. This is of much significance because it helps to bolster a form of unionism that, as indicated above, can genuinely advocate the rights of individuals to political, religious and cultural expression and freedom within Northern Ireland. However, the conception of rights does not allow an extension of these rights to aggregates ('community', 'tradition' etc.). The practical significance of this is that there is no right to an institutional expression of nationalism within Northern Ireland. It is no coincidence that the UUP has advocated a bill of rights as part of a political settlement since this would endorse the concept of individual rights, and of course signal that unionism is not, as its critics often claim, a sectarian, discriminatory or 'triumphalist' set of ideas. It is difficult to gauge if this would be true of all its members, but Robert McCartney's United Kingdom Unionist Party (UKU), the UUP, the PUP and the Ulster Democratic Party (UDP) have all in their literature stressed the rights of individual expression and downplayed the 'protestantism' of unionism.

Without wishing to engage overmuch in philosophical speculation, it is perhaps the case that utilisation of a liberal tradition of individual rights broadly demarcates unionism from a more collective and communalistic political tradition that nationalism can exploit. For example, Jennifer Todd claims that community is one of three inter-related concepts central to northern nationalist ideology.[10] This is not to say that unionism cannot mobilise, or draw strength from, a communal tradition but the invocation of individual rights can help to construct limits to nationalist claims for constitutional and institutional change.

The next term which repays some investigation is that of consent. As with self-determination it is vague and contestable. For example, unionist hostility to the Anglo-Irish Agreement was based in part on the fact that they had not consented to such changes as were effected. Opponents of the unionist position could (and did) invoke two counter arguments. First, the representatives of the British people as a whole overwhelmingly endorsed the Agreement which gave it legitimacy, to which Northern Ireland unionists could counter that, as Northern Ireland was the only constituent part of the UK affected by it, their opinion had a qualitatively different significance. Second, as the constitutional position of Northern Ireland was formally unchanged, with the government of the Republic being granted a consultative role, consent was not required. This hopefully illustrates a particular example of a wider question within political theory; if a government is generally perceived by its subjects/citizens to be legitimate by virtue of its democratic character, is consent needed for specific policies/acts and, if so, which ones?

It is beyond my competence to answer this rhetorical question; however a few observations will be offered concerning consent in the context of Northern Ireland. For the idea of consent to have any meaning then one must have the right not to consent. It is accepted by the two governments and most nationalist representatives that unionists, as long as they constitute a majority, have the right to withhold consent to a change in the constitutional status of Northern Ireland. However, while this formulation seems clear enough, the question is more complex and nuanced than this. Unionists generally would want the right of consent, and conversely the right not to consent, to extend to, for example, involvement in institutions which exceed what they consider to be a legitimate sphere of influence. To take an example which will be discussed more fully below, the *Framework Document* implied a 'duty to serve' by Northern Ireland representatives in putative cross-border institutions which could have executive powers.[11] If one were to argue that consent is only necessary in the event of constitutional change, then it would not be necessary here given these institutions would be compatible with the unchanged status of Northern Ireland within the UK. However, on two grounds one might argue that consent is necessary. First, if one believes such cross-border structures are part of a strategy to remove Northern Ireland from the UK in the longer term, neat distinctions or recognitions of change (or lack of it) in the constitutional position are inadequate, especially given the importance of the idea of 'process' in Northern Ireland talks.[12] This concern is articulated by, among others, Robert McCartney who argues that institutions planned by the British and Irish governments '… will gradually evolve into a factually and economically united Ireland that will render the final consent to the transfer of legal constitutional sovereignty a mere formality'.[13] Second, the existence of cross-border bodies would, presumably, involve representatives in decision-making (for example, members of the Dail) who would not only not be subject to any democratic mandate from the people or electorate of Northern Ireland but would be representatives of a foreign sovereign government. Therefore, there may be good arguments why consent must be forthcoming for changes other than the 'strictly' constitutional. As described below, nationalists generally have a more circumscribed view of what unionists have the right not to consent to and the withholding of consent can be portrayed by nationalists as negativism and intransigence.

Some of these themes will be returned to below and will inform the next section. This will focus more closely on unionist ideas and prescriptions for the political future.

Unionist policies and prescriptions: what they want and what they don't want

The political debate in Northern Ireland in the 1990s has largely taken place within the parameters of the 'three strand' concept introduced in the talks chaired by the then Secretary of State, Peter Brooke, in 1990 although similar ideas were to be found in the Sunningdale talks of 1973. 'Strand 1' involves structures within Northern Ireland, 'strand 2' cross-border institutions and 'strand 3' relations between the two governments. These three broad categories will be used as a framework to examine unionist prescriptions; this section will not exhaustively detail the policies of all parties but attempt to highlight the main features.

i) The internal dimension: possible structures within Northern Ireland

A feature which links the unionist parties is the emphasis on the internal dimension as being a precursor to, and having a role in setting limits to the form and powers of any future 'strand 2' institutions. This is in contrast to a nationalist emphasis which tends to downplay the significance of internal (that is, Northern Ireland-only) structures and does not accept the right of such structures, or the representatives therein, to take precedence over an all-encompassing settlement. This has two facets; that an internal structure, for example an assembly, should not precede the establishment/ development of the other two strands and nor should it be able to constrain or veto these developments. The reason for these divergent positions is clear. Unionists wish political and institutional developments to reflect the integrity and legitimacy of Northern Ireland while nationalists believe an internal solution is not tenable. Hence broad ideological positions are reflected in the degree of emphasis placed on the internal dimension.

Two main emphases are to be found in the recent literature of the largest unionist party, the Ulster Unionist Party (UUP). First, the extent of powers devolved to any regional assembly should be limited. In its 1994 policy statement *A Blueprint for Stability* it advocated that an assembly should have executive powers to deal with departments of government transferred to it by parliament. The paper foresees the possibility of some legislative authority but is not specific about which areas these should cover. In February 1995 the policy statement *A Practical Approach to Problem – Solving in Northern Ireland*, a response to the *Framework Documents*, advocated as an alternative to them the establishment of a fixed period two year assembly. This would constitute part of a transitional process from direct rule to a new devolved assembly. The paper of later that year (November 1995), *Statement of Aims*, seemed to advocate a more minimalist approach to an assembly's responsibility, with an emphasis on administrative powers. One commentator on this paper from within the party has summarised the UUP's focus on government within Northern Ireland as being mainly, if not necessarily solely, administrative.[14] It seems that the precise responsibilities of a future assembly are not fixed; this is because political progress could be part of a process rather than a 'once and for all', static settlement and one important determinant would be the degree of cross-party support. What is clear is that extensive legislative devolution is not advocated by the UUP.

The question of cross-party support constitutes the second point. The UUP advocates 'responsibility sharing' within the executive.[15] The executive envisaged would have a committee structure in which committee membership, chairs and deputies would be broadly proportional to party strengths. Although the term 'power sharing' has been taboo in unionist political discourse since the abortive assembly of 1974, such a formulation implies that the UUP accepts that 'simple' majoritarianism, be it of one party or parties of one 'tradition', is not feasible. There are two possible reasons for this; the knowledge that the British government will not countenance majoritarianism and that a more liberal tendency has emerged within the UUP that accepts the limits of majoritarianism within government and the need to integrate non-unionists within any new structures. I would argue, though somewhat speculatively, it is a combination of the two.

168

The Democratic Unionist Party (DUP) has consistently advocated extensive devolution of powers to a local assembly emphasising the need for legislative devolution and the control of security policy.[16] There is clearly a difference of emphasis between the two main parties in this area and it is worth raising some possible explanations. One suggested reason is that party positions reflect a broader ideological distinction in that those with an 'Ulster' identity are more likely to look to local institutions and advocate that extensive powers be devolved to them, while those with a 'British' identity have a cultural and political identity which predisposes them to look towards Westminster and may also involve a more sanguine view of Westminster's motives regarding Northern Ireland policy.[17] There are some fairly obvious comments to be made regarding these generalisations. First, it can be questioned whether that broad bipolar categorisation of identity does justice to the complexities of identity; a growing literature on which highlights the 'slipperiness' of the concept. Second, to what extent can or has it been demonstrated that there is a correspondence between these two identities and political representation, especially given both the UUP and DUP are fairly 'broad churches'. For example, the UUP has for long periods had integrationist and devolutionist wings within it.[18]

A second possible explanation relates more to party competition than identity. A Westminster-focused strategy, as Molyneaux promoted when leader of the UUP, tends to have fewer rewards for the DUP given the dominance of UUP representation there. The distribution of support within Northern Ireland for a local assembly and the high profile of the leader of the DUP, Dr. Ian Paisley, as evidenced in his electoral success in European elections, may dispose the DUP towards a strategy that gives precedence to a local and regional focus. There is perhaps a feeling within the DUP that a local assembly can act as a bulwark against British machinations but given the power of Westminster to abolish a local assembly, as with Stormont, this seems of limited reassurance.

DUP policy statements are somewhat vague about the question of proportionality. One clue is that the paper *Breaking the Logjam*, presented to the Prime Minister in September 1993, proposed that there should be elections to an assembly which would have the right to put to parliament any proposals for the government of Northern Ireland which had the support of 60% of the assembly. This implies that such a majority might be attained without non-unionist support. However, broader agreement might be required for the actual operation of the assembly so it cannot be assumed that some form of proportionality would not be necessary. The DUP literature is rather vague on this.

The position of the two smaller unionist parties with paramilitary links, the Progressive Unionist Party (PUP) and the Ulster Democratic Party (UDP), seems similarly underdeveloped. The general election manifesto of May 1997 of the PUP advocated 'responsibility sharing', in any future assembly, reiterating a formulation found in its opening statement to the British government in talks of December 1994. Neither short document, however, provides any further details of what this entails or the specifics of its operation. The UDP argues that enforced power-sharing is undemocratic, but like the UUP and PUP, seems to accept the case that a system of proportionality allowing non-unionists a constructive role would be necessary.[19]

ii) The 'North-South Dimension': relations between Northern Ireland and the Republic

The attitude of the UUP towards possible new north-south structures and the wider question of the relation between the two parts of Ireland is summarised in a critical response to the *Framework Documents* of February 1995.

> The *Document* apparently fails to properly reflect the vital difference between the concept of cross-frontier (cross-border) institutions, voluntarily agreed between Northern Ireland and the Irish Republic, and that of all-Ireland institutions with executive powers, agreed by the two governments and imposed by diktat.[20]

The crucial point to be noted here is that cross-border co-operation is not rejected but that a Northern Ireland assembly should determine the extent of the authority of cross-border agencies, the scope of areas covered by such bodies and provide representatives to cross-border bodies. This is advocated (and is acceptable) for three main reasons. First, such agreement would highlight the role of Northern Ireland representatives and the integrity and responsibility of an assembly, thus reinforcing the idea discussed above that the internal dimension is paramount and that Northern Ireland is a legitimate political entity. Second, the structures would be democratic as their powers, responsibility and possible evolution would be determined by elected representatives of the people, north and south. Third, co-operation would be based on mutual interest and benefit and would also acknowledge northern nationalists' empathy with the Republic of Ireland, consistent with the integrity of Northern Ireland as part of the UK.[21]

The position of the DUP is similar though often more forcefully expressed. Relations with the Republic, including possible 'all-Ireland' structures, are subjects for discussions only subsequent to the removal of Articles 2 and 3 and the replacement of the Anglo-Irish Agreement. As with the UUP, such structures or bodies are premised upon the consent of an assembly and not as part of a 'three strand' package to be formulated as of a piece. The question arises of whether either party could accept executive functions for such bodies if an assembly were to assent. The logic of the UUP position suggests it could whereas, in its 1993 local government election manifesto, the DUP asserted that 'under no circumstances' would it consider a north-south body

170

with executive powers and in an interview in September 1997 Peter Robinson, deputy leader of the DUP, argued that such a body would be an embryo of a united Ireland.[22]

In a period of inter-party tensions and recriminations, the above topic is one of frequent contention; in particular with DUP claims that the UUP is inconsistent regarding the question or prepared to 'sell out' unionist interests.[23] As with many developments in recent years, the UUP appears more sanguine and less apocalyptical concerning this area than the DUP (this point will be returned to below). It is the case that the UUP generally (not all MPs and members are of one on the issue) can envisage greater cross-border links than the DUP but the starting-point or premise of their arguments unites them more than it divides. As a Cadogan Group paper indicates, both parties emphasise the concept of statehood, implicitly or explicitly, in their conception of the topic. North-South relations are premised on the political and institutional integrity of two states, and thus must operate within an inter-parliamentary and inter-governmental framework. They are not to be premised or constructed on the basis of 'traditions' which overlap with these; neither can this concept be invoked as a way to supersede or undermine this political integrity.[24]

The position of the smaller unionist parties is broadly similar and would fit with the formulation of the Cadogan group cited above. For example, Robert McCartney has stated that '… few would object to the widest and most comprehensive co-operation with the Republic of Ireland in all areas of mutual benefit'[25] and the UDP response to the *Framework Documents* stated

> The north/south relationship is important and it is in boths (sic) interest to co-operate for mutual benefit. But there is no consent for either the Irish government or the SDLP to circumvent the wishes of the Northern Ireland electorate and pressurise the Northern Ireland assembly into deeper and greater integration.[26]

The PUP also envisages co-operation through the structures of the two sovereign states. Despite inter-party spats and accusations, it can be argued that the positions of the various unionist parties are not fundamentally different. To conclude, the salient points are that the form and pace of North-South co-operation must be premised on the consent of the Northern Ireland people, through their representatives, and must be on the basis of mutual benefit for the two parts of Ireland and not as a part of a mechanism to blur or dissolve the two constituent parts.

iii) The British-Irish dimension

As argued above, recent unionist positions have been struck largely as responses to the 'three strand' concept embodied in the *Framework Documents* of 1994. This does not mean, of course, that either the *Documents* or their conceptualisations are accepted as legitimate. The unionist critique of the existing British -Irish dimension as endorsed by the two governments is twofold. First, it is flawed because it focuses on the relationship between the two parts of Ireland rather than on relations between the constituent parts of the British Isles as a whole. This is, of course, because inter-governmental relations are principally a mechanism for greater involvement by the Republic in the politics of the north with the objective of greater 'all-Ireland' integration. Second, it contains a 'democratic deficit' since the proposals of the successive inter-governmental accords since the Anglo-Irish Agreement of 1985 have lacked an input from the Northern Ireland electorate.

The UUP has sought to supersede this arrangement and also to argue that the second two strands are not distinct but should be conflated. In its submission to the Mayhew talks of 1992, the UUP advocated the creation of a council of the British Isles consisting of representatives of both governments and those of a devolved administration in Northern Ireland. This would reflect the linkages and interactions for example social, economic, cultura- that exist between Northern Ireland and the rest of the UK and those between the Republic and Great Britain. Both of these dimensions are ignored by the current asymmetrical, and hence inadequate, framework of Anglo-Irish relations. A DUP paper of the same period expressed similar ideas, calling for new relationships to be developed on an all-encompassing British-Irish axis. Such a structure would involve the two governments and the leading members of a new Northern Ireland assembly, possibly through an external relations committee.[27]

The conceptual and practical limitations of the current arrangements are well summarised by David Trimble, UUP leader since September 1995. It is worth quoting his formulation at length.

> The reality which Irish nationalists and their soul mates in the NIO try to conceal and evade is that the British Isles is the natural social and economic unit. Its political unity has been fractured by Irish nationalism, but any co-operation that seeks to rise above national boundaries should be based on that natural unity and not try to introduce further artificiality by trying to separate Northern Ireland from its natural, as well as constitutional, unit. In truth the second and third strands of the so-called three strands that are supposed to be the separate elements of any talks process cannot be divided.[28]

There are, therefore, only two strands. The governance of Northern Ireland and friendly relationships throughout the British Isles in which the east-west axis is much more important than the north-south one. If one is serious about 'harmonisation' for economic or technocratic reasons it makes much more sense to focus on the British Isles as the unit in which this should be done.

These ideas get occasional mention by the PUP and DUP but the UDP has developed them furthest. In its 1997 paper, *Council of the British Isles: a*

172

proposal for meaningful co-operation, it advocated the creation of a two-tier council of the British Isles which would embody the worthy principles of subsidiarity and decentralisation by having regional representation. The executive council would be made up of elected representatives from the governing bodies of England, Wales, Scotland, Northern Ireland, the Republic of Ireland, the Isle of Man and the Channel Islands. The councils of the constituent parts would be composed of MPs, MEPs and local councillors. Democracy would be revived by the need for consent and unanimity would be required in decision-making.

The general unionist tactic is clear: it is to critique the not-too-hidden agenda of the governments to use 'strand 3' to push the all-Ireland dimension and to expose the advocacy of harmonisation that ignores the important links, economic and other, between both parts of Ireland and Great Britain. It is interesting that such structures have both a progressive and historic dimension; activity and linkages between devolved regions with local assemblies, as in the UDP scheme, fit well with certain formulations of the European 'vision' while they also draw upon the British Isles structures that predated the settlement of 1920.

Changes in unionism and the question of tactics

Having examined the way in which unionism is articulated and its prescriptions for political progress, two supplementary questions will be addressed. First, what developments can be discerned in unionism over the last decade and, second, how has it tried to prosecute its political vision.

Unionism is by definition a conservative creed in that it is largely concerned with the maintenance of an existing constitutional relationship and to critique those who seek to change it. It thus follows that one would not expect seismic changes within its ideology, and its conservatism is precisely a feature on which its opponents focus accusing it of negativism, defensiveness and an unwillingness to seek accord. However, this does not mean unionism is a static phenomenon. One perhaps needs to distinguish between unionism as ideology which is largely unchanged and the tenor and representational patterns of unionism which have seen developments.

An examination of the literature of various unionist parties reveals this change in tenor. By this I mean that there is more emphasis than in the early period of the 'troubles' on the 'inclusive' and accommodatory character of unionism. The UUP, the UKU and the new, or reconstituted, parties with paramilitary links are keen to emphasise that unionism is a set of political ideas and not an ethno-religious creed and thus one that can embrace all citizens of Northern Ireland. Two cautionary notes should be posted here. This is not to imply that such unionism did not exist before; Carson is often cited as an exemplar of it. Also, it has seemed inadequate to reconcile nationalists to the structures of Northern Ireland. The simple point being made is that much of unionism is less keen to emphasise its protestantism and also more willing to conceive of a role for the minority community within the governance of Northern Ireland (see 'responsibility sharing' above) than was the case in the 1970s and into the 1980s. It is also the case that much of unionism can accommodate cross-border relations and structures, however constrained, to a greater degree than ten or twenty years ago.

With respect to representational patterns, much media attention has focused upon the PUP and UDP as embodying encouraging developments within unionism. Features of these parties include a willingness to criticise the unionism of the Stormont period for failing to take account of the interests of both the Protestant working class and those of the nationalist community. At least one commentator has argued that these parties are more prepared to recognise the legitimacy of the Catholic/nationalist 'tradition' within Northern Ireland than the intellectual, liberal strand of unionism outlined above.[29] However, this development may prove to be of limited significance for two reasons. First, the electoral impact of these parties has been slight; for example the UDP and PUP gained 2.2% and 3.5% of the vote respectively in the Forum elections of May 1996. Second, these parties share with the more established parties the basic tenets of unionism which will probably preclude any rapprochement with elements within nationalism which would change the political landscape within Northern Ireland. A cynic may argue that these parties have gained an attention disproportionate to their influence because unionist self-criticism and tensions within the unionist family makes good 'copy' rather than because of their objective significance.

It would be disingenuous to overplay the decline of a religious identity of unionism despite what I would interpret as sincere 'inclusivist' sentiments emerging from individuals and parties within unionism. Even within the UUP, often seen as the more secular of the two main parties, there are those, activist and MP, whose membership of, and association with, the Orange Order render some unilinear development over-simplistic. Writing in 1996, the Cadogan Group bemoaned the lack of any real evolution in unionism indicated by the maintenance of these links forty years after they were first questioned and Trimble's movement in this area has been marked by caution.[30]

The formulation of a successful political strategy by unionism has proved elusive. This is illustrated by the tensions between (and within) the UUP and DUP over the form and extent of opposition to the Anglo-Irish Agreement in the late 1980s and the attack on the campaign's negativism by other unionists. In the contemporary period the split between the UUP, UDP and PUP and the DUP and Robert McCartney's UKU over the talks process and decommissioning reveals the same uncertainties. If unionists are to achieve a settlement within Northern Ireland and/or prevent the erosion of Northern Ireland's position within the UK there are four possible arenas in which they can attempt to gain support; within the rest of the UK, with nationalists in Northern Ireland, in the Republic and in the international community.

The first arena was central to Molyneaux's minimalist strategy in which he tried to cultivate support at Westminster for the Union and gain incremental improvements to the administration of Northern Ireland. This was lent some credence by the parliamentary arithmetic of the mid-1990s but undermined by the *Framework Documents* of 1995 which signalled to many unionists that faith could not be invested in a Conservative government. The second route or dimension is foreclosed because nationalists are not interested in a 'free standing' internal settlement and it does not seem likely that a unionist/SDLP deal can be reached.

The third and fourth routes depend upon a lobbying and propaganda campaign to explain the unionist argument. There is evidence that unionists have started to realise the gains to be made here with increased visits to Dublin and the USA to explain their position with UUP and the smaller parties' representatives being prominent in such excursions.[31] It is difficult to assess what dividends have resulted from this strategy, but unionists suffer from playing the politics of 'catch-up' since the SDLP, and John Hume in particular, have long been assiduous in prosecuting their views both in Dublin and in international arenas. Unionism is also disadvantaged because most of the international actors with an interest in Ireland, particularly the USA and the European Union, have tended to be disposed towards an 'all-Ireland' settlement and thus concur with a broadly nationalist rather than unionist analysis of the 'problem' and prescription of a resolution.[32]

At the time of writing, the attitude to talks indicates tensions between unionists and a lack of consensus on tactics to be adopted. The UUP and the smaller parties believe that engagement with nationalist representatives, or at least proximity talks, will reveal the unreasonableness of nationalist demands and the conditional nature of the IRA cease-fire. It appears that Trimble's strategy is that by being in the talks his party can avoid accusations of unionist intransigence. Should the British government renege on its commitment to honour the consent principle, unionists would withdraw and the breakdown of talks would not be their responsibility. Therefore, attendance carries no substantial risks. By contrast, the DUP and the UKU have adopted an abstentionist position, informed by a belief that the agenda is skewed towards only one outcome; the erosion of UK sovereignty in Northern Ireland. The lack of any substantive movement can be read as a vindication of either position; unionists have little to fear from participation but also have nothing to gain if Sinn Fein cannot be persuaded of the legitimacy of unionist consent.

The politics of nationalism

The following sections will consider the political language used, and structures advocated, by the two main nationalist parties of Northern Ireland; the Social Democratic and Labour Party (SDLP) and Sinn Fein. This structure is employed for two reasons. First, there are distinctions to be made between them despite the development of 'pan nationalism' (for more on which see below) and, second, because the northern nationalist electorate is overwhelmingly represented by these two parties.

The SDLP: i) political ideas

There are two central assumptions which inform SDLP thinking in the contemporary period. First, in contrast with more traditional nationalist modes of thought, the central question to be addressed in Ireland is not the removal of the malign presence of the British state but the recasting of relations between the Irish people, north and south. This is because the evolution and extension of inter-governmental strategies to manage the problem and frequent British reiteration that it has 'no selfish strategic or economic interest' in Northern Ireland has convinced the SDLP of a basic neutrality, rather than a colonial interest, on the part of the British state. Second, the current constitutional position of Northern Ireland within the UK has not been, and cannot be, the basis for either an equitable or stable settlement.

The belief that an 'internal' solution is inadequate and that is should not be considered separate from, or prior to, a totality of the relationships embodied in the 'three strands' marks a very different conception of relations than that to which unionism adheres. Read in conjunction with unionist thinking outlined above, a discussion of the conception of self-determination, consent and parity of esteem will highlight the broad divisions between the two sets of ideas. One quotation from John Hume will give a flavour of the SDLP thinking.

> We accept that an internal settlement is not a solution because it obviously does not deal with all the relationships at the heart of of the problem. We accept that the Irish people as a whole have a right to national self-determination [...] the exercise of self-determination is a matter for agreement between the people of Ireland.[33]

The phrase 'as a whole' echoes a traditional 'thirty two county' approach to self-determination. However, Hume often emphasises that the Irish people are divided over how to exercise the right to self-determination; the most important project, as indicated above, is how to reach agreement between the people of Ireland rather than focus on an old-fashioned notion of territorial integrity. To paraphrase Hume, people not territories have rights. The problem here is that rather than being divided over its exercise, the people of Ireland do not agree on the legitimate political unit in which self-determination is to be exercised. This is the fundamental division and Hume's reformulation cannot disguise this.

This question feeds into the second term to be considered, that of consent. The logic of Hume's position and that of the SDLP would seem to be that, as Northern Ireland is not a legitimate entity, unionists do not have the right not to consent to constitutional changes or, more prosaically, the development of structures which go beyond or transcend those considered legitimate by unionists. Consent is required for the form which they take and participation necessary for their operation; therefore unionist consent is of a circumscribed form in which unionists can say 'no' to particular forms of change but not to change itself. One can perhaps construct this as the obverse of the unionist formulation above; unionists can accommodate the nationalist identity and tradition(s) on a basis of equality within Northern Ireland but this does not mean there is a right to an institutional representation of nationalism. For the SDLP, the unionist identity – religious, cultural, a sense of 'Britishness' – is valid and to be respected within Ireland but this does not give unionists a right to reject new structures which transcend the current political division of Ireland. As many unionists now stress the 'inclusiveness' of their ideology, so Hume and his party stress the positive republican vision of Parnell and Tone which is not narrow or sectarian but seeks to unite Catholic, Protestant and Dissenter.

The gap between unionist and nationalist perceptions can also be viewed through the prism of 'parity of esteem'.[34] The precise meaning of this somewhat gnomic phrase is a matter of contention but that does not preclude drawing some conclusions about differing perceptions about rights and equality from discussions around it. In the SDLP representation to the Forum for Peace and Reconciliation, Brid Rogers stated

> … parity of esteem must relate not just to social and economic life, it must also relate to political life, and it must be built into the very structures under which we are governed, and it must deal with the fundamental question of allegiance.

Denis Haughey, in the same Forum, concurred

> … I think Brid Rogers was absolutely right to say that equality of rights doesn't just mean proportional representation, it doesn't just mean even power sharing, it means *absolute* equality of political and national rights for both communities in the North …[35]

It is clear that such a conception goes far beyond the rights and claims for Northern nationalists that unionism would deem legitimate. This is summarised by Robert McCartney of the UKU's view of such claims.

> Gradually I came to realise that what they [nationalists] mean by 'parity of esteem' is not parity of esteem for the individual but parity of esteem for the constitutional identity of the state. I don't know of any democracy which says that the minority shall be allowed the same rights as the majority in determining the constitutional and political identity of the state itself, [for] that seems to me to be a concept that has nothing to do with civil rights, protection of individual rights or protection against majoritarianism ...[36]

McCartney may not, of course, cover all unionist conceptions of parity of esteem but he highlights again a basic division between nationalist and unionist positions. For nationalists Northern Ireland is not a legitimate entity; therefore as long as it exists it should at least, as Haughey argues, recognise the political equivalence or parity of the two communities; for unionists there is no grounded claim for such a demand.

Having outlined the basic tenets of nationalism, the question of the extent of its 'modernisation' will be considered. Hume and the SDLP often speak of a 'new' or 'agreed' Ireland as their objective. This can be read in at least three ways, which are not mutually exclusive. First, it signals the progressive and forward-looking nature of the party which has gone beyond a vision of territorial unity for nationalism. Second, it is an attempt to reassure unionists that their identity, culture and traditions are valid and their agreement is sought for change. Third, and in possible conflict with the second, is that those who do not seek agreement are the obstacles to progress and may be implicitly contrasted with the conciliatory politics of the SDLP. This 'forward-looking' aspect of SDLP thinking is bolstered by the use of the concept of 'post nationalism' and the European dimension to promote its agenda.[37]

The broad implications of post nationalism are as follows. The nation state and the territorial formulations of self-determination associated with it are (becoming) outdated. Both individual and communal identities are being forged at both sub-national and supra-national levels and the way forward is to give political and structural recognition to this and move beyond historical Britain versus Ireland polarities. The existing structure in which this process can be furthered is the European Union (EU), embodying as it does both the concepts of regionalism and subsidiarity and supra-national co-operation. It also provides a possible venue for the supersession of national antagonisms. As Hume has often rhetorically asked; if European integration has fostered the co-operation of France and Germany, why cannot the disputes of one small island be resolved through this framework?

The extent to which there is a functional and economic logic to greater all-Ireland integration within the context of the EU is a question of debate.[38] The important point here is that while unionists accept such linkages may be of mutual benefit, they suspect that the espousal of these two interrelated concepts has a political agenda in that both post nationalism and the European dimension are seen as concepts designed to underpin the advocacy of all-

Ireland structures which will weaken the Union. Again, the question of process is important here. If functional co-operation is not engaged within strict limits, unionists are likely only to interpret such changes as manifestations of 'nationalism by stealth' or by the 'back door' as set out in *The McCartney Report on the Framework Documents*.[39] I would contend that the 'modernisation' process of appealing to post-nationalist developments and the European context is underwritten by broad nationalist assumptions; the likely outcome being the undermining of the union. The point here is not whether this is 'right' or 'wrong'; rather that the SDLP remains a nationalist party in which post nationalism is something of a tactical gloss.

The SDLP: ii) structures and tactics

The future structures for an 'agreed Ireland' are largely implicit in the discussion above so will be briefly summarised here. Since the late 1970s the SDLP has placed little emphasis on the internal aspect or 'strand 1'. It is clear that any assembly for Northern Ireland must be considered only in the context of the three strands together; this was a principal stumbling-block between the SDLP and the unionist parties in the Mayhew talks of 1992. Also, power-sharing would be a necessary, though not sufficient, requirement in the absence of agreement on the other two strands. The extent to which the SDLP views the internal dimension as secondary, and as a delaying-tactic for more substantial negotiations, was revealed in its hostility to elections to a new Forum announced by John Major in January 1996 from which parties would choose negotiating teams.

The SDLP proposes a 'strong' version of north-south bodies. In representation to the Forum for Peace and Reconciliation, Sean Farren reiterated the point that north-south bodies must possess executive powers and should not be considered subsequent to the operation of structures within Northern Ireland. Two fundamental principles underlay this prescription; that there needs to be an expression in institutional form of the affinity nationalists in Northern Ireland have for the rest of Ireland and that such structures should embrace economic, social and cultural matters.[40]

The third strand is conceived of as essentially being composed of intergovernmental structures which will help to foster the second. The increasing formalisation of intergovernmental management from the establishment of the Anglo-Irish Intergovernmental Council in 1981, through the Conference established by the Anglo-Irish Agreement of 1985 to the *Framework Documents* of 1995 largely accords with the SDLP view of the future, in that these developments are likely to increase the all-Ireland dimension of any resolution. The 'British dimension' of east-west relations, as advocated by unionists, is recognised but is emphasised less in SDLP formulations.

The question remains as to what precisely the SDLP envisages for a future Ireland, for example is an 'agreed Ireland' a united Ireland? The implication of respecting unionist consent to the form of changes to take place would seem to rule this out and it is possible that a form of joint authority may be considered as at least a medium term objective. However unification remains an aspiration for most of the party and the opacity of the cross-border institutions outlined in the *Framework Documents* gives rise to the hope that the blurring of national identities and functional integration will gradually undermine the union. Such structures can be viewed as part of a process rather than an end-state which is why they can foster both nationalist aspirations and unionist alarms.

The main plank of SDLP strategy has been, since at least the late 1970s, the cultivation of external agencies and an attempt to build an international coalition which shares its conception of the problem; fundamentally that any settlement must transcend the internal. Those who now share this broad approach include the British and Irish governments, the US administration and the EU. It may be the case that there are different motivations and imperatives at work here and these positions are not solely attributable to SDLP influence. However its influence, and in particular the personal campaigning and networking of John Hume, is significant. It would scarcely be an exaggeration to state that the northern policy of the Dublin administration is not formulated without recourse to SDLP opinion. In the American context, attempts both to marginalise Irish-American groups supportive of the 'armed struggle' and to involve the administration in Irish affairs (Clinton has been much more closely concerned with the issue than any of his predecessors) have proved successful. As argued above, much of the international community's view of the Irish question tends to be one that is disposed, on whatever grounds, towards nationalism rather than unionism and this has been assiduously cultivated.

The other important strategic dimension has been negotiation and discussion with Sinn Fein since 1988. It is too early to state definitively if this will pay dividends in terms of an indefinite cessation of violence. However, it seems clear that this is a 'high risk' strategy. It has provoked internal party tensions and, periodically, much criticism from elements within Irish society. Such is Hume's personal status that he has been able to 'ride this out'. Perhaps more significantly, it has had two implications within Northern Ireland. It has helped to bolster the legitimacy and electoral performance of Sinn Fein, whose general election performance of May 1997 was their best ever, which makes the SDLP's electoral hegemony less secure and leads to contradictions in which a vote for a party with which the SDLP has had long negotiations can be termed a 'vote for murder'. Association with Sinn Fein may also make accommodation with unionists in the north more difficult to achieve; making more complex a process already strained by the relative indifference of the SDLP to the internal dimension.

180

A provisional assessment of SDLP strategy would indicate its success given that its conception of the problem and prescriptions for the future are shared, in substance if not in detail, by the all the major protagonists except the unionists.

Sinn Fein: i) key positions

Limitations of space preclude a comprehensive review of the welter of papers and documents associated with the Hume-Adams talks and the 'peace process' in general.[41] The focus here will be to highlight the main themes in Sinn Fein thinking, cutting through some of the convolution and dissembling found in the texts. As with the parties previously discussed, a useful starting-point is perceptions of Britain's role and the concepts of self-determination and consent.

A notable difference between Sinn Fein and the SDLP is the perception of Britain's role. Although the tone has softened to an extent, Sinn Fein sees the British presence as the fundamental cause of the conflict and rejects the notion that Britain can play the role of arbiter. The main shift concerns the time scale of British withdrawal and its role in the interim. In 1988 a policy document argued that '...a definite date within the lifetime of a British government would need to be set for the completion of [this] withdrawal'.[42] By 1992 and the publication of the discussion paper, *Towards a Lasting Peace in Ireland,* the focus on a time scale had been dropped and the call on the British government to become 'persuaders' for unionist accommodation with the rest of the Irish people was established. Mallie and McKittrick [43] and O' Brien[44] detect shifts in republican thinking in this period but it can be interpreted as a tactical move and not evidence of any serious rethinking. Certainly the view of British rule as malign and biased towards unionism persists as the following extracts indicate.

> The refusal to allow the Irish people to exercise their right of self-determination has been and remains British government policy. ... British government policy in Ireland arbitrarily and by coercive force upholds the political allegiance of the unionist community as a national minority against the national and democratic rights of the national majority.[45]

All texts and statements obviously have to be read in context and it could be counter argued that this emphasis on Britain's role was aimed at republican activists to whom it was presented at the ard fheis. Some commentators have argued that the leadership at least have re-appraised the traditional imperialist conception of Britain's role, particularly that of a strategic interest.[46] However the refusal to concede British neutrality indicates a qualitatively different analysis from that of the SDLP.

The problems with the concept of, and divisions over, self-determination have been a recurring theme of this chapter and the Sinn Fein position can be illustrated by two short statements found in recent publications. The 1994 European election manifesto argues that the '... way forward to lasting peace lies in the exercise by the Irish people as a whole of the right to self-determination. There can be no internal solution in the six counties'.[47] Later that year in the *Submission to the British Government* paper, Sinn Fein called for the restoration of the right to national self-determination with agreement on how that right is to be exercised being a matter for the Irish people alone.

The Sinn Fein position is that Northern Ireland is not a legitimate entity. Therefore, the majority within that unit do not have the right to self-determination. As a minority of a national grouping they have rights but not of self-determination. This equation sums up the Sinn Fein position. Whether the formulation 'democratic right to self-determination' or 'right to national self-determination' is employed (both are to be found in Hume-Adams drafts) and arguably the former is more conciliatory, it does not seem to me this alters the case fundamentally. As with the SDLP formulation concerning division over the exercise of self-determination, the Sinn Fein position cannot be reconciled with the unionist one. Similarly O' Brien detects a shift in the republican movement circa 1993 in coming to see self-determination in terms of groups of people rather than territorial rights. This is questionable and, as with the SDLP formulation, it does not make a fundamental difference to the issue.

Related to the question of self-determination is that of consent and this is the crux of any future settlement and of more concern to some unionists than the question of decommissioning. It thus requires a lengthy analysis. The method employed will be to cite a selection of Sinn Fein statements chronologically and then to offer some reflections of commentators on the use of consent.

a) The requirements for peace include a commitment by both governments to the ending of partition and 'democracy and practicality demands that this be done in consultation and co-operation with the representatives of the Irish minority'.[48]

b) '... the democratic right of self-determination by the people of Ireland as a whole must be achieved and exercised with the agreement and consent of the people of Northern Ireland ...'[49]

c) 'We need a strategy for change and peace. A lasting settlement must seek an end to partition in the shortest possible time, consistent with obtaining maximum consent to the process and minimising cost'.[50]

d) '... the consent and allegiance of unionists, expressed through an accommodation with the rest of the Irish people, are essential ingredients if a lasting peace is to be established'.[51]

e)   'The argument that the consent of the unionist population is a pre-condition for any political movement is entirely bogus and without democratic basis'.[52]

f)   'Arguments in favour of a unionist veto are a subversion of the concept of consent'.[53]

What can be discerned from these statements? First, a lack of clarity and precision is evident. This is presumably the result of simultaneously trying to project a conciliatory tone towards unionism (see below), to fashion joint statements with the SDLP, to maintain dialogue with the Irish government and to reassure republican supporters that fundamental tenets are not being abandoned. Consider in the above extracts: in (a) is 'consultation and co-operation' the same as consent; if not how does it differ? In (c) what does the term 'maximum' mean? Possibly that some or a majority of unionists are needed for the process or that a majority in Ireland as a whole is sufficient? The inference to be drawn from (e) and (f) is that unionist consent is not needed (unless political movement is distinguished from the ending of partition). As discussed in the section on unionism above, if consent is the cornerstone to progress than it is devoid of meaning if one does not have the right not to consent. It is questionable if the term has meaning, or any practical political application, unless it can be withheld – which republicans construe as a veto and impermissible. The last two extracts contradict the sentiment expressed in (b). This is the strongest formulation of the necessity of unionist consent and was, according to Mallie and McKittrick, the first time republicans had conceded this position.[54]

The balance of positions struck would indicate that republicans do not accept the right of unionists not to consent and therefore new structures of an all-Ireland nature and, in the longer run, a unitary state should be progressed if consent is not forthcoming, though such consent would be preferred. There is agreement among the majority of commentators on this question. Tonge argues that the position is unchanged and that a unitary state could only be successful with unionist allegiance but prior consent was not necessary.[55] In effect, Sinn Fein's historical view appeared to remain intact, namely that unionist consent and allegiance would be a consequence of the creation of Irish unity. Denial of a qualitative shift is also found in Smith[56] and in Power. Power, writing of the period following the *Downing Street Declaration* of 1993, argues that

> … Sinn Fein did nod publicly towards securing northern majority consent to unity as the best road to achieving the goal; but Sinn Fein did not openly accept the consent doctrine, antipodal to republicanism.[57]

This position remains unchanged.

The previous section has hinted at the limitations of Sinn Fein's changes. Many core positions remain although the characterisation of Britain's position as simply imperialist has been reassessed. However, it is unclear why Sinn Fein think it possible or likely that Britain would act as 'persuaders' for unification if it is basically pro-unionist and biased towards them. Another area of change is the emphasis on the 'inclusive' nature of the republican vision, in which the rights and identities of the Protestant tradition are respected (as in the benign vision of republican historically). The problem with this attempt at rapprochement, even if sincere, is that unionists are unlikely to find it reassuring because it does not allow adequate expression of their British identity – in the sense that they may have a British identity or its recognition through some institutional link with the UK. Republicanism can accommodate protestantism but not unionism. The problem is the two are not easily separable. Therefore, such solicitude is likely to fall on deaf ears as is the tactic of including 'peace' in the title of virtually every document and pronouncement.

The evolution of Sinn Fein strategy can be dated back to 1986 and the dropping of abstentionism within the Republic. The process which was given further momentum by the discussions with Hume in 1988 and the so-called 'pan nationalist' front was outlined by Adams in the same year in *A Pathway to Peace*. Prior to this, in 1986 and 1987, two internal conferences had discussed a broad front of coalition with smaller parties and groups which advocated British withdrawal.

The risks of association with other actors, principally the Irish government and the SDLP, were high. These included the possibility of splits, pressure to moderate, if not abandon, republican shibboleths (which underlies the tortuous and inconsistent framing of statements considered above) in order to carry potential allies who had often been formerly denounced as stooges or collaborators and the longer-term abandonment of violence if Sinn Fein were to be included in talks, thus jettisoning an important bargaining chip. On the other side of the equation were the limitations of Sinn Fein strategy without changes. The bolstering of the SDLP by the Anglo-Irish Agreement of 1985 and the links with the IRA were barriers to further electoral gains and the 'armed struggle' looked increasingly unlikely to effect British withdrawal. According to O'Brien, although not publicly acknowledged by Sinn Fein, loyalist attacks on members were taking their toll and provided another argument.[58]

An interim judgement on this strategy must be one of success from the point of view of Sinn Fein. Despite the breaking of one cease-fire Sinn Fein have been included in talks and the return to violence for seventeen months in 1996 was largely judged by nationalist Ireland to have been the result of British procrastination on including Sinn Fein in negotiations. Also, the electoral performance of Sinn Fein has improved and the movement (at the time of writing) has not splintered. The legitimacy of Sinn Fein has increased in both the Republic and the USA. This is not to say that Sinn Fein will 'win'; it is highly unlikely that a united Ireland will emerge from any political process.

Sinn Fein   iii) possible structures

The aim of Sinn Fein remains a thirty two county unitary state. However, there has been a recognition that this is a long-term aspiration and that 'interim' measures may be necessary as a route to this. This recognition, or 'historic shift' in O' Brien's phrase, dates from a speech given by Martin McGuinness in June 1993.[59] For example, the 1992 document *Towards a Lasting Peace* does not endorse interim arrangements, such as joint authority. It is clear that Sinn Fein seeks the widest possible powers for any all-Ireland bodies and sees them as evolutionary and to promote the transition towards the ending of partition. One difference between their ideas and those of the SDLP was revealed in the Forum for Peace and Reconciliation when Jim Gibney maintained that all-Ireland institutions did not have to be derived from elected forums, north or south, and could thus proceed without 'strand 1' agreement, which Seamus Mallon of the SDLP considered to be an undemocratic prescription. Elsewhere, Gibney has argued that joint sovereignty or a federal Ireland would have to be staging posts towards an all-Ireland democracy.[60] The 'third strand' is of residual interest to Sinn Fein and the question of whether any formal structures are needed between the two sovereign states would be decided by the people of Ireland.

In conclusion, it would seem that the objective of Sinn Fein remains unchanged but there has been a recognition of the unreality of either a rapid move towards unification or its achievement without interim institutional change. The move from absolutist language was indicated above and is to be found in Adams' adoption of the Hume formulation of a 'new and agreed Ireland' in the USA in March 1995[61] and his indication in August 1997 to Mo Mowlam, Secretary of State for Northern Ireland, that joint sovereignty would be an acceptable down payment for the objective of a united Ireland.[62]

Afterword

The Agreement of 10 April 1998, which was subsequently endorsed by the Ulster Unionist Council later that month and the special Sinn Fein *ard fheis* in May, suggests a more flexible approach by these protagonists compared with the positions adopted between the late 1980s and 1997 as outlined in the discussion above. However, it remains to be seen if the shifts have been significant enough to allow the successful operation of the institutions to be established. Although Sinn Fein has dropped its abstentionist position with respect to participation within a Northern Ireland Assembly, it has stopped short of fully endorsing the legitimacy of Northern Ireland as a political entity and embracing the 'northern majority consent principle'; in addition the unresolved question of decommissioning may still prevent it from being allowed to participate in the executive of the assembly.

Second, at the time of writing, the precise powers and responsibilities of the north/ south body have still to be determined and the Agreement is somewhat opaque concerning this area. Given the difference in emphasis which remains between the majority of representatives of the traditions of nationalism and unionism in this area, its functioning may prove contentious. Whether or not peace holds, it remains likely that nationalists will continue to press for the extension in scope and powers of cross-border institutions (reflecting Adams' view of the settlement as transitional) and unionists for their limitation; thus underlining the differing constructions of political legitimacy which still remain.

References

1. See S. Bruce, *God Save Ulster: The Religion and Politics of Paisleyism*, Oxford University Press, Oxford, 1986; J. Todd, 'Northern Irish nationalist political culture', *Irish Political Studies*, vol. 2, 1987, pp. 31–44; J. Todd, 'Two traditions in unionist political culture', *Irish Political Culture*, vol. 5, 1990, pp. 1–26; A. Aughey, *Under Siege: Ulster Unionism and the Anglo-Irish Agreement*, Blackstaff, Belfast, 1989; C. Coulter, 'The character of unionism', *Irish Political Studies*, vol. 9, 1994, pp. 1–24; J.W. Foster, (ed), *The Idea of the Union:*, Belcouver Press, Vancouver, 1995; N. Porter, *Rethinking Unionism: An Alternative Vision for Northern Ireland*, Blackstaff, Belfast, 1996; C. O'Halloran, *Partition and the Limits of Irish Nationalism: An Ideology Under Stress*, Gill and Macmillan, 1987; F. O'Connor, *In Search of a State: Catholics in Northern Ireland*, Blackstaff, Belfast, 1993.
2. P. Shirlow and M. McGovern (eds), *Who are the 'people'?*, Pluto, London, 1997; F. O'Connor. op. cit.
3. N. Porter, op. cit.
4. M. Gallagher, 'Do unionists have a right to self-determination?', *Irish Political Studies*, vol. 5, 1990, pp. 11–30; M. Gallagher, 'How many nations are there in Ireland?', *Ethnic and Racial Studies*, vol. 18(4), 1995, pp. 715–39.
5. Documents using the phrase 'greater number' include, *Submission by the Right Honourable J. Molyneau MP to the First Plenary Session of Strand 1 Talks*, Ulster Unionist Party, Belfast, 16 June 1991; *A Blueprint for Stability*, Ulster Unionist Party, Belfast, 1994; *Building your future within the Union*, Ulster Unionist Party Manifesto for the Forum Election, Belfast, 30 May 1996; J. Molyneau, *Text of a speech to Ulster Unionist Council*, Belfast, 19 March 1994; *Progressive Unionist Party's opening statement to the British government*, Belfast, 15 December 1994.
6. *Submission by the Right Honourable J. Molyneau MP to the First Plenary Session of Strand 1 Talks*, UUP, 16 June 1991.

7.	A. Aughey, op. cit., and Robert McCartney, *Liberty and Authority in Ireland,* Field Day Pamphlet 9, Londonderry, 1985; Robert McCartney, *The McCartney Report on Consent,* Belfast, 1998.
8.	Cadogan Group, *Square Circles,* Belfast, 1996.
9.	A. Aughey, op. cit., and A. Aughey, 'Unionism and self-determination', in P. Roche and B. Barton (eds), *The Northern Ireland Question: Myth and Reality,* Avebury, Aldershott, 1991, pp. 1–16.
10.	J. Todd, 'Two traditions in unionist political culture'. *Irish Political Studies,* vol. 5, 1990, pp. 1–26.
11.	Although Major tried to reassure unionists with the 'triple lock' guarantee – that is, that any proposal would have to have support form the Northern Ireland parties, the Northern Ireland people in a referendum and be approved by the Westminster parliament.
12.	P. Arthur, 'Dialogue between Sinn Fein and the British government', *Irish Political Studies,* vol. 10, 1995, pp. 195–91.
13.	Robert McCartney, *The McCartney Report on Consent,* Belfast, 1998, p. 2.
14.	D. Nesbitt, *Unionism Restated: an analysis of the Ulster Unionist Party's 'Statement of Aims',* Ulster Unionist Information Institute, Belfast, 1995.
15.	*A practical approach to problem-solving in Northern Ireland,* Ulster Unionist Party, Belfast, 1995.
16.	*What's the British government up to? Tampering with Ulster's constitutional position,* Democratic Unionist Party Policy Document, Belfast, 1994.
17.	J. Todd, 'Northern Irish nationalist political culture', *Irish Political Studies,* vol. 2, 1987, pp. 31–44.
18.	A. Aughey, *Under Siege: Ulster Unionism and the Anglo-Irish Agreement,* Blackstaff, Belfast, 1989; F. Cochrane, *Unionist Politics and the Politics of Unionism since the Anglo-Irish Agreement,* Cork University Press, Cork, 1997.
19.	A. White, *The development of working-class loyalist thought (1985–95) and the rise of the PUP and the UDP,* MA thesis, The Queen's University of Belfast, Belfast, 1995.
20.	*A practical approach to problem-solving in Northern Ireland,* Ulster Unionist Party, Belfast, 1995.
21.	*The democratic imperative: proposals for an elected body for Northern Ireland,* Unionist Party, 1996.
22.	*Unionists alienated – answer back! Get mad with Mayhew* Democratic Unionist Party Local government manifesto, p. 2 Belfast, 1993 and *Belfast Telegraph,* 2 September 1997.
23.	*What's the British government up to? Tampering with Ulster's constitutional position,* Democratic Unionist Party Policy Document, Belfast, 1994: *Democracy not Dublin rule,* Democratic Unionist Party general election manifesto, Belfast, 1997.
24.	Cadogan Group, op. cit., p. 23.
25.	Robert McCartney, *The McCartney Report on Consent,* Belfast, 1998, p. 24.
26.	*Response to the Government Framework Documents Belfast,* Ulster Democratic Party, Belfast, nd 1995?
27.	*A new start,* Democratic Unionist Party, Belfast 28 August 1992, p. 1.
28.	D. Nesbitt, op. cit., pp. vii–viii.
29.	F. Cochrane, op. cit., p. 38.
30.	Cadogan Group, op. cit., p. 38.
31.	P. Bew and G. Gillespie, *The Northern Ireland Peace Process, 1993–96:* A Chronology, Serif, London, 1996, pp. 73, 74, 92, 101, 126, 147, 158, 166, 174, 175.
32.	A. Guelke, *Northern Ireland: The International Perspective,* Gill and Macmillan, Dublin, 1988; J. Ruane and J. Todd, *The Dynamics of Conflict in Northern Ireland: Power, Conflict and Emancipation* Cambridge University Press, Cambridge, 1996, chapter 10.
33.	J. Hume, 'Joint statement issued with Gerry Adams', *Belfast Telegraph,* 23 April 1993.

34. T. Hennessey and R. Wilson, 'With all due respect: pluralism and parity of esteem', *Democratic Dialogue Report,* no. 7, Belfast, 1997.
35. *Debate on parity of esteem,* Forum for Peace and Reconciliation, Report of Proceedings, vol. 5, Dublin, 10 February 1995, pp. 81, 87.
36. T. Hennessey and R. Wilson, op. cit., p. 50.
37. M. Cunningham 'The political language of John Hume', *Irish Political Studies,* vol. 12, 1997, pp. 13–22.
38. It is of course contestable whether there is a movement towards post nationalist identities. For the question of the implication of cross-border co-operation within the European context see J. Anderson and J. Goodman, 'European and Irish integration: contradictions of regionalism and nationalism', *Journal of European and Regional Studies,* vol. 1, 1994, pp. 49–62. See also E. Tannam, 'The European Union and Northern Ireland politics', *Ethnic and Racial Studies,* vol. 18(4), 1995, pp. 797–817, 1998.
39. Robert McCartney, *The McCartney Report on the Framework Document,* Belfast, 1997.
40. *Statements on North-South structures in the light of the Joint Framework Documents and other documents,* Forum for Peace and Reconciliation, Report of Proceedings, vol. 16, Dublin, 15 May 1995, p. 24.
41. E. Mallie and D. McKittrick, *The Fight for Peace: the Secret Story Behind the Irish Peace Process,* Heinemann, London, 1996; P. Bew and G. Gillespie, op. cit. p. 48.
42. *Sinn Fein Policy Statement,* Dublin, 1988, p. 2.
43. E. Mallie and D. McKittrick, op. cit., p. 138.
44. B. O'Brien, *The Long War,* The O'Brien Press, Dublin, 1995, pp. 222–223.
45. Sinn Fein, *Towards a lasting peace in Ireland,* 1992, pp. 1–2.
46. J. Tonge, 'The political agenda of Sinn Fein; change without change?' in J. Stanyer and G. Stoker (eds), *Contemporary Political Studies,* vol. 2, Political Studies Association of the UK, Nottingham, 1997, pp. 750–60.
47. *A democratic Ireland in a democratic Europe: peace in Ireland – a European issue,* Sinn Fein European election manifesto, Belfast, 1994, p. 3.
48. *Towards a lasting peace in Ireland,* Sinn Fein, Belfast, 1992.
49. Hume-Adams draft of 1992 cited in E. Mallie and D. McKittick, op. cit., p. 376.
50. *Strengthening the nationalist agenda,* Sinn Fein local government election manifesto, Belfast, 1993, p. 2.
51. *Sinn Fein Peace Commission,* nd 1994?, p. 12.
52. *Ibid,* p. 11.
53. *Statements on constitutional issues in the light of A New Framework for Agreement and other documents,* Forum for Peace and Reconciliation, Report of Proceedings, vol. 16, Dublin, 25 May 1995, p. 24.
54. E. Mallie and D. McKittrick, op. cit., p. 150.
55. J. Tonge, op. cit., p. 111.
56. M.R.L. Smith, *Fighting for Ireland? The Military Strategy of the Irish Republican Movement,* Routledge, London, 1995, p. 211.
57. P. Power, 'Revisionist nationalism's consolidation, republicanism's marginalisation, and the peace process', *Eire-Ireland,* vol. 31(1–2), 1996, pp. 89–122.
58. B. O'Brien, op. cit., p. 322.
59. Ibid., p. 322.
60. T. Hennessey and R. Wilson, op. cit., pp. 74–75.
61. B. O.'Brien, op. cit., p. 342.
62. *Guardian,* 7 August 1997.

Notes on Contributors

Brian Barton is a research fellow in the Department of Politics at The Queen's University of Belfast. He has extensive publications on the political history of Northern Ireland, including *Brookeborough: The Making of a Prime Minister,* Institute of Irish Studies, 1988 and a contribution to *A New History of Ireland,* vol. 8, Clarendon Press, forthcoming 1999.

J. Esmond Birnie is a member of the Northern Ireland Assembly and was a lecturer in economics at The Queen's University of Belfast 1989–98. He has extensive publications on aspects of the economics of industry, the European Union and environmental regulation and co-author (with Patrick J. Roche) of *An Economics Lesson for Irish Nationalists*, Belfast, 1995.

D. George Boyce is professor in the Department of Politics, University of Wales. He has extensive publications on Irish nationalism and on unionism, including *Nationalism in Ireland,* Gill and Macmillan, 1991 and his study of British decolonisation will be published by Macmillan in 1999.

Michael Cunningham is a senior lecturer in politics at the University of Wolverhampton. He has extensive publications on Northern Ireland politics including *British Government Policy in Northern Ireland, 1969–1989*, Manchester University Press, 1991.

Sydney Elliott is a senior lecturer in politics at The Queen's University of Belfast. He has extensive publications on electoral issues in Northern Ireland and is co-author (with W.D. Flackes) of *Northern Ireland: A Political Directory, 1968–1998,* Blackstaff Press, fifth edition forthcoming 1999.

Brian Girvan is a senior lecturer in politics at the University of Glasgow. He has extensive publications on Ireland, the United States, nationalism and conservatism including *Between Two Worlds: Politics and Society in Independent Ireland,* Gill and Macmillan, 1989 and *The Right in the Twentieth Century: Conservatism and Democracy*, Pinter, 1994.

Graham Gudgin is Special Advisor to the First Minister of the Northern Ireland Executive. He was previously Director of the Northern Ireland Economic Research Centre and has published extensively on economic matters in Northern Ireland. His contribution to this book is written in a personal capacity.

Dennis Kennedy is a lecturer in the Institute of European Studies at The Queen's University of Belfast. He was Representative of the European Commission in Northern Ireland, 1985–91, former deputy editor of the *Irish Times* and author of *The Widening Gulf: Northern Attitudes to the Independent Irish State,* Blackstaff Press, 1988.

Patrick J. Roche is a member of the Northern Ireland Assembly and was a lecturer in economics at the University of Ulster until 1995. He is co-editor (with Brian Barton) of *The Northern Ireland Question: Myth and Reality,* Avebury, 1991 and *The Northern Ireland Question: Perspectives and Policies,* Avebury 1995.

Index